BELOVED &
DARLING CHILD

BELOVED &
DARLING CHILD

Last Letters Between Queen Victoria
& Her Eldest Daughter 1886–1901

Edited by AGATHA RAMM

SUTTON PUBLISHING

First published in 1990 by Alan Sutton Publishing Limited,
an imprint of Sutton Publishing Limited
Phoenix Mill · Thrupp · Stroud · Gloucestershire · GL5 2BU

This edition first published in 1998 by Sutton Publishing Limited

British Library Cataloguing in Publication Data
A catalogue record for this book is available from the British
Library

ISBN 0 7509 1825 X

Cover illustration: Queen Victoria and her Family, *(detail) 1887 by
Laurits Tuxen (The Royal Collection © Her Majesty the Queen)*

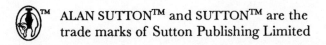
Typset in Baskerville 11/12.
Typesetting and origination by
Sutton Publishing Limited.
Printed in Great Britain by
WBC Limited, Bridgend, Mid-Glamorgan.

Contents

List of Illustrations

The illustrations are reproduced by gracious permission of Her Majesty the Queen, from the Royal Archives, Windsor Castle (4–14), and the Royal Collection (1, 2). Illustration no. 3 is reproduced by courtesy of John Van der Kiste.

Foreword

The letters are published by the gracious permission of Her Majesty the Queen from the letters of the Princess Victoria in the Royal Archives at Windsor and from those of Queen Victoria in the possession of Prince Wolfgang of Hesse. I wish to express my grateful thanks that the same facility was given to me as to the late Roger Fulford to use the latter in this country (see Roger Fulford, ed., *Dearest Mama*, Evans Brothers, 1964, p. ix). The originals have been returned to Friedrichshof.

I gratefully acknowledge the help of the Queen's Librarian and of the Registrar of the Royal Archives (successively Miss Jane Langton, Miss Elizabeth Cuthbert and Lady de Bellaigue) and of her assistants, and also the kindness of Sir Oliver Millar in answering my questions about paintings in the Royal Collections.

A.R.

Prefatory Note

The Queen normally wrote and sent her letters on a Saturday or a Sunday by post and on a Wednesday by messenger. Her daughter frequently wrote three times or even oftener in the week. If the Queen 'misses her day' she sometimes has as many as six letters to thank for.

The Queen usually begins her letters 'Darling Child'; if much moved she will use stronger terms of affection and the beginning has been printed with the letter; one such phrase has been used as the title for this book. She ends her letters 'Your devoted Mama' or 'Ever your devoted Mama'. Her daughter begins her letters 'My Beloved Mama' and usually ends 'Your most dutiful and devoted Daughter'. Towards the end of the correspondence she more often writes, 'Kissing your dear hand I remain your most dutiful . . .'

No attempt has been made to reproduce exactly the original punctuation, capital letters, underlining and spelling. As much has been reproduced as seemed compatible with ease of reading and consistency. Underlining is represented by italic type. Anything in square brackets is the editor's addition.

Individuals and houses can be identified from the index, not usually from the notes. The most useful genealogical tables are the set printed at the back of volume three of *Queen Victoria's Letters*, 3rd series, edited by G.E. Buckle (1930–2), abbreviated *QVL*. The set is called *Descendants of Queen Victoria*. There is a good table in the more easily obtained *Victoria R.I.* by Elizabeth Longford (Weidenfeld & Nicolson, 1964).

Bescherung	Presentation of gifts. This was made on Christmas Eve, following the German custom in the Queen's Household. As on birthdays presents were arranged on several tables one for each recipient.
D.V.	*Deo volente* – God willing. Very frequently used by the older generation well into the twentieth century, when notifying a time of arrival or arranging a journey.
unberufen	Equivalent of the English slang phrase 'touch wood'.
Verlobungstag	Betrothal day

Introduction

This selection of letters omits much that is characteristic of
the correspondents. The Queen writes a lot about the
comings and goings of herself and her many children,
relations and friends between Windsor, Balmoral, Osborne
and their own homes. It becomes tedious reading so it has
been omitted. Both writers in nearly every letter report the
weather and comment on natural phenomena. A little but not
much of this has been retained. The Queen has a wealth of
phrase and metaphor to express distress and only some of this
has been kept. Both notice every anniversary and only a few of
these comments remain. The selection, however, reflects
many shared interests. Both are interested in the particulars
of illnesses and deaths and in the increasing possibilities of
medical relief. The Queen writes with natural pleasure of
music. She had a good ear and was well trained in singing. She
appreciated good acting and liked tableaux vivants. Her
daughter is more interested in portrait and landscape
painting and in the history of art. Both delight in what they
call 'the South', meaning especially the Mediterranean
countries. Both notice the Nelson and the Cromwell cults of
the 1890s; indeed, both show a strong historical sense,
though that of the Queen's daughter was rather concentrated
on Charles I. All of these interests are fully reflected in this
selection. Yet German, British and international politics
were the stuff of life, and so of their letters, for both writers.

The German Background

The political background to which both constantly refer is
so entangled with personal emotions that it is difficult to tell

I

from their letters what is actually happening. The German background is especially confusing. In 1886 the Crown Prince and Princess were the centre of a liberal circle critical of the existing regime in the sixteen-year-old German Empire. Political criticism was mixed with resentment at the personal tyranny over them of Emperor William I and the Empress Augusta. Unfortunately, the Emperor and Empress found ready support in the ultimate heir to the throne, the Crown Princess's eldest son, William, then twenty-seven, and his younger sister Charlotte and, because of his affection for Charlotte, in the second son, Henry. It was a situation exacerbated by William's poor judgement, by his mother's pain at William's want of consideration and outward signs of affection for her and, worst of all, by the willingness of Bismarck, still Chancellor, to encourage, for his own political purposes, the children's marked preference for their grandparents over their parents.

The trouble came to a climax when Queen Victoria was reluctant to invite William and his wife to her jubilee celebrations. She consulted her daughter, took her advice and sent an invitation, whereupon William telegraphed his pleasure at having been honoured with the duty of 'representing' the German Emperor at his grandmother's jubilee. It was characteristic of the Queen's extraordinary tact that she succeeded without offence in conveying to William that there was no question of 'representation', nor of the relative importance of himself and his parents, and equally without offence in protecting the Emperor's authority and saving the sensitive feelings of the Crown Prince and Princess.

But the trouble with William continued after June 1888 when he himself became Emperor. From 1889 up to and including 1895 he annually visited his grandmother at Osborne and attended Cowes Regatta, though until 1891, not being a member of the Royal Yacht Club, he could not race. Just as regularly he succeeded in giving offence to the Prince of Wales. Apart from this the trouble with William was entangled with Anglo–German relations and must for the moment be left while something is said of the Crown

Princess's personal tragedy in 1887–8. It is not fully covered by this selection of letters. It is better covered by Frederick Ponsonby in *Letters of the Empress Frederick* (Macmillan, 1928). But even this cannot convey the full poignancy of her letters, when she was fighting against the rational diagnosis of her husband's trouble with voice and throat as cancer, and of the doctor's daily telegrams to the Queen from San Remo and later from Berlin during Frederick's hundred days as Emperor. The present selection of letters shows, however, something of the attitude of Germany to the Crown Prince and Princess during the illness and of the controversies centred upon it, all of which seemed to degenerate into arguments about the superiority of German over English medicine.

The first symptom of Frederick's fatal illness was the hoarseness recorded in the Queen's letter of 26 February 1887. On 15 March the Crown Princess wrote the first of her many letters largely concerned with her husband's illness (not printed). On 16 April the Queen hoped the hoarseness was better for she was 'worried at its lasting so long'. By then the couple were at Ems and he was taking the cure. His general health seemed to improve but the growth in the throat was still there. There was next dispute between the German doctors over whether there should be surgery or no surgery. Before the use of X-rays a dangerous operation would have to be performed blind from the outside. Since Frederick was heir to the throne and the ruling Emperor was ninety, both a fatal operation and a fatal illness were of the utmost political importance, so Bismarck insisted on further consultations. These took place and a recommendation to operate resulted. Bismarck was still not satisfied and insisted on the best throat specialist in Europe being summoned.

On 17 May the Crown Princess, not knowing the outcome of the consultations, telegraphed that Morell Mackenzie of London had been asked for. This is the unintelligible cipher mentioned in the Queen's letter of 18 May. The falsehood soon established itself in Germany that the Princess's

English prejudices had led her to distrust the German doctors and to send for Mackenzie. Morell Mackenzie arrived at Berlin on 20 May. He, with the support of the German, Professor Virchow, denied that the growth was malignant. This is the explanation of the Queen's emotion in her letter of 27 May. It was now arranged that the Crown Prince and Princess, with German doctors in attendance, should go to England – to Norwood, then a quiet suburb near Dulwich – to take part in the jubilee celebrations and for Frederick to be treated in Mackenzie's London clinic. Afterwards, in August, the Crown Prince went to Braemar while the Queen was at Balmoral and the Princess stayed with English friends, visited Waddesdon and toured country houses in Devon. The Prince's general health continued to improve. But already pressure to return to Berlin because of William I's age had begun. There was now dispute in Germany over whether the Prince should or should not return and it continued after he and the Princess went to San Remo on the Italian Riviera. Their absence from Berlin led to young William's increasing political activity and the Princess gives full rein to her anxiety lest intrigue centring on him should succeed in setting Frederick aside in favour of William. But William and Henry paid a visit to Baveno without untoward incident. On 6 November 1887, Morell Mackenzie, though still refusing to be certain, diagnosed cancer, but an operation was deferred until 9 February 1888. The postponement of the operation was the cause of further charges against the Crown Princess and further controversy. She still resisted the notion of cancer and wrote even on 9 February 'that the malignant illness does not exist'. Then in March there was fresh dispute between English and German doctors over the insertion of a canula in Fritz's throat, indeed over the best device, German or English. By now Fritz was Emperor Frederick III. William I had died on 9 March 1888, and the Crown Prince and Princess travelled at once to Berlin which they reached on 11 March. Frederick III acted with great energy publishing a proclamation and a letter asking

Bismarck to remain as Chancellor almost at once. On 13 March he was back in bed. In mid-April the Queen visited the Emperor and Empress at Charlottenburg which made up for her earlier disappointment when a proposed meeting in Florence had been cancelled in March. On 15 June 1888 Frederick died.

In 1888/9 the treatment of Frederick III's illness was debated in Germany with even more bitterness than in 1887/8. William, now Emperor William II, called for a report from the doctors and published extracts in the *National Zeitung* and then published the whole as a pamphlet. With the Empress's permission Morell Mackenzie, now Sir Morell Mackenzie, published his view in *The Fatal Illness of Frederick the Noble* (October 1888). Much to the indignation of both correspondents the book was at once banned in Germany. This did not stop the newspaper articles. Nothing could be sounder than the Queen's advice: 'Now let me tell you that I hope you won't read nasty newspapers. They should be burnt and no one should let you see them. It only irritates and does no good. I never read nasty things for that very reason' (unprinted letter of 8 August 1888).

The Empress was by 1889 the Empress Frederick. Her laments shifted to more direct complaint against William. He announced that Friedrichskron, so called while the Crown Prince lived there, was again to be called Neues Palais; he decorated Puttkamer, the minister whom Frederick III had asked to resign; he pointedly thanked Heinrich Treitschke for his account, which the Empress Frederick disliked, of Frederick's reign; he embarked on a visit to the Tsar and a Baltic sea voyage which his mother thought incompatible with mourning for his father; he renewed the ban (referred to below on p. 11) on her second daughter's marriage with Prince·Alexander. This last was fortunately now irrelevant since Alexander no longer wished for it anyway. The Empress Frederick had reason for complaint on less personal grounds when on 17 December 1889 Maximilian von Lynckner, a court official, suddenly sent to her a letter written to him by Frederick III but unopened, in which the Emperor had stated his wishes about funeral arrangements. The Queen's letter of 27 December, referring to this, was typical of her mixture of sympathy and common sense which relaxed her daughter's tension without encouraging her criticism. She was at pains to explain that William's mistakes were ones of manner, thoughtlessness and youth, not of heartlessness, though she was ready enough 'to put him in his place' and ridicule him when he addressed her as 'dear colleague'. She only once (18 June 1889) seriously remonstrated with her daughter when, in a letter (unprinted) of 14 June, she wrote of the wrongs inflicted upon her by the court at Berlin as ones she 'could never forget or forgive'. When William paid his first visit to Osborne, 2–8 August 1889, the Queen realizing she could not put him off determined to make it a success. William made her *Chef* of Frederick's former regiment of dragoons and she conferred on him the title of Admiral of the Fleet.

The turning-point came with the fall of Bismarck in March 1890. Under General Caprivi William was no longer the son used against his mother by a hostile party. William's first exploit, the summoning of an international conference to consider the social question was, as the Queen hastens to explain, a step in a direction to which Frederick III would have been sympathetic. Moreover, Caprivi embarked upon a policy of reconciliation, seeking to harmonize the classes and parties that the political tension in which Bismarck worked best, had set against each other. He survived all Bismarck's attempts to discredit him and all the 'interviews' and articles Bismarck published in the newspapers. By 1893 Caprivi and Bismarck had each driven the other into untenable positions. The reinstatement of Bismarck into court and society at Berlin was unlikely, therefore, to have any political consequences and seemed only fair and civil. Caprivi's trade treaties, relaxing and diversifying Bismarck's more rigid protective duties, were the most successful part of his policy. The Empress Frederick comments on these and also on some of the reforms which he encouraged

6

in Prussia. The principle he applied in finance was the old one of using direct taxes to provide the revenue of the states (Miquel introduced an income tax for Prussia in 1891) and indirect taxes to provide the revenue for the Empire but the Reichstag opposed most of the indirect taxes which Miquel had wished to introduce, and the Empress Frederick's fears about a tax on works of art were not realized.

The worst part of Caprivi's policy badly divided Prussia and William's intervention in it did his reputation no good. This related to schools. By its School Bill his government attempted to strengthen the power of the churches in education but was defeated and had to withdraw its bill. Both correspondents were interested also in Caprivi's Army Bill. A small increase in the army had been made in 1889 to enable it to accommodate the increasing number of men liable for military service as the German population rose. But the bill of 1892 increased the army by 84,000 men, with proportionate increases in officers and NCOs costing an extra sixty-four million marks a year. The bill failed in the Reichstag where Caprivi had mismanaged his negotiations with the parties. The Empress Frederick knows nothing of these political details and reports only the general feeling of discontent. Caprivi dissolved the Reichstag. The elections of June 1893 brought an increase in the strength of extremist parties: right conservatives and social democrats. The bill nevertheless was passed on 15 July 1893. After that the chancellorship of Hohenlohe brought an interval of political peace or inactivity in domestic affairs.

The Empress Frederick had by this time achieved a better relationship with William, or, rather, she had been deflected from her bad relationship with him by fresh interests. She took comfort in her younger children and in the next generation. Henry had married Irène of Hesse Darmstadt, third daughter of Princess Alice, in 1888 and the Empress Frederick was with them at Kiel for the birth of her first grandchild outside William's family (which she complained was kept from her). Her third daughter (Sophie) married the younger son of the King of Greece (Tino) at Athens in

7

October 1889. Her second daughter, Victoria or Moretta, married Prince Adolf of Schaumburg-Lippe in November 1890 and her youngest daughter, Mossy, married her Fischy, Frederick Charles of Hesse Kassel, in January 1893. All her children were now married and the birth of grand-children became increasingly important to her. From 1889 the house she was building, Friedrichshof near Homburg, then furnishing and later filling with her guests, occupied another part of her mind.

A further reason why she could think of the affronts which William inflicted upon her less personally was that she had now taken his measure. She knew he had no application, no capacity for sustained effort or for continuity. She knew after 1890 his settled pattern of life: the spring in Berlin would be followed by the *Nordlandreise* in the summer, the manoeuvres in the early autumn and hunting parties in the late autumn and winter, ending perhaps with a visit to Corfu. She resented William's quarrel with Sophie over her entry into the Orthodox Church (December 1890–2). She resented his sending his own doctor to enquire when Sophie's first child was born prematurely. She resented his unexpected visits to Friedrichshof with numbers of attend-ants. But in each case she accepted the Queen's common sense and conciliatory explanations and advice.

William's unfortunate speeches and telegrams, his ill-judged incursions into policy and their disastrous effect on Anglo–German relations seriously troubled both correspon-dents to the end. The most notorious speeches began in 1891 with his reference to Napoleon as the 'Corsican upstart' (September) and his observation in taking the oath from army recruits that they might be called upon to shoot their own relatives (November). Then in February 1892 at a banquet given by its president to the members of the provincial diet at Brandenburg, he made a bombastic reference to his responsibility 'to God, our former ally of Rossbach and Dennwitz who will not leave me in the lurch'. He made another unfortunate speech on the anniversary of Sedan in September 1895 and at Kiel in 1897 and, in seeing

8

General von Waldersee off to command the international force in China, he bade him behave like the Huns of old and give no quarter. He disapproved of Ernst of Lippe Biesterfeld taking over Detmold from Prince Adolf and telegraphed his dislike of Ernst's tone, beginning: 'To Regents what is due to regents, nothing more'. His visit to Rome in 1893 and journey to Palestine in 1898 worried both the Queen and her daughter, but passed without dangerous consequences.

After 1890 the Empress Frederick's principal complaint is her exclusion from the political world in Germany. She writes with pleasure that the King of Italy or Willy of Greece (i.e. King George) will still talk politics with her and respect her political judgement. Worst of all she feels her powerlessness to stop the growing hostility to Britain in Germany after 1896 and the corresponding hostility to Germany in Britain. She is, however, sufficiently detached to put in coolly and calmly her contribution towards better feeling. When she met William at Strassburg after the celebrations at Wörth on 18 October 1895, she had a long conversation with him which she renewed on 21 November at Rumpenheim, sounding him out about a possible concerted Anglo–German policy in relation to Turkey. The substance of the last conversation was sent to Hatzfeldt, the ambassador in London. Again in August 1898 when William visited her at Friedrichshof the Empress Frederick invited Sir Frank Lascelles, the British ambassador at Berlin, to lunch and his conversation with William was important enough for him to report it to Balfour. Her intervention was, of course, fruitless.

Soon afterwards the Empress Frederick's sources of relief from the pain William caused her were themselves turned to dust and ashes when she too succumbed to the same disease that had killed her husband. The reader suspects something when she reports to her mother from Dalmeny in November 1898 fits of giddiness and pain in the ear. But the allusions in the surviving letters are cryptic and covered up by full details of painful lumbago. The nearest one gets to allusion to the incurable illness is a remark in the Queen's letters that she had given this or that detail about her daughter's health to someone but 'said nothing more'. The Empress Frederick had asked for correspondence about her illness to be burnt and the end of the personal tragedy, like its beginning, is barely reflected in the preserved letters.

The International Background

The first incident in international affairs which is touched on in the correspondence relates to the union of the two Bulgarias. In 1876 the Bulgarians had rebelled against their Turkish ruler and a Bulgarian state independent of Turkey, except for the payment of tribute, and Eastern Roumelia, a Bulgarian province still part of the Turkish Empire, were the outcome of the Russo–Turkish war and the Treaty of Berlin. In September 1885 Eastern Roumelia had proclaimed its reunion with Bulgaria and its allegiance to Prince Alexander – the Sandro of the letters – Prince of Bulgaria. Between 1876 and 1878 Russia had supported a Bulgaria that should include all Bulgarians, whereas Britain, especially Salisbury, had worked for a small Bulgaria leaving the Balkan mountain range as a defence for Turkey. This policy had largely failed and in 1885–7 they reversed their support: Russia opposed the union under Prince Alexander and Britain, with Salisbury as foreign secretary, supported the union and Alexander.

This policy suited both the Queen's anti-Russian and her pro-Battenberg feelings. There were four Battenberg brothers and one sister. The eldest Ludwig (Louis) had married Victoria Alberta (Victoria B. or Battenberg), daughter of Princess Alice (d. 1878) and the Queen's granddaughter. The second was the Prince of Bulgaria and a favourite of the Queen. The third, Henry, the Liko of the letters, married Princess Beatrice in 1885. The fourth, Franzjos, and his marriage to Anna of Montenegro, also play a part in the correspondence, and the sister, Marie Erbach, was often the Queen's guest. Yet another Battenberg link was planned. Moretta, second daughter of the Crown Prince and Princess, had met Prince Alexander in 1879 when she was thirteen and in 1885 accepted him as her future husband. This love match, which the Queen believed she had been the first to suggest, was postponed in deference to the wishes of the Emperor William I and the Empress Augusta. But the political opposition of Bismarck who had recognized the primacy of Russian influence in Bulgaria in the Three Emperors' Alliance (1881) was even more important. Confrontation between Britain and Russia was successfully avoided at diplomatic level while first Salisbury, then Rosebery and then Salisbury again concentrated on working through the European Concert to restrain the territorial ambitions of Bulgaria's neighbours, Serbia and Greece, who were both preparing to assert their claims to Macedonia lest Bulgaria should get there first. Serbian peace with Bulgaria (3 March 1886), a naval blockade of Greece ending with her submission (June 1886) and a Bulgarian–Turkish agreement (February 1886) were the fruits of this policy.

While politics worked for Britain and against Russia, a personal calamity destroyed dynastic and family peace. Russian Panslavists took the law into their own hands and on the night of 20/21 August 1886, officers of the Bulgarian army inspired by them kidnapped Prince Alexander. Their object was to cause such chaos in Bulgaria as to justify a Russian occupation, so they released their prisoner on Russian territory near the Russo–Roumanian border, where he was met by his brothers Louis and Franzjos. Alexander, on Louis's advice, appealed by telegram in what the Queen called 'that fatal message' to Tsar Alexander III. The 'brutal' Tsar replied by counselling Alexander to abdicate. This he did on 7 September. Bulgaria remained for ten months under a three-man regency of Stambulov, Mutkarov and Karavelov. Russian policy in Bulgaria was then represented by General Kaulbars while Bulgarian patriots concentrated on finding a ruler to replace Prince Alexander. For this purpose delegates from the Bulgarian parliament made the rounds of the European capitals. They were not welcomed in St Petersburg but the Prince of Mingrelia, the Russian candidate, was not pressed. Ferdinand of Coburg in 1887 offered himself to the Bulgarian Delegates and was elected Prince by the Bulgarian parliament in July. Thus, the Bulgarian Prince was still among Queen Victoria's family connections.

This dynastic link with Bulgaria proved to be the nucleus of an extensive Balkan network. The marriage of Sophie to Tino, the future King Constantine of Greece, was the most notable contribution to this. The old patronizing attitude to Greece which allowed her to be blockaded in Rosebery's time (1886) disappears from the correspondence and the Empress Frederick shows much interest and concern about internal developments and finally much sympathy for Greece at the time of the Greek war with Turkey over Crete (see Arthur Gould Lee, ed., *The Empress Frederick Writes to Sophie*, Faber and Faber, 1955). Greece was eventually to return this sympathy by offering volunteers and other help during the British South African War. Moreover, the Empress Frederick was to promote an understanding between Bulgaria and Greece by bringing Ferdinand and Tino together. But the next link was achieved by the marriage of Missy, the eldest daughter of Prince Alfred, the Duke of Edinburgh, to another Ferdinand, the heir to King Carol (Charles) of Roumania. This brought the Queen into close contact with the affairs of Elisabeth of Wied, wife of Charles, a wayward and temperamental character, known later as Carmen Sylva, who was sent back to her mother's care in Neuwied when a *mauvaise passion* for Hélène Vacaresco threatened scandal in Bucharest.

The last link was with Montenegro with whose Prince the Queen made acquaintance in 1897. His daughter Anna in that year married Francis Joseph, the youngest Battenberg brother. The Queen's comment on the engagement is one of two or three reflections in the correspondence on the European alliances and alignments which once so preoccupied historians of the origins of the First World War.

The Queen commented on its importance for British relations with Italy and Russia since other daughters of the
Prince of Montenegro had married into their royal houses.
This comment reflected two elements of Salisbury's alignments. It was his policy to seek a European base for Britain
in close relations with Italy, Austria-Hungary and, if possible, Germany. For this purpose, ten years before, in 1887,
he had signed the Mediterranean Agreements with the first
two. At that time the Queen had justly noticed his important conversations with Corti of Italy and Hatzfeldt of
Germany in her letters and most interestingly repeated to
her daughter Salisbury's wish for alliance but refusal of it in
accordance with Castlereagh's principle fifty years earlier of
not committing Britain on speculative contingencies. The
Crown Princess, on her side, in an unprinted letter of
17 October 1887, had repeated to the Queen the gist of what
was in fact the secret Re-insurance Treaty signed between
Germany and Russia in that year. The other element of
Salisbury's policy which the Queen's 1897 comment reflects
is the dropping of anti-Russian precautions (the Russo-
phobia of Palmerston and Disraeli) and the attempt to
improve relations with Russia which followed the accession
of Nicholas II in 1894. Nicky in that year had married
Alicky, the youngest child of Princess Alice and a granddaughter of the Queen. This not only brought the pair to
Balmoral as guests of the Queen but did in fact ease the
improvement of Anglo–Russian relations, for Salisbury had
important if not immediately fruitful conversations with the
new Tsar there. In 1898 he was to make a formal but equally
fruitless overture to Russia for general cooperation in
China.

Neither writer of course ever refers to the specific terms of
treaties but both were acutely aware of the deterioration in
Anglo–German relations from about 1894 onwards, with the
lowest point in 1896 at the time of William II's telegram to
President Kruger congratulating him on the Transvaal's
defeat of the Jameson raid. The Empress Frederick deplores
the German adoption of a colonial policy at the time of the

dispute over Zanzibar but neither writer notices the clearing up of colonial disputes by the treaty of 1893. She again deplored Germany's interference in the Congo in 1894. A more persistent lament was the building up of German influence in Turkey and the policy of isolated assertion pursued by Germany, apart from the five other members of the European Concert, when the Cretan and Armenian questions arose in the 1890s.

In order to understand the Empress Frederick's comments on Greek affairs it is important to realize just how small the political world in Greece was, so that power virtually oscillated there between Charilaos Tricoupis, brought up in London and Paris, with ideas of economic development and polarized party politics, and Theodore Deligiannis, or Delyannos as the Empress Frederick consistently spells his name, with his more relaxed attitude to finance and clientele politics and a sharper voice when it came to Greek claims on Macedonia or Crete. She champions Tricoupis and laments the harm done by Delyannos. He was in power in 1891 when there was restlessness in Crete and Greek agitation to support the Cretans in their wish for union with Greece or, at least, independence from Turkey. The Queen echoes Salisbury in blaming Greeks as well as Turks for the troubles and, though she passes on to Salisbury the Empress Frederick's pleas for British intervention, she was not moved by them. Delyannos was again in power in 1895 when Greek claims on Macedonia were agitated. There were revolutionary committees at work within Macedonia; Serbia was founding schools for Macedonian Serbs; and Bulgaria, encouraged by European recognition in 1896 of Ferdinand as her legitimate ruler, procured from Turkey the founding of fresh bishoprics for the Bulgarian church there. Crete erupted first: in January 1897 there was a full rising against Turkish rule and fresh supportive agitation in Athens.

King George of Greece (Willy) was restraining, but a naval expedition under Prince George, Tino's elder brother, went off to Crete in February and General Vassos landed with 1,500 men and proclaimed the occupation of the island in the King's name. Salisbury had organized the presence of an international naval force off Crete and a force of five ships' companies occupied the capital with Turkey's consent. William II pursued an isolated policy, holding aloof from the international action already begun, and it became Germany's policy to press for the international coercion of Greece (not Crete). The diplomatic deadlock was broken by Turkey's declaration of war on Greece on 18 April and the Greek defeat in Thessaly at the battle of Domokos. Greco–Turk negotiations, armistice in May and peace in December 1897 secured self-government for Crete and a high war indemnity for Turkey. William II still pursued an anti-Greek and pro-Turk policy when it came to the question of negotiating for the withdrawal of Turkish troops from Thessaly, as Greece struggled to pay her indemnity with the help of European banks, and of finding a Christian governor for Crete. Before the peace was finally ratified and Turkish troops withdrawn there was a further phase of international pressure upon Crete from which William II again held aloof. But in November 1898 Turkey withdrew and Prince George of Greece entered upon a three-year (reduced from five years to pacify opposition) period as governor of Crete, having been elected by the Cretan parliament.

In November 1894 the newspapers in England and the Empress Frederick from Germany were already writing about Turkish massacres of Armenians. Because of their dispersal from Erzerum to Cilicia the Armenians could not claim at this time an independent Armenian state. The Armenian patriarch sought from Turkey, not independence, but protection for the lives, religion and property of Armenians wherever they lived. The situation was characterized by local and spontaneous killing and looting, arising from the age-old hatred between Muslims and Christians, incapable Turkish governors and an army which, sent in to maintain law and order, soon joined in the looting. Internationally the situation was affected by humanitarian agitation in England and France, reaching peak points in

1896 and 1898 – Gladstone's last crusade – and by the cooperation of Britain, France and Russia, acting under Article 61 of the Treaty of Berlin, in putting pressure upon Turkey to enquire, to appoint capable governors and organize effective military control. Germany joined in none of this. On the contrary, when Turkey sent a Turkish commission to conduct an enquiry it was made up of generals who had done three years' military service in Germany and General von der Goltz was attached to it. If it was odd for Britain and Russia to be acting together in an eastern question, it was still odder for William II to blame the Armenian massacres on Armenian provocation and the English humanitarians.

The South African War, as both correspondents constantly notice, was fought against a background of German and French criticism and of general continental suspicion. Indeed the Queen even went to the extent of avoiding her annual continental journey because of it. But by then the scope of international relations had much widened. To the continent of Europe, the Middle East and Africa, had been added the Pacific, China, Japan and the United States. This widening had begun already in 1895. In that year Britain held aloof from the international pressure, in which Germany and Russia took a lead, to compel Japan to restore to China the Liaotung Peninsula which she had taken as spoils of war. The Empress Frederick writes of the wisdom of the British policy. Henry's posting to Chinese waters with the German navy in 1897 is a reminder of the leasing of Kiao Chiou to Germany. Russia had leased Port Arthur and Britain Wei-Hai-Wei. The settlement of the Samoan dispute with Germany in 1899 by a partition of the islands is a sign of a partial improvement in Anglo–German relations that immediately preceded the fresh outburst of Anglophobia stimulated by the South African War. But the correspondence of course shows no inkling of the soundings for a German alliance that Chamberlain took in 1898/9.

Meanwhile, from April to July 1898 the Spanish–American War was fought. The Queen saw no justification at all for this war and both correspondents deplored it. The Spanish were defeated and America took Cuba (given independence in 1902), Puerto Rico and the Philippines from them. The war remained for the Queen a war to relieve Spain of Cuba because she misgoverned it. The last international action of the Queen's reign arose out of China's inability to pay the war indemnity demanded of her by Japan. She could only do so by the aid of European loans, and Russia on one side and Britain and Germany on the other were rivals for her custom. China was right to tell Russia and Britain, as the Queen noticed (on 9 February 1898), that they did so at the pistol point. By a misunderstanding and a mistranslation of a Chinese term the young men who served in the militia were popularly known as the Boxers and the anti-foreign riots which eventually ensued became known as the Boxer rising. By 17 June 1900 Russia, Germany and Britain were committed to military operations in China. Two days later the German minister, von Ketteler, was killed in a street in Peking where the foreign legations were under siege. By the time the international force under von Waldersee had been organized, the Boxer movement was over and only a fresh ruffling of Anglo–German relations had resulted.

The British Background

The Queen's ideal government was a quiet one. She liked ministers who cared for stability and social harmony. She did not like change and uncertainty. She 'felt safe' with Lord Salisbury. He had come in as prime minister in June 1885 without a general election. When the new registers – they had to be revised after the Reform Acts of 1884 and 1885 – were complete, the general election was held. The Queen was disturbed by the Irish vote, wherever there was one, going to the Conservative candidates, but took comfort in Salisbury's having been persuaded by two cabinet collea- gues to try out the Home Rule issue with the electorate and, when it proved to be no attraction, in his reversion to the more orthodox Conservative disdain for the Parnellites. Later (in June 1886) she admired his speech at Leeds explaining his view that Home Rule for Ireland was impracticable.

The Queen disliked Gladstone because he stirred up the country, 'setting class against class' as she was to notice in July 1886, and she protested at his conduct during the election when he treated all Britain as his constituency and did not confine himself to Midlothian, his actual constituency. In January 1886 the Queen had to accept a Gladstone government. The Liberals (333), however, only had a majority over the Conservatives (251) if the Parnellites (86) in the Commons supported them. She opened parliament in person, something she had declined to do between Prince Albert's death and 1874, on 21 January 1886. Salisbury resigned and Gladstone replaced him with Lord Rosebery as foreign secretary. The Queen was much disturbed by the uncertainty when Gladstone refused to declare his hand over Home Rule for Ireland. He had not been able to retain the Whig wing of his 1880–5 cabinet and was afraid he would lose the Chamberlainites if he came out for Home Rule too soon. The Queen came to admire Chamberlain's ability (she was to visit Birmingham in 1887 and 1897) and was shrewd enough or well enough briefed, to understand that in 1886 Chamberlain was out to destroy the Home Rule Bill which Gladstone had at last introduced on 8 April, and that no amount of manoeuvring on Gladstone's part at the second reading (10 May) would keep him in the Liberal party (he had already resigned from the government). She never seems to have coupled Chamberlain with Dilke, who had been his ally in 1880–5. Her animus against Dilke went back to his early republicanism and was only strengthened by the two lawsuits of 1886 in which he was involved. In the first he was cited as co-respondent in a divorce case, pleaded not guilty but would not go into the witness box. The second, which he brought in order to clear his name, since the plaintiff in the first had got her divorce despite the case against himself being dismissed, resulted in a verdict virtually convicting him of perjury.

Gladstone's Home Rule Bill failed, though not as quickly as the Queen had expected. It was not defeated until 8 June. Gladstone did not resign but asked for a dissolution of parliament and appealed to the country. The general election began on 1 July. The country deliberately declared against the Liberals and on 21 July 1886, Gladstone and his government resigned. The change of government was completed by the end of the month and with Salisbury as prime minister the Queen was comfortable again. Lord Iddesleigh was at the foreign office until his death led to Salisbury's taking it on. Lord Randolph Churchill was chancellor of the exchequer and a number of new men, such as W.H. Smith at the war office and H. Matthews at the home office, completed the cabinet. Churchill was leader of the House of Commons and came into regular contact with the Queen as the writer each evening of the report to her of the day's proceedings. He was the chancellor who never presented a budget for he resigned at the end of the year hoping to be accepted back on his own terms. In this he was disappointed for Salisbury had a successor ready in G.J. Goschen. He and particularly his wife, because of their German connections, were known to and liked by the Empress Frederick.

The Salisbury government carried the Queen through her golden jubilee (in 1887) and remained in office until 1892 with a firm policy in Ireland and few domestic incidents. The Queen appreciated the importance of the Commons' strengthening its power to close debate by new rules of procedure and commented on the passing of these. She wrote to her daughter about the so-called 'Bloody Sunday', 13 November 1887, when the Social Democratic Federation defied a police attempt to stop Trafalgar Square being used for open-air meetings. The Queen was shocked that of the two ringleaders arrested one (R. Cunninghame Graham) should have been an MP, but takes no notice of John Burns, the other. She was not much disturbed by it. Another incident or series of incidents which drew comment from her related to the decline in the government's popularity when the tribunal investigating the Pigott forgeries showed

up the wrong done to Parnell, and the recovery of its
fortunes at the end of the same year (1890) when Parnell
was revealed to be no hero after all by the O'Shea divorce
case. The Queen's chief comment related to the consequent
breach (26 November 1890) between Gladstone and the
Parnellites from which she augured well for the future. She
did not understand that by breaking with Parnell Gladstone
was merely safeguarding a future Home Rule Bill.

The so-called 'dull parliament', acceptably dull to the
Queen, completed its term and was dissolved on 28 June
1892. The general election began on 4 July and by 13 July,
when most of the returns were known, a Liberal victory was
foreseen. The Queen wrote on that day (unprinted letter)
rightly recognizing that there had been no real swing in the
country towards the Liberals and regretting the 'disagreeable ordeal' of having to accept a Gladstone government.
The Liberal majority against Conservatives and Unionists
combined, even including their Irish supporters, was only
forty – Lady Salisbury's 'forty thieves'. Salisbury resigned
on 11 August and 'the best government of the century', as
the Queen described it (20 August), was over. Gladstone
was prime minister with Lord Rosebery again foreign
secretary, but only four others (Spencer, Kimberley, Harcourt and Ripon) were familiar faces to the Queen. 'These
horrid new people' included Asquith at the home office,
Campbell Bannerman at the war office, Lord Herschel as
lord chancellor and H.H. Fowler at the local government
board. These last three the Queen came to like. Meanwhile,
she reconciled herself to Gladstone's fresh attempt to carry
Home Rule, but yielded nothing to his clumsy effort in the
long 'essay' of 27 October to persuade her of its desirability.
The bill introduced in February 1893 was rejected by the
Lords in September. The Queen was to end her life with her
conviction unshaken that Home Rule as a remedy for Irish
grievances was an illusion. Gladstone lasted as prime
minister only six months longer. Her final verdict on him
was not without justice: 'a clever man, full of talent . . . a
good and very religious man . . . but he never tried to keep

up the honour and prestige of England'. Rosebery succeeded him in March 1894. The Queen soon believed she
had exchanged bad for worse. Rosebery as foreign secretary
'could restrain the others'; as prime minister he either
couldn't or wouldn't. He lacked authority. The crisis in their
relations came in October, when Rosebery announced his
policy of reforming the House of Lords. The Queen formally
complained to him as she told her daughter (30 October)
that he had 'entirely ignored the opinion of the sovereign'.
Rosebery fell in 1895. Her verdict on him, that he did not
believe what he said, hit off the particularly unconvincing
quality of Rosebery the politician.

By 26 June Salisbury was again her prime minister and
was foreign secretary as well. The Queen might exchange
with regret Rosebery's personal warmth for Salisbury's
more aloof demeanour, but she had been early informed of
the likelihood of Conservative and Unionist coalescence
under him and welcomed it. The new ministry had few
surprises for her. Its life was dominated by Africa. It
organized the successful Ashanti expedition (on which
Prince Henry died) to defend the British colony on the Gold
Coast (Ghana) and the reconquest of the Sudan, thus in the
Queen's eyes atoning for Gordon's murder. In the end, in
1899/1900, it found itself engaged in the South African War
as well as in defending foreign interests in China by war and
by contributing to the international force. This government
carried the Queen through her diamond jubilee (1897) and
tumultuous demonstrations in London in 1900 as well as
her visit to Ireland in 1899. Domestic politics drop out of the
correspondence except for praise of Chamberlain's parlia-
mentary performance in 1900. In foreign policy she plays
her part by entertaining Nicholas II in 1896 at Balmoral and
William II in 1898 at Windsor and by transmitting to her
daughter ideas with which Salisbury had imbued her mind.
But as has been already suggested her attitude to foreign
questions was personal and unintellectual. Whereas the
Empress Frederick was speculative and delighted in entertaining probabilities and positing ideal solutions, the Queen

was guided by Salisbury's general principle of 'not promising help when we don't know what for' and her instinct for defending British possessions and power. She was spared any further change of government because the so-called khaki election of October 1900, when the campaign cry of 'a vote for the Liberals is a vote for the Boers', confirmed the Conservatives in power until her death in 1901.

Queen Victoria's Indian Servants

(in order of arrival)

Abdul Karim (the Munshi, or Indian secretary, literally 'language teacher')

Mahmoud Bakhutschina

Karim al Ali, March 1888 to October 1889

Ahmed Hussein, arrived 1888 but did not stay after 1889

Yussuf Bey, from October 1889

Harmet Ali

Mustafa Chedra

The Families

(with familiar names; the first named
parent being a child of Queen Victoria)

**Princess Victoria (Vicky) and Prince Frederick (Fritz)
(Crown Prince and Princess of Prussia until March
1888, then German Emperor and Empress from March
to June 1888, and she was Empress Frederick from
then until 1901)**

William II, German Emperor (Willie)
Charlotte
Henry
Sigismund (Siggie, who had died in 1866)
Victoria (Vicky or Moretta)
Waldemar (Waldie, who had died in 1879)
Sophie
Margaret (Mossy)

**Albert Edward, Prince of Wales, King Edward VII
(Bertie) and Princess, later Queen, Alexandra (Alix)**

Albert Victor, Duke of Clarence (Eddy)
George, later King George V (Georgie)
Louise (who married the Duke of Fife)
Victoria Alexandra
Maud (who married Prince Charles of Denmark, later
King Haakon of Norway)

24

Princess Alice and Grand Duke Louis IV
of Hesse Darmstadt

Victoria Alberta (Victoria B., after marriage to Prince
Louis of Battenberg)
Elizabeth (Ella)
Irène (Ninny)
Ernest (Ernie)
Alix (Alicky)

Alfred, Duke of Edinburgh, and, after 1893,
of Saxe-Coburg-Gotha (Affie) and Marie,
Grand Duchess of Russia (Marie E.)

Alfred (Young Alfred or Young Affie)
Marie (Missy)
Victoria Melita (Ducky)
Alexandra (Sandra)
Beatrice (Baby Bee)

Princess Helena (Lenchen) and Christian,
Prince of Schleswig-Holstein

Christian Victor (Christle)
Albert (Abbat or Abby)
Helena Victoria (Tora or Thora)
Marie Louise (Louise Holstein or Louie)

Princess Louise and the Marquess of Lorne

No children

Arthur, Duke of Connaught, and Louise,
Princess of Prussia (Louischen)

Margaret (Daisy)
Arthur (Young Arthur)
Victoria Patricia (Patsy)

Leopold, Duke of Albany, and Helen, Princess of Waldeck-Pyrmont

Alice
Charles Edward (Charlie)

Princess Beatrice (Baby) and Henry, Prince of Battenberg (Liko)

Alexander (Drino or Sandrino)
Victoria Eugenie (Ena)
Leopold
Maurice

The Battenberg Princes and Princess

Louis or Ludwig
Alexander (Sandro)
Henry (Liko)
Marie (Marie Erbach)
Francis Joseph (Franzjos)

Emperor William II and Empress Augusta (Dona)

William
Eitel Friedrich (Fritz)
Adalbert
Augustus William
Oscar
Joachim
Victoria Louise

The Letters

The story begins with a crisis in Bulgaria where Alexander of Battenberg (Sandro), a favourite of Queen Victoria, was Prince. His elder brother had married a granddaughter of the Queen, while a younger brother,Prince Henry (Liko), had married the Queen's youngest daughter, Princess Beatrice. Liko and Beatrice as well as Sandro are prominent characters in the story which the letters tell. Another prominent character, Moretta, the Crown Princess's second daughter, hoped to marry Sandro, but encountered the opposition of the German Crown. The Queen's letter of 21 May 1888 gives the story. But the crisis of 1885/6 was political. Bulgaria had only just achieved independence from the Sultan of Turkey and still paid tribute to Constantinople. Also, Queen Victoria's liking was more than matched by the enmity of Tsar Alexander. He hated Sandro's refusal to be dominated or to be politically Slav. He hated even more Sandro's acquisition of the southern Bulgarian province then called Eastern Roumelia. The introduction to this book explains how this came about and how it set Greece and other Balkan countries with frustrated territorial desires, on the march and the European blockade of Greece which resulted.

From the Queen
OSBORNE, JANUARY 23, 1886

... We have encouraging accounts from Constantinople and as Mr Gladstone has stated his approval of Lord Salisbury's conduct in foreign affairs and especially of the Roumelian question which was in accordance with the feelings of the country, Russia has nothing to hope from any change. And the stupid Tsar cannot depose Sandro who I am sure will never and ought never to desert his people; *that* after all is his first duty and object. The pressure on Greece will please the Sultan who is now very well disposed towards Sandro. . . . Mr Gladstone will not speak out [i.e. about Home Rule for Ireland] and he has been called upon to do so. His speech was received in silence the other day except by the Parnellites who cheered him and seemed to be in agreement with him. The debate is adjourned till Monday. I am a good deal tired – by what really is a great exertion [opening parliament] – the long journey there and back, the quantities of things to do, the dressing so early in grande toilette, and the drive there and back with perpetual cheering, and getting four times in and out of the carriage was really a great exertion at my age when you have to attend to so many things besides. . . .

From the Queen
OSBORNE, JANUARY 30, 1886

Only two words to reassure you that nothing dreadful as regards foreign affairs will happen. I have been forced to confide the formation of a Government to that old crazy man Merrypebble [Gladstone], as Louis calls him. . . . And I made it a condition that Pussy [Lord Granville] should not go to the F.O. which he had to own he was not surprised at, as well as that the foreign policy should not be changed. But the bother and nuisance is dreadful. I am well, but most bothered and wretched and it is a great misfortune to lose such a man as Lord Salisbury who is one of the most intelligent and large minded and unprejudiced statesmen I ever saw, besides being so good, so loyal and so courageous. He was overruled about Ireland by two of his own colleagues [Ashbourne and Carnarvon] and this has shaken the faith of those who would have supported him as to his views about Ireland. . . .

From the Crown Princess
BERLIN, FEBRUARY 2, 1886

We hear that the arrangement between the Porte and Sandro is concluded on the basis of his being Governor General of East Roumelia for five years – I think it was wise of him to accept this. It is now said Russia is using this fact against him in Bulgaria and trying to make people believe they (the Russians) could have wrung more concessions from the Turks – in favour of Bulgaria – than Sandro was able, and that his being their Ruler was a bad disadvantage to them. I trust these intrigues will take no effect and if England does not change her policy the young Bulgarian State will steer through the rocks and shoals and breakers into smoother water where it will be plain sailing.

From the Queen
WINDSOR CASTLE, FEBRUARY 17, 1886

... I wish you would not believe what you hear about England. There never was the slightest idea of Sir C. Dilke's coming in. You speak as if I were *pour rien* – or a mere puppet to accept all proposals whereas I never accept people I know won't do – and as for Sir C. Dilke who has got off for a technicality, – his silence when the gravest charges were brought against him, has utterly condemned and ruined him. Look only at the trial. I insisted on Lord Rosebery for the F.O. who is doing remarkably well. I refused to accept Mr Childers at the War Office or Admiralty and Lord Ripon for the India Office. You speak of your hope of the ablest men joining bye and bye and this I believe and hope is not very far distant. Lord Salisbury is doubtless the brightest light I think in the country; but there are some very able younger men amongst the Conservatives as Lord G. Hamilton and Mr Stanhope; and Lord R. Churchill, if he sobers

down, is extremely clever. Then Sir R. Cross and Mr Smith
are two excellent, able men and the latter wonderfully
looked up to in the country. The new Government is firm
about Greece and the three Powers join in agreeing to
blockade the Greek fleet. We hear Russia will probably join
too and even France. Then Servia is being pressed hard and
the Sultan is very friendly to Sandro and the settlement will
I think be very shortly settled. Sandro is thoroughly warned
of, I fear, the danger his life may be in, and every precaution
taken. It is instructive to think that in these days such
things can exist. . . . I send you two books which I think you
will find very interesting and very powerfully written. The
author (whose real name I do not know) is only 21 – and I
must say I think the writing worthy of George Eliot and
Curra Bell [so written, Currer Bell, pseudonym of Charlotte
Brontë]. 'Donovan' should be read first. I have not yet read
'We Two', but Beatrice has and many others and men of
intellect who are immensely struck by it. I hope you like
them.[1] Today is poor Helen's birthday and she came here
yesterday and is going to stay till after little Alice's birthday
on the 25th. . . .

From the Crown Princess
BERLIN, MARCH 19, 1886

Let me again congratulate you on the birth of your
twentieth granddaughter [Victoria Patricia or Patsy]. I am
very sorry to hear that all was not quite normal, but thank
God, the dear baby came into the world all right, and now
all is going on all right; with the first the position of the baby
would have been even more dangerous. You remember me
and William and what a dreadful business it was and with
the result of his poor arm.[2] These insufferable Greeks will
be quiet now soon I hope. They have made such fools of
themselves – I mean neither the King nor his people but the
Government, the press and the chauvinists. There are
sensible Greeks living here who wanted to write to the

Greek newspapers to point out how the Greek people were being deluded but the newspapers would not take the articles.

From the Crown Princess
BERLIN, APRIL 5, 1886

. . . As to my being 'misled' about England, dearest Mama, I never make the pretension of being always right. There are so many things on the spot you are so much more likely to know better and quicker than I do. I can only tell you what I hear, when the source I have it from is such as to make it worth notice! I am always very grateful when you can correct the information, and show it to be imperfect, or mistaken. It is good to hear what is thought by important people on all sides. I am not one given to gleaning views in general as you know, and I have such firm belief in British commonsense and experience – in the firm-rooted loyalty and the prosperity and content which in spite of all dark sides of the picture exist in a greater degree in England than in any other country in the world, that I feel confident of our finding our way safely out of all the stormy days which may be in store. Questions so intricate and huge have to be dealt with that one cannot be astonished at the noise they make. There are more sound and cool heads in England than on the continent and if they keep the upper hand and are not careless, I am sure all will be well. Please do not be angry with me for so crudely putting things. You know how I mean them and that I am the last person to doubt the genuine and affectionate loyalty you are so fortunate as to possess – naturally enough – to so high a degree, and that you will always possess to our happiness and our pride.

From the Queen

WINDSOR CASTLE, APRIL 7, 1886

Dear Leopold's birthday

... Mr Gladstone only thinks of Irish affairs and nothing else. We have just heard Liszt who is such a fine old man. He came down here and played four pieces beautifully. What an exquisite touch.

From the Queen

NEWSHAM HOUSE, LIVERPOOL, MAY 11, 1886

One more line to say that everything went off admirably – excepting that it rained when we drove back. But the crowds, though we only drove through the outskirts of the town [i.e. Liverpool], were marvellous, and the enthusiasm and the perfectly deafening cheering inside the Exhibition as well as outside was more than I have ever seen or heard almost, excepting occasionally in Edinburgh. But such countless numbers you never saw. And they behaved so well – never pushed or crowded. And they looked so delighted only to see their little old Queen. I knighted the Mayor on the steps of the high throne just after the opening was announced – quite a theatrical effect and the burst of cheering was tremendous. I wonder how many people were in the Exhibition. It seems a good one; international machinery, carriages down to the little basket carriages which you children were dragged about in – very large *chars à bancs*, also old travelling post chaises etc. Then boats etc. and poor Grace Darling's own boat. There were 80,000 school children drawn up near the Exhibition who sang 'God Save The Queen'. We drove back here and the Gentlemen changed their uniforms – and we drove to Croxteth and took tea (endless good things) there. The Seftons were much pleased. I recognised the house at once.

Constance Stanley and her very tall nice-looking son, Lord Derby (who told me he considerd the H[ome] R[ule] Bill 'as dead') were there. Today Arthur and Liko dine at a great civic banquet in St George's Hall; tomorrow there will be nothing for me till the afternoon and then the reception in driving through the town will I hear be marvellous after which we go on board a steamer down the river and in the evening Beatrice, Arthur and Liko will go to a Ball given on purpose. I am very tired. Will you kindly let Bertie see this and then send it to Lenchen.

Ps. The music was weak and played too low.

From the Crown Princess
BUCKINGHAM PALACE, MAY 11, 1886

... I am still so miserable and unhappy at parting and nothing would have induced me to shorten the precious time I could spend with you but the feeling that my presence [in Berlin] is needed for so many reasons just now. It is a far harder sacrifice than I can say, or than you can know, not to be able to accept your dear kind offer to stay another few days, a short twelve days in two years is indeed little ... I went to *Faust*[3] yesterday evening. All that artistic taste, arrangement and effect can do to reproduce an impression is wonderfully studied and carried out, and Irving is a very good Mephistopheles, Miss Terry a good Gretchen, but the grand work of art, the real *Faust* is sadly mutilated and difficult to recognise. ...

From the Crown Princess
HOMBURG, MAY 15, 1886

... The Russians are agitating most violently and behind Sandro's back they are treating with the Turks – for the cession of the harbour of Burgos to Russia. It is a thing which his own country would never forgive if he allowed the best harbour to be ceded to the Russians. This seems the method they are adopting to upset him and drive him away. Besides it is also said that his Ministers are more or less playing him false and that the form in which the union has been obtained is considered by them *ein Misserfolg, eine Niederlage* [a failure, a defeat] and that they wish to make him alone answerable before the country for this. They wish to take away all the Roumelian officers before the Elections, as they are all so much for Sandro. Meanwhile the Greeks seem coming to their senses and one hears Alfred [Commander-in-Chief of the Mediterranean Squadron] spoken of with much praise as understanding his work so well. The blockade is already having good effect.

From the Crown Princess
POTSDAM, MAY 22, 1886

These lines are to wish you joy with all my heart and soul of your dear birthday. We hope you will like the picture we send you. It is painted by Schadow. He is no longer alive and his works are rare but he was full of talent. This picture[4] was painted twenty-six years ago. We thought it might find a place at Osborne. The upper rooms are not quite full of pictures yet. May this difficult crisis in England come to a good result and may good sense and enlightened patriotism triumph over this unaccountable confusion of ideas. Nothing is worse than to set class against class, the essence of peace, prosperity and liberty – of true progress, is that the classes should trust one another and work with one another. Their interests are the same, the goals the same, but the parts they have to play are very different, though each necessary for the health of the community. Those who toil with their heads cannot toil with their hands – to sow discord between them is to do harm to both. . . .

[Ps.] We are so glad you liked the picture. It has never been reproduced either by lithograph or photograph or engraved. We are so glad to be able to contribute to your collection of modern German Art; and Osborne is the very place for these pictures, the light is good and they suit the style of the House. As dear Papa is no longer there to give you pictures, they must come from us.

From the Queen
BALMORAL CASTLE, JUNE 15, 1886

... I must first repeat what my telegram told you of our horror at this awful tragedy of poor crazy Ludwig of Bavaria's sad and tragic end.[5] And now the accession of his totally mad brother! The whole is like some dreadful story in a sensational novel. Poor young man (for 41 is still young), how full of promise, how gifted, talented and handsome he was when he came to the throne. What could be the reason of his extreme eccentricity which was ever increasing and of the total madness of poor Otto? Poor King Ludwig was in many ways clever, and he was not bigotted or narrow-minded which I fear his uncle Luitpold is. His sons [Luitpold's], however, I hear are not so. Poor, poor Queen Mariechen! Can anything be more awful for a mother? Only the other day she offered to give up all she had to pay his [Ludwig's] debts. But he refused to see her even. Here various manifestos and addresses [in connection with the General Election after the defeat of Home Rule] have already appeared and Mr Gladstone's I am sure you will think very weak and inaccurate even, as regards what he said before the last Election. The papers are down upon him, including the *Scotsman*. Mr Chamberlain's is a very strong one and Mr Trevelyan's is very good. Mr Gladstone would have done far better for himself and far more loyally towards his country if he had resigned and Lord Rosebery, who was here for two days at the end of the week, told me he would have preferred it, but that he knew Mr Gladstone never would do so till he was completely beaten which (though others expect he will) Lord Rosebery does not, which is not dignified. 'He is so pugnacious on this subject', Lord Rosebery said and that his age made him so tenacious as he thought no one but himself could settle the Irish question – a most unfortunate delusion. . . .

From the Queen
BALMORAL CASTLE, JUNE 22, 1886

. . . What you told me of Uncle E[rnest] and that pamphlet[6] is simply monstrous. I assure you I felt great difficulty in writing to him for his birthday but I wrote it as short and cool as I could consistently with civility. He is a misfortune like the G.O.M. I send you an excellent article from the *Observer* (a very independent paper) about his (Mr G's) wild and illogical speech. He behaves in such an undignified way and really stumping the country. The dissolution was considered by Lord Salisbury (who spoke so well at Leeds), Lord Hartington and Mr Goschen as the least evil and they all advised me to grant it but *at once.* And that is the case for it takes place D.V. on Saturday, 26th. I heard from a good judge, a Scotchman, living in Edinburgh, that his [Gladstone's] reception [in his Midlothian constituency] was not spontaneous as formerly, but 'organised' and composed of numbers of the Irish and of the lowest people in the town. I cannot refrain from sending you two other articles, one from the same *Observer* and the other from the *St James's* about my beginning my fiftieth Jubilee year. *The Times* and *Standard* of Saturday had equally very kind ones. I received quantities of telegrams from people of all kinds in England. I don't like flattery but I am pleased to see loyalty and *Anerkennung* [appreciation]. To dear Papa do I owe the greatest part of what the people praise in me. . . .

From the Crown Princess
NEUES PALAIS, JUNE 25, 1886

So many thanks for your dear letter of the 22nd and the newspaper cuttings! It gave me such pleasure to read all the nice articles in all the newspapers about your Jubilee Year! They were not flattery or fine speeches – they seemed to me true and sincere and just; as I am sure they are well meant! Years of labour and care and anxiety of doing one's best deserve to find their acknowledgement, and I did not think the papers said a word too much. . . .

From the Crown Princess
JULY 3, 1886

I return the papers about the Schmalkalden Forest with many thanks. Uncle [Ernest] is entirely mistaken in calling it a dotation. It was never given to him as a reward for his military services, but merely ceded as he had been an ally.[7] His letter is certainly very gracious. His pamphlet has done all the mischief possible, it has been much read in France, is translated even into Russian and is read in Russia. They say it has especially done me harm. Considering how I have always stuck up for Uncle Ernest here where he has always been very unpopular and often unjustly so, I think it not very nice or kind of him and cannot quite get over it.

AFTER THE LIBERAL DEFEAT IN THE ELECTIONS AND ACCESSION OF A CONSERVATIVE GOVERNMENT

From the Queen
OSBORNE, AUGUST 4, 1886

. . . Though Lord Iddesleigh's health cannot inspire one with confidence, he is thoroughly to be trusted [as foreign secretary] and will not be taken in and is very able; besides Lord Salisbury [as prime minister] will superintend everything. The new Home Secretary, a Mr Matthews, is said to be a very clever man, a lawyer and an admirable speaker. . . . The two Councils yesterday were very fatiguing and long and you will see it all in the Court Circular. Bertie and Arthur were both with me. Tomorrow I have some or the greater part of the new Household, most of them the same as before, only the young Duke of Portland instead of Lord Bradford. Parliament meets tomorrow to elect the Speaker and to swear in the Members and then there will be a sort of Queen's Speech, after which it will be prorogued, if possible, beyond the Autumn. I am very tired and my head aches and is much over taxed. . . . Swoboda, Angeli's pupil and recommendation, who did that pretty picture of Patricia, has done some charming heads of the Indians and one of the handsome Singalee woman for me and is doing more.[8] They are beautifully done. . . .

From the Queen
OSBORNE, AUGUST 12, 1886

. . . I also forgot in each letter saying how grieved we were at old Liszt's death. Such a distinguished man and so sad that he should be taken after all his successes. But I fear his visit here and all the parties he was asked to killed him. I have been interrupted by the arrival of thirteen of the Indians, some Singalese, Malays and two Cypriots (who speak English) who have come with Dr Tyler and another gentleman. I saw them on the Terrace and shall see them again in the Council Room to wish them all goodbye. . . .

AFTER THE KIDNAPPING OF ALEXANDER OF BULGARIA

From the Queen
BALMORAL CASTLE, AUGUST 24, 1886

On arriving here on the 21st I found your dear letter of the 17th all about Willie and Fritz.... And, oh, what has happened since! It is too, too awful! But today we hear every moment fresh news. Dear Sandro is safe and on his way to Bucharest. There are great counter revolutions in his favour and the Russian villainy and monstrosity are as clear as day and the Russians have been far too open monsters not to show what *they* have done alone and what is intended against us. Sandro, it is now said, has refused to abdicate. You always warned against a *coup d'état*. I have written very strongly to Lord Salisbury and Lord Iddesleigh yesterday and today and ciphered about our being very firm and getting Morier and Sir E. Thornton removed, especially the former, and Sir William White employed. *He* will have picked other people's brains and opened eyes and ears at Gastein. The quiet and rest I so needed is of course utterly gone and I have more to write and cipher than ever. But the pure air and absence of all visits etc, which is, as you say, a terrible aggravation of everything, is a great thing.... Poor dear Liko's distress was heartrending on Sunday and yesterday, but today he is better and cheerful. Bismarck, Sir E. Malet telegraphs, was 'not sorry for dear Sandro's fall' as it would remove a danger to the peace of Europe! This cannot be true and is utterly wrong, for it is just the reverse.... I am exhausted by all my writing. Up to the last our visit to Edinburgh was a great success. We have lovely complete summer weather since we came and I wear the same things as I did at Osborne which I have not been able to do for years. Only just at sunset one requires a shawl or cloak. Fritz must be firm and insist on going to Russia and not Master Willie.

From the Queen
BALMORAL, SEPTEMBER 11, 1886

What terrible events! Poor dear Sandro is safe at home but I hear terribly broken and terribly aged and altered and Franzjos too. But how nobly he has behaved and with what dignity! Many thanks for your dear last letter of the 3rd or did I answer it? I am really so confused, so absorbed in this terrible affair, I forget what I have done. What ovations Sandro has received all along the road [back to Bulgaria from Bucharest]. In Austria Hungary and in his own country, Bulgaria and Hesse! Somehow I always cling to the idea that he will some day come back triumphant. I am sorry he has a further anxious time. I feel as if we were culpable and yet what could we do? Lord Iddesleigh thinks amiable Sir Edward Thornton did act stupidly and that if Sir Wm White had remained (which he ought) this might have been prevented. If Turkey had been firm we should have backed her up, but with Turkey weak and almost Russian, Germany and Austria refusing to do anything (shamefully) what could we do? For we could not send an army to Bulgaria! It is too dreadful! And what is to happen? *I* think there will have to be a conference anyhow. We shall object to any and every Russian candidate. What do *you* think should be done? You are so wise and so full of resource. I enclose first the telegraphic account of Sandro's interview with Sir F. Lascelles (a cipher), second the copy of a sad touching letter from Ella of Roumania (they are so friendly and so was King Milan) and lastly Sandro's touching and painful letter about Sandro's kidnapping and the journey. It will make you shudder. I have had also an explanation about the message to the Tsar. He did it as a last resource, when the Russian Consul at Rustchuk came to tell him Prince Dolgorouki was on his way (which was untrue) to take possession of the country, to save his country. And it was a private cipher which the horrid Tsar answered *en clair* so brutally and had both messages sent to Sofia to be published and circulated in order to injure him. What perfidy! I can understand and admire that Moretta should remain faithful to dear Sandro and now it signifies but little if he is freed or not. Two years ago his marrying would have been of great use to him. But now you could not, I fear, get over the Emperor's and Empress's prejudices? We heard dear Arthur and Louischen reached Malta this afternoon and embarked this evening on board the Bengal P. & O. steamer and go straight to Bombay [where he was to be Commander-in-Chief].

From the Crown Princess
VILLA CARNARVON, PORTOFINO, GENOA, OCTOBER 5, 1886

. . . Henry is coming here now instead of his going to Balmoral as you did not wish him to come. I suppose he will try to go to Darmstadt in January, if only the Empress does not prevent it. He is very much attached to Irène. The Empress says she knows he is not. He wrote so nicely about her – and said if he was only worthy of her. The Empress's caprices, supported by Louise of Baden, are a very great misfortune for us. Was ever anything so exasperating as the way Kaulbars goes on in Bulgaria – one did not give the Russians credit for so much stupidity in spite of all their slyness and wiliness. They will set the whole population against them, which would be a very good thing!

From the Queen
WINDSOR CASTLE, DECEMBER 15, 1886
Confidential, to be kept

I had a long conversation with dear Sandro last night and spoke to him about his personal plans. He said he did not think of marrying now – the object for doing so no longer existing now – but if he ever did marry he [would] like to take Moretta as his wife. He knew she had a good heart, and that she remained true to him, through evil and good report and therefore thought she would make him happy. But that he had been so grossly insulted, messages being sent to him when he had never asked for Vicky's hand, that *he* could never make any advances – and that if ever anything was to come of this idea, Fritz must take the first step. His intention for the present is to travel to distant parts. I write this to you, as you some weeks ago wrote to me – that if he could wait, you thought all would come right. But no advances must be made, till you are quite sure of dear Sandro's being treated with that respect and that cordiality which he has a right to expect and which he so fully deserves. There must be no mysteries and no secret dealings as all those have caused him so much suffering. It must all be open and straightforward.

[Ps.] Sandro only leaves on the 23rd so if you have anything you wish me to say to him, there will be ample time to do so.

From the Queen
WINDSOR CASTLE, DECEMBER 15, 1886

. . . Let me, before doing anything else, thank you for the very valuable packets of letters you have sent me of dear old Stockmar to you, for which I am very grateful. Those about poor Princess Charlotte are especially interesting and the letters from Lady Liverpool, a very true, dear old friend, much devoted to the Baron, Papa and me, are also very interesting to me. I will sort them. I keep up the collections of papers dear Papa used to be so interested in, most carefully, but I fear there are too many almost, and yet I have constantly to refer to things and sometimes just something is wanting. . . .

From the Queen
WINDSOR CASTLE, DECEMBER 22, 1886

... The [Bulgarian] Delegates [touring Europe in search of a new prince] are not pleased with Herbert Bismarck's answer which is indeed an insult considering that the whole of Bulgaria is against Mingrelia, a creature of Russia and if he is pressed, Sandro will be at once re-elected. Some middle course will then have to be found till enough time has passed to enable the passions to cool and the Emperor of Russia to come to his senses. *I* am, and always have been, of the decided opinion that the Tsar is merely saying he won't have Sandro as he dislikes him, which is not a reason for Europe, or part of it, humbly to submit. I think he ought to be asked categorically what are the accusations he has to bring against him. He should answer and Sandro says he knows he could answer them all. No sovereign or country has a right to say they won't have a person without giving reasons, especially when the country wishes to have their ruler back again. I will however another day (soon) tell you more of what I think possibly might be done. Ferdinand Coburg proposed *himself*!! He is clever – but sickly, very effeminate, a fop and not good-natured who would not remain there a year. He is besides very ultramontane. I am so sorry dear Sandro could not remain here a little longer, but he has promised to come soon again. He is quiet and unwatched here which, alas, he is not in Germany. He is quite charming – so clever, so dispassionate, so amiable and kind – and so handsome. I am quite devoted to him and am as proud of him as if he were my own son. ...

From the Queen
OSBORNE, FEBRUARY 11, 1887

... Beatrice sends you some important extracts about France. Many thanks for your letter of the 5th and the enclosure. I am most grateful for what Fritz sends me. It tallies exactly with what Sir E. Malet has written and Lord Salisbury has had several important interviews with Count Hatzfeldt and Count Corti. What England cannot do, and never could, is to promise assistance without knowing what for. Nor could we ever join in any attack on France unless she quarrelled with or threatened us. That we should not see Austria crushed without acting is sure, as also that we could not see Russia or France have any footing in the Black Sea, the Aegean or Mediterranean [*sic*, though she cannot mean Mediterranean in relation to France]. I hope some tacit sort of understanding will be come to. Lord Salisbury offers alliance of which he is quite alive to the dangers, but Parliament is a great difficulty. If you would some time write in this sense to your friend Mr Goschen, it would do good, for he has a great regard for you and your views and I think he is a little timid in foreign politics, quite right, but just a little timid. Our accounts from Bulgaria are favourable. It would be madness to make war at the poor, old Emperor's age. Monstrous! I do feel so much for dear, noble-hearted, brave Fritz and wish I could do anything to help him. You have never told me what the Empress says about Henry's engagement. I fear he had great difficulty with her. Pray tell me. I have had a very radiant and quite enthusiastic letter from Henry and two from Irène who seems very happy. This devotion to him, far more than from, is very touching. Arthur's little darlings are very well. . . . Sir E. Malet wrote that he thought the Emperor looking very ill and changed since New Year. A war would I think kill him. Is Marie Anna [of Prussia, mother-in-law of Prince Arthur] at Berlin or gone again to Italy? Do tell me who was Count Robilant's mother. I remember your telling me all about it. He is the son of Charles Albert I know. His resignation would I know be very unfortunate. . . .

From the Queen
WINDSOR CASTLE, FEBRUARY 26, 1887

... I am sure you and poor, dear Moretta must be very anxious and distressed about our beloved Sandro who is a martyr as well as a hero. On Saturday night (or Sunday I think) he was very ill: temperature 107, but that soon fell and these last two or three days the temperature is almost normal. ... He was ill before from worry and annoyance; and God knows, was ever a noble, brave, excellent young man more tried than he has been? And in that he was, therefore, predisposed to catch anything, for else he must have been so much exposed everywhere that it seems incredible this should happen now. He is supposed to have got it at Marseilles. But I fear he has never been vaccinated. Still I thought in the German Army that was regularly done? I am so glad that the ball etc. are over and Vicky must try to get out of the Empress's teas etc. She ought not to be exposed to unkindness and insult. I feel much for her just now. I send some more interesting letters [from Prince Arthur] for you to forward to Marie Anna. Count Hatzfeldt and Count Corti dined here last night. But under the circumstances I avoided politics with the former. ...

[Ps.] I hope dear Fritz's hoarseness is better and Mossy quite well?

From the Crown Princess
BERLIN, MARCH 7, 1887

... The state of internal affairs here is most distressing and deplorable and our position most painful. We have to keep as quiet as mice and not express any opinions, while William is used as a tool by the Government and conservative party and the Emperor's Court. We want him to have a regiment in the provinces, but all these people will not allow the Emperor to let him go. And he fancies himself consequently of immense importance, and that he is of more use to the country than his papa, who in his eyes does not keep up Prussian traditions enough and is *suspected* of a little leaning towards a more liberal and modern tendency! It is such rubbish, but the waves of party feeling, excitement and intrigue run very high. The Emperor and William are cards in the hands of very unprincipled and violent people. It is very sad for us; we are so isolated and can do nothing. Thank God, dear Sandro is doing well. . . .

From the Queen
BUCKINGHAM PALACE, MARCH 19, 1887

I give these lines to Bertie and hope all will go off well.[9] How you can squeeze so many into your house I cannot imagine. . . . We are going back to Windsor in an hour. All six children were with us here, but the litle Albanys return to Claremont today, where Helen will arrive at seven this evening. She has been soothed and comforted by her visit to Cannes. . . .[10] I have written to the Emperor a few lines by Bertie. The principal rule of procedure was at last carried [in the House of Commons] last night which will help very much. But the language of the Irish Members inciting to rebellion and violence is quite atrocious. Austria is behaving extremely well and drawing nearer and nearer to us. . . .

From the Queen
WINDSOR CASTLE, MARCH 21 [sc. 20], 1887

As we shall be away all Wednesday at Birmingham, my messenger letter must be written tomorrow, but I wish to write a few lines . . . on a subject I am in a difficulty about. I did not intend asking Willie and Dona for the Jubilee, first because Fritz and you come, and secondly because I must lodge them and thirdly because you know how ill he behaved, how rude, to me, to Liko . . . and how shamefully he calumniated dear, excellent, noble Sandro and how shamefully he behaves to you both, his parents. I thought if he wished to pay his respects to his Grandmama that he could have come a little later when 'the mob' would be gone. We shall be awfully squeezed at Buckingham Palace, though only for two nights: Leopold and Marie of B[elgium], Uncle Ernest, Rudolph and possibly Stéphanie, Louis and three children, Serge and Ella I hope (on account of the latter) then Lenchen and Christian, Arthur and Louischen and poor Helen. More I don't believe we could get in. This excludes Beatrice, Liko and myself. No suites, only one of my own Ladies, to be in the house. Here [i.e. at Windsor Castle] I will try and avoid having all at once if possible. Bertie wants me to invite William and Dona, but I can't invite them when I can't lodge them and I fear he may show his dislikes and be disagreeable. Tell me what you think. *I* can't put him up and I don't think Bertie or Affie can. Besides I think he at least should remain [in Germany] on account of the Emperor. Then [i.e. if William was invited] Charlotte would wish to come and much as I should like seeing her, I don't think *she* ought to go to Marlborough House. I don't know if Affie could take them or her in. Bertie says Germany won't understand it, but I think Germany would understand his remaining in the country when you are away on account of the Emperor at his age. Would you answer me as soon as possible. Poor little Irène was looking forward in terror to this ordeal of upwards of ninety *Fürstlichkeiten* [princely people] to be stared at.

From the Crown Princess
BERLIN, MARCH 23, 1887

. . . Yesterday was such a day of worry, bustle and confusion that I could not find a moment's time to write. Since three days I have neuralgia so that the very few moments I spend in my room are employed in lying down. The announcement of the engagement [i.e. of Henry and Irène] went off very well. Irène and Henry were much overcome, but very happy. The crush of the ninety-five *Fürstlichkeiten* was tremendous, the heat in the Emperor's Palace and the Schloss was asphyxiating. The Empress was frigid, as was to be expected, the Emperor very kind and everyone else most cordial. Here in the house and in the town great rejoicing. I am so glad to have Bertie and Lenchen here. It is impossible in this crush and rush to collect my thoughts to write you the interesting things I have heard and observations I have made, but I will do so very soon. Please excuse me . . . I feel as if I had spent a few days in the Tower of Babel. One most important thing I must not forget. The King of Saxony told me that as he was the head of the Saxon House, you had always been so kind to him and had given him the Garter, it was his wish to go and pay his respects to you for your Jubilee. I own I was very glad to hear it and think it not only right and proper, but very nice of him. I know it will be frightfully inconvenient and uncomfortable for you, but if I may be allowed humbly to express an opinion, it is that King Albert may not be refused as I think it very important his offer should be kindly accepted. Rather would we be stuffed [in] anywhere than that he should not appear on an occasion when he proposes himself. Would you kindly telegraph to me or to him?

[Ps.] How very glad we are that Carlos of Portugal has a son!

From the Queen
WINDSOR CASTLE, MARCH 28, 1887

. . . After what you say I will ask Willie and Dona and Charlotte and Bernhard for the Jubilee and ask you to tell them so from me. I cannot lodge them in the Palace, but Bertie will try and manage what you suggested. The King of Saxony's wish to come is very amiable and of course I could not refuse. But I shall [dread?] all this 'Royal Mob' as Louis calls these tremendous royal assemblages than which I dislike nothing more. But I personally cannot do much entertaining. I am not able for much. I can't stand hardly at all any more and hot dinners and standing about after dinner and much talking are impossibilities. I am very grateful for the enclosure and the telegram. If you send your letters through Sir E. Malet to Sir Henry Ponsonby, or Major Bigge or to Harriet Phipps or to Emilie Dittweiler, it will be quite safe ... [The Queen gives her address at Cannes and at Aix, travelling as the Countess of Balmoral].

From the Crown Princess
BERLIN, APRIL 2, 1887

... It is very kind of you to invite William and Dona and Charlotte and Bernhard to your Jubilee. I will tell them this evening. Do not worry yourself, dearest Mama, about the guests and fatigue, etc. The apprehension is worse than the reality and everybody will try and save you all possible trouble and fatigue. The fact that all want to shew their sympathy, affection and respect is gratifying and satisfying though I completely agree with you that such gatherings are a very great plague and bore and no one hates them more than I do. However London is so vast and there is so much to do and to see that your visitors will be quite happy and well employed. ... It is far worse here where there are such impossible hours and where Berlin sights are exhausted in a day ... On Monday Sophie and Mossy are to pass an examination before the Emperor and Empress. On Tuesday the Confirmation takes place at twelve. There is a great deal now in the newspapers about Sandro going back to Bulgaria. ... I had so hoped the Regents would continue on for some time and then later he could return as King. Now he would only have to continue the struggle with Russian intrigue which brought about his fall. ... The idea for the *future* of an independent United Kingdom under him seems the only sensible solution, does it not? But it is too early now. The Tsar's hatred, the Panslavist opposition and the unfriendly coldness of the German Government would not be counterbalanced as yet by the support of the others [i.e. other Powers] would it? I own I am in terror of his fate taking a bad turn. Still, of course, he himself must know best and what he thinks, of course, one does not know.

From the Queen
MAISON MOTTET, AIX-LES-BAINS, APRIL 23, 1887

I can only write you a few lines tonight as I am tired and sleepy, having been to the Grande Chartreuse today, an expedition of ten hours, but well worth the exertion! The drive up the Gorge de Chaillet on an excellent road with those enormous mountains towering over and almost closing over you is simply magnificent. And the monastery itself which is very large stands in a marvellous position protected by the high rocks and surrounded by fine meadows. Lovely small gentians were growing all over the grass round the monastery. The Révérends Pères were most kind and amiable and showed us about. It is most curious. You know, it is a most unusual and extraordinary exception which was made to the rule to allow me to go. . . . We found a very good looking young Englishman there, only 23, having gone there at 18, but he assured me he was 'very happy'. . . .

April 24 I finish this today sitting out and writing in the garden. . . . We leave on the 28th. We shall be very sorry to go and I especially who have hosts of fatiguing troublesome things awaiting me. I don't feel at all equal to them. Certainly I can bear less and less fatigue. I feel the difference from year to year. The great quiet and the very fine air are doing me decided good.

From the Queen
WINDSOR CASTLE, MAY 18, 1887

... We are busy with preparations and have questions without end. But Bertie and darling Beatrice and Lenchen are very helpful and Sir H. Ponsonby and Lord Lathom are most clever and active. We are sadly distressed by the illness of darling Victoria of Darmstadt of that terrible typhoid which we know too well. . . . Your cipher [see p. 3] is quite unintelligible. Every effort has been made to try and decipher it, but in vain. The Danish artist[11] will shortly present himself at Potsdam and I am sure you will be charmed with the sketch for the family picture. It is so prettily grouped and the effect is so sunny and bright. He is very quiet and gentlemanlike and speaks French and English. I can only repeat that Sandro must not move now. But if even politically it were wise, his health would not admit of it. . . . Though Fritz is not to go into hot rooms and parties, perhaps he would just go to the one State Ball, given on the 24th, and the State Concert on the 27th June. My labours are: 1st, the reception of the Royal guests, on the 20th afternoon, Family Dinner in the evening; 2nd, Thanksgiving, 21st June morning, again large Family and Princely Dinner; after it Corps Diplomatique, Indian Princes and all the suites; 3rd Wednesday, 22nd, music, presents and at 5 pm back to Windsor where my statue is to be unveiled by Christian as High Steward of Windsor. A *Fackelzug* [torchlight procession] is in the evening. There are Ball and parties in London. But nothing for me, beyond, if coming, some of the guests coming down [to Windsor] each day till 2nd July when I go up to Buckingham Palace to see the Volunteers march past the Palace, returning here afterwards. I made a mistake for on the 29th I go up for my Garden Party and come back here directly afterwards. On the 4th July I am to lay the first stone of the Imperial Institute. I saw old Mr Bright, who has behaved so well and who has been so firm a Unionist, on Monday after the

Address had been brought, and found him very much aged and broken, and his voice feeble.[12] He said he could not trust himself to speak of Mr Gladstone.

From the Queen
BALMORAL CASTLE, MAY 27, 1887

Darling and Beloved Child, Truly, earnestly and most gratefully do I thank God that the (unnecessary though perhaps not unavoidable) alarm about our precious Fritz has been dispelled and that your agony of uncertainty and suspense has been removed. I wish I could fly to you and clasp you in my arms and tell you just how I suffered for and with you. . . . The one thing I am so anxious for, is that you should come over for the Jubilee, as now you can, and that you and your girls at any rate could be with me and I pray that dear Fritz may just be able to go to Westminster Abbey. It will not be long and I do so wish he could just ride with my sons, sons-in-law, grandsons and grandsons-in-law in front of my open carriage in which I should drive with you and dear Alix, who is quite a daughter to me. . . .

From the Crown Princess
NEUES PALAIS, POTSDAM, JUNE 9, 1887

I can write to you today with a much lighter heart as Dr M. Mackenzie sees no unfavourable symptoms in my darling Fritz's throat since he last examined it. He has removed two tiny particles of the growth and Virchow will again examine them. . . . The children are so looking forward to their visit. They are in great excitement. Sophie hopes to appear at a ball, the first in her life. The toilettes are also of course a subject of serious consideration. Much care has been bestowed on them and I trust my dear little people's appearance will find favour with their Grandmama. How fine and striking is Algernon Swinburne's 'Ode on the Jubilee' in the June number of the *Nineteenth Century*![13] I hope it has been read to you.

From the Queen
WINDSOR CASTLE, JULY 5, 1887

... I think much the same as you tell me was in today's papers. Philippe[14] is dreadfully annoyed about his absurd, conceited, but in some ways clever, brother. I am sure if they saw and knew him, who can't ride or fight etc., he will be sure to be sent away or killed before long. Lord Salisbury does not believe he will be elected. I hope dear Fritz's throat is going on satisfactorily and that you will soon find an improvement in his voice. I was dreadfully tired last night and the heat all day including the very fine ceremony[15] of yesterday was quite overpowering. I could do nothing but pant. Today is a great relief but I feel now the effect of the great fatigue of this last fortnight which has been incessant. Tomorrow I have again Addresses. Today I go to Aldershot, Saturday, the Review. Charlotte is coming to dinner tonight and sweet little Feo [Charlotte's daughter], who is so good and I think grown so pretty. We were delighted to have her and I think the dear child has enjoyed herself. ...

From the Queen
ON THE TRAIN AFTER BASINGSTOKE, AUGUST 24, 1887

Darling, Beloved Child, I must write you a few lines and say how truly grieved I was to part from you again. I only pray it may not be very long. The older one grows, especially at my age, one feels it more and more. To feel that this memorable time, this large family meeting, is all over is sad. And to part from you, knowing you in the midst of such uncertainty and difficulties, though thank God, without any real cause for alarm, distresses me doubly. Only be firm. Don't on any account let Fritz go to Potsdam or Baden, or take those two useless doctors with you who will counteract all Mackenzie's treatment. He must write a letter which can be shown the Emperor and, if necessary, the wicked man [i.e. Bismarck]. I feel very sad to have parted from you. I can hardly believe it. It was nice to see the five cousins so happy together. I could not go out this afternoon and was soon then so hurried. You would have been amused to see me take my tea with little children[16] alone in my room, only two good Indians waiting on me. They follow tomorrow. The welcome tomorrow at dear Balmoral will be full of very *vorherundjetze* [then and now] feelings, such kind, true, loving ones, who would so have rejoiced to see it and join, are no longer in this world. I hope you will get this tomorrow or next morning. How beautiful the evening was! And now there is a lovely moon. Forgive this writing, but the train shakes.

From the Crown Princess

ON BOARD THE *VICTORIA AND ALBERT*, PLYMOUTH, AUGUST 28, 1887

... Yesterday we made the most delightful expedition, and the girls did not go with us as they wanted to do some shopping in the town and to walk about the place. The *Vivid* took our party early outside the harbour to the mouth of the little river up which one has to go to Membland, Emily Revelstoke's place. It was very rough outside and the *Vivid* tumbled about a good deal, so that getting into the steam-launch was quite a matter of dexterity. Her river is so pretty and the drive to Membland from the shore quite short but very pretty. Lady Revelstoke drove me in a pony carriage to Flete. The country is quite lovely and the house very fine, half new and half old, done with great taste and skill and refinement, all beautifully finished and I should say (to use

Christian's favourite phrase) regardless of expense. The situation of the house is charming. Membland is just as attractive in its way, of course, not nearly so important in size or style, but so comfortable and in such good taste. It interests and amuses me immensely to see beautiful English homes. . . . We got home rather late as we went back by carriage. It was a great pleasure on getting back to find your dear letter. So many thanks for copying out what Fritz wrote. He seems in very good spirits about himself, which is the chief thing. . . . Wegner had begged to be allowed to go home as he does not feel well. We shall, therefore, I think have Schröder and Dr Hovell with us. . . .

From the Queen
BALMORAL CASTLE, AUGUST 29, 1887

We have just taken leave of beloved Fritz who is looking so well and his dear voice so much better! To think that he should have recovered his dear health so much in England and still more in dear Scotland is an indescribable source of joy and thankfulness to us. May God bless and protect him and may he go on improving more and more. . . . Poor Ferdinand seems in a great plight [in Bulgaria] and they say his manners are much disapproved for their haughtiness, so unlike dear Sandro. Italy and Austria behave very well, not so Bismarck. You will hear that Fritz is travelling with a little family, his dog having got three little puppies since he was at Braemar. . . .

From the Queen
BALMORAL CASTLE, SEPTEMBER 6, 1887

. . . I am so glad you saw again all those places which you saw with us at Plymouth thirty years ago. Membland and Flete I never saw. How annoying and unfortunate the bad weather was and I wonder it did not thoroughly disgust you with the yacht. The very smell of everything gives me a disagreeable feeling. I will see if the improvements you mention can be introduced.[17] I dislike electric light in rooms, as it hurts one's eyes so. . . . Arthur arrived at Bombay yesterday, so nice and quick. . . . Affairs in the East are not satisfactory. The three Powers, Austria, England and Italy, are all of one mind against the great man [Bismarck], the Bear [Russia] and the Turk who is too miserably weak. . . . Dr M. Mackenzie comes here to be knighted on the 8th.

From the Queen
BALMORAL CASTLE, OCTOBER 7, 1887

I asked dear Emily Ampthill to write you an account of the unveiling of my statue, which was a very pretty, touching sight, favoured, as every single event which took place and ceremony I have had to perform during this year, by beautiful weather, which, indeed, we have enjoyed, with hardly any exception, since the 17th September. I put in an article from the *Aberdeen Journal* as it gives Bertie's very pretty speech, the nice Address of the good people and my answer. . . . I can quite understand all the difficulties about dear Fritz's keeping quiet or rather talking very little. I wish he could have stayed a month longer here. It did him so much good. Bertie has been here since the 2nd and in the best of spirits and humours, very kind and friendly to Liko, quite as it should be, which is a great relief. Altogether he is quite like former days. He complains you have not written to him. . . .

From the Crown Princess
VILLA CLARA, BAVENO, OCTOBER 17, 1887

. . . William has arrived and until now he is very nice, amiable and friendly. Henry comes tonight and I hope will be nice too. . . . Fritz promises to be good and not to speak. He is dreadfully annoyed by all the foolish articles about himself in the German newspapers. . . . It is very unfair and ungrateful and unkind to abuse me at Berlin for having an English doctor for Fritz and even going so far as to abuse me for bringing Fritz to an English house instead of a German one in Italy. Really people are too narrow-minded. In politics I have heard from very good sources, but not through my usual ones, that there is a rapprochement between Germany and Austria and that the special point on which the Emperor of Austria and Prince Bismarck do not agree is Bulgaria. Prince Bismarck wishes the Russians not to be opposed in making a military occupation of the country. He thinks Russia will be occupied there and will weaken herself. Granted! if Prince Bismarck can guarantee Russia marching in with an insufficient force and being beaten, but this is not likely and if Russia occupy Bulgaria with a very large army, of course the Bulgarians have not the power or the numbers to resist and an occupation of Servia and of Roumania would be almost sure to follow. This Austria could not allow; therefore I really do not see how Germany and Austria are to agree about Bulgaria. Bismarck has, I think, been wrong from first to last about it and has led the Russians to believe and wished them to believe, which they do, that their road to Constantinople lies through Berlin and that it is therefore worth their while to behave well to Germany and not to make an alliance with the French or make war singly on Germany. Prince Bismarck wants peace at all hazards and will strain every nerve and fibre to maintain it. He has perhaps entered a slightly, very slightly, new phase, i.e. he admits the possibility, though not the probability of all his love-making to Russia being fruitless, so he is looking about in other directions more seriously and earnestly than hithertofore for allies, and Crispi's visit to Friedrichsruhe is a clear proof of this. Had this policy been adopted a year ago, indeed if now, had Sandro only received the smallest support and the Russians only a warning to let him alone, we should not have all these intricacies, difficulties and dangers surrounding European peace and we should have perhaps Sandro King of a united and independent Bulgaria. I said it often enough at the time. If Germany had made fast her other alliances she might have defied Russia and France and they would have quickly drawn in their horns. Now much time has been wasted in running after Russia and trying to win her good graces by sacrificing Sandro and Bulgaria. It was both wrong and short-sighted. All this is in strictest confidence. An enormous deal now depends on the influence England, i.e. Sir William White, can gain on the Sultan. If the Porte can be got to refuse the Russian proposals, a great deal would be won. The Tsar hates war and will think twice before he sends an army of occupation into Bulgaria. But he is still under the terrorism of the Panslavist and National party and must do something to content them. This is all only in strict confidence to you. I hope I shall not have bored you too much with these remarks on politics. I had a visit yesterday from poor Madame Minghetti. It was a mournful meeting. I had not seen her since her husband's death. I also saw Morelli, who is still so delighted at having been presented to you and at having seen Windsor. He says you have some great treasures at Hampton Court which are but little known. . . .

From the Queen
BALMORAL CASTLE, NOVEMBER 14, 1887

. . . I have endless enquiries and the interest shown is quite indescribable. Such admiration for our darling Fritz! Lily of H[anover] who is here wishes me to say everything most kind and sympathising and how much she feels for you. Many friends write, all in the same very kind strain. . . . There was a riot in London last night and the troops were called out to relieve and support the police, but it was all very successfully put down and two of the ringleaders, one an M.P., were arrested. What can you say when Mr Gladstone himself preaches to the people to resist the police. . . .

From the Crown Princess
VILLA ZIRIO, SAN REMO, NOVEMBER 21, 1887

On opening my eyes this morning I received your dear letter and read it with tears of joy and gratitude. In anxiety such as mine what can be more soothing, comforting and supporting than a mother's love. Later I found the sweet little brooch on my table with the pictures of my two lost darlings. It is so pretty and will be so precious to me. . . .

From the Queen
WINDSOR CASTLE, DECEMBER 5, 1887

. . . *Unberufen* and thank God! our beloved Fritz, whom everybody enquires after, is going on so well. I think this will continue and Sir William Jenner is strongly of the opinion that it is not the really malignant growth which, indeed, Sir M. Mackenzie told me it was just possible it might not be. One hopes in trembling but one *should* hope. I am anxiously waiting to hear from Mary P[onsonby] from whom I had a telegram on the 2nd. I cannot say how shocked I am about Henry. It is abominable. I shall not say a word to Irène as that would do no good. . . . I wish now to tell you about my interview [with Count Hatzfeldt, the German ambassador] which was quite satisfactory in many ways, in fact in every way, except his powerlessness to prevent these dreaful mistakes or this constant interference. He spoke more openly than he did before and knows Willie's faults and the way in which he is toadied. I did not mention you, but he assured me that no one dreams seriously of making Fritz resign his rights and that he was sure Fritz never would dream of yielding to such a mad proposal. We had a very interesting visit from the Gaikwar of Baruda and the Maharani on the 2nd. He is enormously rich, very clever and well-informed and does a great deal for his country. In fact he has overworked his brain and is obliged to keep very quiet. He is small and not at all good-looking and his costume is not very pretty. She is a pretty little thing but quite like a child. . . . The Gaikwar came in the same train but not in the same carriage. Nor does she ever be in the same room with him in the presence of a stranger and this is the custom all over India. Every man was kept out of the way; only one, the Lord in Waiting, took her over the Castle. Lady Waterpark, Lady Cross and the wife of the gentleman who came with him, Mrs Elliot, brought her to the Audience Room and her (the Maharani's) sister accompanied her. Beatrice was with her. The Maharani was just like a bit of India taken out of a picture, for she and her sister had trousers and no petticoat and only a gauze veil, light red and quite wrapped round her, covering her head. She had splendid jewels on. When *he* was invested with the Star of India, she sat behind a glass screen which was hung with Indian stuffs and saw it all and no one saw her. They went away before dinner. I thought all this would interest you and dear Fritz. . . .

From the Queen
WINDSOR CASTLE, DECEMBER 15, 1887

. . . Bertie and I got a little alarmed at the report and at Sir Morell's leaving so hastily. But your answer yesterday reassured us. But you must have traitors in the camp who telegraph behind your back everything. I wish you would try and find out. For everything is known. Any telegrams to Sir M. Mackenzie is immediately known. And everything sent here by cipher is not. I fear Sir M.M. is not reticent enough. Bertie, Alix and their three dear girls, Lenchen, Louise and Lorne, Helen and ourselves all went to the mausoleum yesterday morning. It was a stormy, almost April day, as it is again today. I enclose the [order] of the music and service. The music was beautiful. Alix is looking very well and the girls are really charming. . . . With respect to Lord

Lyons, I believe the correct version to be this from what a reliable friend said. He was, unfortunately, what is called an agnostic and latterly very unhappy and very unsettled. He felt his sister, the Duchess of Norfolk's death terribly. She, I believe, said to him on her deathbed, she hoped he would consider it. Then in his sorrow and his doubt he read a good many books and at last saw the Roman Catholic Bishop of Southwell and was, alas, not entirely satisfied with what he said. Very soon after, he had the severe stroke from which he never even partially recovered and was never really conscious. There was therefore enough to justify them in burying him according to the rites of the Roman Catholic Church. The Duke of Norfolk is no proselytiser, at all, though a fervent Catholic.

From the Crown Princess
VILLA ZIRIO, SAN REMO, DECEMBER 24, 1887

Let me hasten to thank you a thousand times and with all my heart for all the beautiful and charming things with which you made our Christmas table and Christmas Eve bright, so many tokens of your love and care. . . . Fritz was charmed with his stick, with the watch, and with the beautiful book and Landseer etchings, and I with my beautiful silver lamp candlesticks. I have often wished for a pair and admired them in other people's houses in England. . . . Mons. de Launay, Italian Ambassador at Berlin, brought lovely gifts from the King and Queen of Italy. . . .

From the Queen
OSBORNE, JANUARY 1, 1888

. . . All you say and Mary P[onsonby] tells me of all your troubles and worries grieves me much. It is very hard. I hope that you will send away anyone whom you find telegraphing behind your back and I am sure the Italian Government would help in stopping the [copying] and watching telegrams. Mary P[onsonby] wrote to me you were going to do something of the kind. . . . The good accounts of darling Fritz gladden our hearts and made yesterday and today far brighter than they would otherwise have been, though to me all such days are sad now except in the pleasure of giving others pleasure and that is the greatest I can have. I am so pleased that my gifts gave satisfaction and that you admired the Jubilee album. To Annie McDonald, superintended by me, the merit of the arrangement is due. I hope that the little performance today comes off well? We are to have tableaux, the subject of which I am not to know, on Twelfth Night. Jubilee presents still come in and I am tired, so tired, never being two or three days without some audience, etc. since we came back from Scotland, five weeks ago. . . .

From the Crown Princess
VILLA ZIRIO, SAN REMO, JANUARY 1, 1888

. . . We have much reason to be thankful for being able to begin 1888 with our burden of anxiety lessened. Fritz is going on all right, though of course it is still a serious and anxious business. . . . . Yesterday evening Henry and Vicky acted two little pieces very nicely indeed, as a surprise for their Papa to amuse him a little. It succeeded very well and all were much amused. . . . Might I ask you to be so very kind as to thank dear Aunt Clém for this kind telegram. I dare not answer it as I should be accused by Prince Bismarck of dangerous intrigues, etc. and I am so fond of Aunt,[18] I should be so sorry if she thought me uncivil. I hear that the Empress is comparatively quite well again and the Emperor, William says, 'as fresh as a daisy'.

From the Queen
OSBORNE, FEBRUARY 2, 1888

... I take a little lesson every evening in Hindustani and
sometimes I miss writing by post in consequence. It is a great
interest and amusement to me. Young Abdul (who is in fact
no servant and just as little one as Mr Bell is) teaches me and
is a very strict master and a perfect gentleman. He has learnt
English wonderfully and can now copy beautifully and with
hardly any faults. He will I hope remain and be very useful in
writng and looking after my books and things. A third[19] is
coming to wait at meals and Mahmoud, the stout one, is going
on four months leave and the new one will arrive before he
goes. When he returns Abdul will no longer wait at meals
which is what he feels a good deal. I hope you will not be
wearied by this account, but I know they interest you. It is
indeed an immense pleasure to think I shall see you soon,
beloved child, and our very dear, precious Fritz. I do hope you
will come and see us for a few hours at Florence D.V. Short,
alas, as it will be, it will be such a comfort after all you have
gone through to be able to speak to one another. . . .

*IMMEDIATELY AFTER FRITZ BECAME FREDERICK III,
GERMAN EMPEROR*

From the Queen
BUCKINGHAM PALACE, MARCH 10, 1888

It is difficult for me to know how to begin my letter. My
heart is very, very full. May every blessing be yours and may
you *now* be able to see the right thing done for beloved Fritz
as it should be, and every possible help and care that is
needed afforded. While I write I know you are on your
journey [to Berlin] – an anxious one, but I will hope that
with *great care* it may be easily accomplished. The arrival will
be very trying. How suddenly this all comes! Doubtless

beloved Fritz must feel deeply the loss of his beloved father, my kind old friend, who was always most kind to me. But, on the other hand, the relief from the extraordinary and incomprehensible thraldom and tyranny and from the worries etc. must and will be enormous. I know how kind and good and forgiving you are, but I beg you both to be firm and put your foot down and especially to make those of your children, who were always speaking of the Emperor and Empress to remember who they are now. Many there are who will have to learn this and I fancy that you will be firm. My own dear Empress Victoria – it does seem an impossible dream – may God bless her. You know how little I care for rank or titles, but I cannot deny that after all that has been done and said, I am thankful and proud that dear Fritz and you should have come to the throne. The poor old Empress, what will she do? Alas, how many enemies she had made. I hope Hedwig [Countess Brühl] will be made to feel how ill she has behaved and will be somewhat *éloignée* [set at a distance]. We went over to Bertie and Alix this morning and presented our jug [silver wedding present] with which they were delighted. Alix looks as young as this day twenty-five years ago. They have received beautiful presents. They all lunched with me. We dine *en famille* with them tonight quite quietly and we go back tonight to Windsor at a quarter to eleven from [Bertie at] Marlborough House. . . .

From the Empress
CHARLOTTENBURG, MARCH 14, 1888

. . . Fritz has had a better night and Sir Morell Mackenzie was better satisfied with the state of his throat. . . . But alas, Fritz has had so much to do and with all the previous excitement and emotion it is impossible he should be as well as he might be if his health were the only consideration.

March 15 I could not get further than this yesterday, there were so many people to see. The cold is intense, the wind howls and the windows are quite frozen up. Yesterday evening the Empress [Augusta] came out here at 7 to see Fritz. It was most trying to them both, but they tried to be as calm as possible as it is very bad for both to give way to any emotion. We saw Uncle Ernest, Anna of Hesse and her sister Louise, Abbat and Marie, Addy, Princes George and Alexander. But Fritz could not see them all. How it will be with all the guests, I really do not know. I think Fritz's proclamation and also his letter to Prince Bismarck produced the right impression. I think Bismarck was surprised at receiving these papers all ready for publication and written out in Fritz's own hand. . . . It is of course very uncomfortable to have the dear girls in town and not here, also all my things are at our house at Berlin, so that this is more or less of an encampment. Today we shall see dearest Bertie we trust. . . .

From the Queen
ON BOARD THE *VICTORIA AND ALBERT*, MARCH 22, 1888

We are just starting. And I wish to write one line in this ship which I know you like so much and where I have thought so much of you and dear Fritz. We had an excellent smooth passage and now it pours and is beginning to blow again. We miss good Kanné's familiar face to which we were accustomed on every journey abroad for thirty years. It is too sad! We take Schobert and another good courier called Hermann though an inferior man, besides.

From the Queen
VILLA PALMIERI, FLORENCE, MARCH 29, 1888

We are comfortably installed here and have not found it [at] all cold. The last two days were most overpoweringly hot. I drove each day till yesterday through the beautiful town which I delight to do. The Duomo (I have only seen the outside of it) is simply glorious and quite took one's breath away, when we came suddenly upon it on arriving. We went on Tuesday to the Palazzo Pitti by the Boboli Gardens and were delighted with it. What treasures and what old acquaintances there are. My favourite is the Madonna della Seggiola, but there are numbers of beauties. Saturday [i.e. 24 March] we drove to Quarto to visit the King and Queen of Württemberg. Both most kind and pleased to see me again after thirty-five years. He had been to see us already on Monday. I gave your message. She asked most particularly after you and dear Fritz and wished I should say everything most kind to you and express every possible good wish. The Queen of Servia is also here and I shall see her soon. Many loving thanks for your two dear letters of the 23rd and 25th. I wish I could get a good and detailed account of the *Trauer Cour*.[20] Could Mlle de Perpignan not write one? The accounts of beloved Fritz and the wonderfully improved ones are very encouraging and, though, alas, one can as yet feel no certainty as to the improvement, the present is an inestimable blessing for which we must all be thankful. . . . Since I began this letter I have been to the Uffizi where I was again delighted with the treasures of art which are there seen to such great advantage. The crowd on getting in and out of the carriage was tremendous, but very friendly and the streets were swarming with people who were walking about and going in and out of the churches. I am very anxious to hear how things are going on, with Prince Bismarck and his son etc. . . .

From the Queen
VILLA PALMIERI, FLORENCE, APRIL 10, 1888

. . . You are quite wrong if you think I do not care for art. I delight in it. Only I can't spend hours upon it, as you can, or go about everywhere. I am enchanted with the pictures. . . . I have been, as I told you, to the Santa Croce, which is most

interesting, then to the Bargello and today we are going
to the Santa Maria da Novella. Beatrice has been about
of course much more and delights in it all. They all say
that Florence is so much more interesting than Rome, that
the collection of pictures is finer and the country here is
so lovely. I drive about every day, have been to see Fiesole
and round by Vimiglialegata, though not yet into the
Cathedral or the Villa. I will certainly go to the Palazzo
Vecchio, but my leg is a great hindrance. I shall also visit
the Duomo and the Battisteria, *all* I *can* see, for I enjoy it. I
have asked Beatrice to write about some arrangements
which I hope you can manage [at the Charlottenburg Palace
for her visit].

From the Queen

ON BOARD THE *VICTORIA AND ALBERT*, APRIL 27, 1888

A quarter past four, on our way to Queensburgh

Most beloved and darling child, How dreadful our separ-
ation was I cannot say or *how* my whole heart and soul go out
in love and sympathy towards you and our most dearly
beloved suffering Fritz. I cannot express in words what I felt
and feel. I would not give way before you. I wished to assure
you both that my heart was wrung with grief and pity and
yet not devoid of the hope which God mercifully implants
into our souls and hearts to enable us to go on. All the time I
had the happiness (for it was happiness still) to be under
your dear hospitable roof for the first time, I felt this. Could
I have only remained to be a little help, a little comfort! My
poor, dear, darling child! You are so good and brave. I hope
I have done a little good and that my visit has had a good
and beneficial effect in Berlin and elsewhere. The English
papers wrote well, though *The Times* correspondent tried a
little to depreciate the first day (with little success) of my
reception. If I can be of any further use in any way, only tell
me, and I would even run risks, papers and all if I could be

of any use. Do not, let me implore you, listen to too many reports of ill-natured observations and remarks and childish, loose observations of your own children. Believe me, there are people who wish to fan the flame, but pray also be firm, put down your foot and don't lose courage and rather have it out with your children if you hear anything. You have Germany with you. The journey was dreadfully cold. The carriage, in which some of the servants were, caught fire and delayed us and had to be taken off, not two hours after we left. On arriving here we were told that the passage would be fair and that we should go. So after breakfast, at a quarter to nine we started. In the first hour there was but little motion but for three hours after that it was very rough. I was, however, not at all ill or nervous and since the last hour and a half or more it has been quite smooth, but it is very thick, damp and cold. . . .

[Ps.] I am anxious to know what the Chancellor thought of our interview. I have not said how truly comfortably you had lodged me and how admirably *everything* was done. Sir Henry [Ponsonby] was so touched and equally so dear Jane Churchill that darling Fritz saw them.

From the Empress
CHARLOTTENBURG, MAY 4, 1888

So many most loving thanks for your dear letter by messenger, for the Order for my little Mossy of which she will be justly proud, and for the photos, the one for Princess Hatzfeldt which I have sent her, and the other for Miss Inglis with which she was quite delighted. I have had bad neuralgia for three days, in spite of which I started yesterday at half past seven on my tour, and was back again at half past ten in the evening. The weather was bad. It blew and there were heavy showers of hail and rain and the air very cold. You will see the whole account in the newspapers. The destruction wrought by the inundations is frightful: large districts laid waste, 15,000 people deprived of either homes or property. Everywhere I was most kindly received and people pleased that Fritz had sent me to look after them, and full of sympathy for him and enquiries after him. It touched and interested me so much to see in the Town Hall at Lüneburg (in a room which was given me) a banner your father [Edward, Duke of Kent] had given to a corporation. It is rather like the standard of the Life Guards, only of white satin with a rich blue fringe round and E and the Garter embroidered in the four corners. I gave it a kiss for your sake when I was alone. The *Rathaus* [Town Hall] is most interesting. If I had not felt so unwell it would have been quite enjoyable to see the old place. As it is, I was delighted to have been there. The *Oberbürgermeister* [chief mayor] made a charming speech at dinner. All the many presentations were very fatiguing and, of course, they made me terribly shy all alone. I send you some newspaper articles and a little poem which many interest you. Fritz passed a very good day yesterday and again today, sat up in a chair and has no fever ... much more himself and has been able to read and write. Today the neuralgia was so bad ... that I had to go to bed and remain there for half the day, such a bore when there is so much to do. . . . I saw different Hanoverian gentlemen of the Guelph Party[21] who do not normally show themselves. They were very nice and I am sure bore me as little malice as I did them. Of course the spiteful clique say here that I have no business to be civil to Poles or to Hanoverians. They are bent on finding fault and I cannot please them as my very existence is gall and wormwood to them and all I do is wrong. And they hate me all the more for being popular with others without their permission. The chief of all my sins is not being afraid of them, not being crushed by their calumnies and attacks. I was much struck by the honest, kind faces of the old clergymen I saw at Lüneburg. They seemed such nice simple people, so different to the affected, ambitious, scheming *Hofprediger* [court preachers] at Berlin, who are bent on rivalry with the Roman Catholic Church as to power and ascendancy over the minds of their flock; as if the influence they ought to have ought not to be due to higher motives and spring from the superiority of their souls and minds and lives and their large and noble acceptance of Christianity in its best form, instead of the subtleness and 'orthodoxy' of their doctrine. Their sway ought to be the sway of love and goodness. Then how readily would they be followed and listened to. When I see the mischief that Stöcker and his party do, I think of the passage 'Woe unto you, ye scribes and pharisees, hypocrites'. . . .

From the Empress
CHARLOTTENBURG, MAY 12, 1888

. . . Affairs are very unsatisfactory in some ways and good in others. William fancies himself completely the Emperor and an absolute and an autocratic one. Personally we get on very well, because I avoid all subjects of any importance. If dearest Fritz pulls up again things will alter materially and he (William) too will be more ready to listen. What you say about Moretta and Sandro I completely agree with. *Now* is not a favourable moment to talk to William or to take up the subject and so at present I let it completely rest and shall refuse to discuss it with anyone. I have an immense deal to do and so many people to see, there is so much to be settled and so many questions turn up. Today I went to the market at Berlin with the *Oberbürgermeister* [chief mayor] and authorities of the town. The people seemed beside themselves and we were really nearly carried off our feet. I think it right to go about a little as Fritz cannot, so the people may at least see one of us.

From the Empress
CHARLOTTENBURG, MAY 16, 1888

I am happy to say Fritz is doing nicely though progressing very, very slowly. He sits up dressed now for some time and is able to see different people and sign papers. . . . I gave your message to Prince Bismarck yesterday. He has gone to Friedrichsruhe. With next messenger I will send you some letters of your father to a Herr Ribock at Lüneburg. I heard that these letters existed and the daughter sent them kindly for me to see. . . .

From the Queen
WINDSOR CASTLE, MAY 21, 1888

I enclose a letter for dear Irène which pray give her on the morning of the 24th, which will I fear be a very trying and anxious one for you, but also, I trust, the source of future comfort and satisfaction. I must thank you for . . . the letters of my father. I have had to buy numbers of his letters but often only to burn them, as I did not wish that records of them should remain. But I should like to buy them. I send you today the photograph of my dear old [dog] Noble which you admired and will send you some others of different kinds soon. What a blessing that darling Fritz is so much better and that he may be able to be present at the wedding. It is a real *crève coeur* [grievance] to me not to be able to be present at the marriage of my two dear grandchildren. It does seem hard. But once it had to be in May, it was impossible. I am most grateful beforehand [i.e. before it arrives] for the bust of the Emperor which had better be sent on here. I am indeed grieved to hear that you have still so much annoyance. But I must always repeat that you should not allow it. You are the masters and as long as you are, you must be determined and *not* allow it. Willie telegraphed to me to express his sorrow at Sir William Hewett's death which I am sure has grieved you. You say you have had a letter from Ludwig B[attenberg] and I only hope you will see your way to put an end to a state of things which is quite ruinous and that for unlucky Sandro. Unfortunately, there is no denying that this unfortunate project [i.e. of the marriage of Prince Alexander (Sandro) with Victoria (Vicky or Moretta)], which in itself was so natural, has been the indirect cause of all his misfortunes. I know your one wish was to help him and therefore I feel if you and Vicky really love him, you ought to set him free and spare his honourable name being assailed as it is now being, even by his friends. A man's honour is after all the one thing in life which he is bound to guard and without which his existence would be misery. And it would be misery for your child too. As I was the first person who mentioned the project to you, five years ago, when I thought it would bring happiness to both, I feel bound to speak as strongly to you as I can, and for your sake, Vicky's and poor unhappy, persecuted Sandro's. . . .

From the Empress
FRIEDRICHSKRON, JUNE 5, 1888

I send you a little present today which I hope you will like. It is your father's watch which he wore and gave to an acquaintance at Lüneburg from whose daughter I have now succeeded in obtaining it. I thought you might like to have it, and have certainly a greater claim than I have. If you will accept it from me it will give me the greatest pleasure. Fritz is doing pretty well today. . . .

IMMEDIATELY AFTER FRITZ'S DEATH

From the Queen
BALMORAL CASTLE, JUNE 15, 1888

Darling, darling, unhappy Child, I clasp you in my arms and to a heart that bleeds, for this is a double, dreadful grief, a misfortune untold and to the world at large. You are far more sorely tried than me. I had not the agony of seeing another fill the place of my angel husband which I always felt I never could have borne. May God help and support you as He did me and may your children be some help, some comfort, as so many of mine were. Though at that time there *was bitterness*. I can't write what I feel. I can't collect my thoughts. I feel stunned. I would wish to do anything and everything to help you, even to go to you if you wished. Do come to us. You should get quite away with the girls for a time. Your health will require it after such a long strain. Darling beloved Fritz, I loved him so dearly. He was so kind to me always and in *'61*. I see him always before me with those beautiful, loving blue eyes. How well he was here last year still. *Here* you were engaged and *here* I received the dreadful news. I am so thankful other people who would have aggravated all were not there. . . . God in His mercy help and support you.

From the Queen
WINDSOR CASTLE, JULY 7, 1888

. . . How well I know that feeling when the months change and the years. *I* have now been a widow four years and a half more than I was a wife. And I hoped for a year or two, and more, to be taken to join him! After a time the sense of being of use to others made me wish again to live on. For your three dear girls' sakes you must struggle on bravely. Why had you to give up the uniform which your darling husband wore? Is it a rule?[22] When I had to give up Orders and things, I had them [i.e. replicas] made and *kept* the originals. I am sorry you could not keep his little pet dogs. The two little ones here are looking very well and growing nicely. They are under the special kind care of the Taits. Is there any bust of darling Fritz you like and any cast of his dear hands? I thought both existed. I shall be too glad to contribute to the building of the addition to the *Friedenskirche* [at Potsdam]. Those receptions must be cruel but the veil is a great comfort. We have terribly wet weather almost like tropical rains. Would the small sum I mentioned be of any use for the purchase of what you mention [i.e. a house of her own]? Is Bornsted private property? Oh, how dreadful is the thought that all goes on and we remain alone, as you so truly say. We shall stay here till the 17th and then go to Osborne. How, oh how shall I think of last year! Here and at Frogmore where he came to tea or to breakfast, how I thought of him and of you all! I have just had a letter from darling Arthur, who had heard by telegram the dreadful news three days before [i.e. before the date of this letter, or some three weeks earlier than the Queen's receipt of it. It had taken this time to come from Bombay]. I send you again Lord Rosslyn's sonnets, written by himself and with some difficulty, as he has a numbness in one hand, I don't know why. I still hope and pray that this controversy between the doctors may not be pursued further.

From the Queen
WINDSOR CASTLE, JULY 17, 1888

... Your quotation from *King John* of Queen Constance's words are very appropriate.[23] She was not Queen, but the widow of Geoffrey, brother to King John. . . . Is there a chance of Sophie's marrying Tino of Greece? It would be very nice for her, for he is very good. . . . I saw Böhm's sketch for the statue of beloved Fritz which I thought very fine. Lenchen saw it and can tell you. You will find her very quiet, I think. . . . I am so glad to see that your title has been officially settled as Empress Queen Frederick. It must be such a satisfaction and pride to bear his loved name.

From the Queen
OSBORNE, AUGUST 13, 1888

I must write again to tell you that Count Robilant [natural son of Charles Albert of Savoy] came here on Saturday to dine and sleep. It is thirty-three years since I saw him and I should never have known him again. He was dark then and [full?] and now he is terribly thin, quite white and looks fearfully ill and of a death-like colour. But he has been very ill. He is, as you know, most amiable, agreeable and very clever and sensible. It did my heart good to hear him speak of our darling Fritz with tears in his eyes with such admiration and love. He has known him, he says, from his childhood, *quand j'étais avec ma mère*. Do tell me again who she was. He does not like or trust Crispi and indeed he is *très difficile* and has been giving a great deal of trouble.

From the Empress Frederick
FRIEDRICHSKRON, AUGUST 16, 1888

... I am so glad you saw Count Robilant. He was an old friend of Fritz's and I like him so much. One must not forget that he is a thorough Piedmontese and conservative and therefore not at all disposed to do justice to Crispi, though I doubt not he is most difficult as *Chef*, being a Sicilian and not belonging to the aristocracy and at one time a republican. I am sure Robilant will make an excellent ambassador. His mother, whom I knew well, was a Countess Truckses or Trugses, a Prussian. She was very tall and ladylike looking. Her sister was a Countess Dohna, in Ostpreussen. Count Robilant's wife is a Clary, first cousin to the Radziwills at Berlin. I went to the Tennsberg. Uncle was very kind and civil and took me all over the place, but, alas, it will not do for me. It is nearly a ruin and would have to be entirely rebuilt which would, of course, far exceed my means, so that this would be impossible. I regret it immensely. The position, the view are so lovely and the air delicious and what walks and drives all around! I have given up the idea – much to my discomfiture – and must try to see the place near Kronberg at the end of the month. Perhaps it will do. Of course it will be less lonely, not being far from Frankfurt, but it is very small and the price is rather high. Still I could add on to the little modern house which stands there, and there is a small garden and a field belonging to it. I thought so much of former days when I saw the old Gotha Schloss again and had a short glimpse of the Thürringer Wald. But everything I look at seems to give me pain and remind me of happiness lost and gone. I am much hurt that [William's] new baby is not to be called after me. The last one I was told must be August on account of the Empress Augusta and this one I am told can only be called Oscar after the King of Sweden, who is after all no relation. Surely I might have been considered first and out of five grandsons *one* might have been called Victor as well as Oscar. It is really not kind. And I wished for Victor on account of you. It annoys me also that William is going to Austria and Italy to pay great official visits before ever asking whether he could pay you one, who are his grandmama and longer on the throne than any other sovereign. My own darling Fritz always said *erst will ich Mama besuchen* [first, I will visit Mama] but alas, he was never allowed to carry out his intentions. It is however no use being annoyed as one would not know where to stop, there is so much that hurts my feelings.

From the Queen
BALMORAL CASTLE, AUGUST 25, 1888

I meant to write from Blythswood, but it was impossible and tonight I fear my letter can only be short. I received your dear, very sad and most painful one of the 22nd this afternoon which I will answer properly by messenger. It makes my blood boil and I cannot say how furious I am, and what an insult and abomination I think it all is. The article is very nice and the other on your present title, you sent me the other day, I thought apt, really pretty. Our visit to Glasgow was a great success. Over a million of people [were] in the streets when we went there on Wednesday and great enthusiasm. We went there in state and then went to a portion of the Exhibiton. The next day we went to Paisley, also full of people, profusely decorated and most enthusiastic. We likewise passed several times through the little town of Renfrew which is quite close to Blythswood. Renfrew and Paisley are the cradle of our family as the Baron of Renfrew took the name of Stewart from being made the Royal Steward and married Margery, Robert Bruce's daughter. King Robert the Third and his wife are buried in Paisley Cathedral. Yesterday morning we went (not in state) again to the Exhibition and saw the foreign courts and the Indian and Canadian, etc. The people were out in numbers again and the same loyal enthusiasm. I looked with sad interest at your contribution, your dear pictures and the one representing darling Fritz's entry into Jerusalem.[24] I could but think that he now had entered into a far brighter and greater Kingdom than that one. The things are all much admired. Blythswood, though too much surrounded by factories, is a very pretty place with pine trees and a lovely garden and a very comfortable house, the exterior of which reminds us much of Claremont. Sir A. and Lady Campbell (she is Lord and Colonel Carrington's sister) are charming people and he is a wonderful mechanic. I thought much of you both, especially as Louis, Ernie and Alicky were with us.

From the Queen
BALMORAL CASTLE, SEPTEMBER 4, 1888

. . . But before I say anything more let me wish you joy (or I ought not to say *that* for I can never feel it) but satisfaction over dear Sophie's engagement. Tino is a good, steady young man and Sophie likes him very much and he comes from, and belongs to, loving parents and a very united, loving family. And this is a priceless blessing. A good heart and good character after all go far beyond great cleverness. Olga of Greece is a sweet, dear creature and will be kindness itself to Sophie. You will like to go to that celebrated country with all its antiquities to see Sophie. It is a fine position. I am so glad you went to Homburg and only wish you had stayed on there a little longer. I grieve to hear from both you and Bertie that Lenchen is not looking well. I know that she has to go to Wiesbaden for Pagenstecher to treat her poor eyes. I think they are weak and bad for her general health and I think the cure [at Homburg] is too strong for her. But I don't quite understand why she can't come to you at Potsdam, for it was to Coburg she could not go and she was going to you after that. How I pity you having to go to the christening [of William II's fifth son]. I think it cruel, but in Germany, or rather in Prussia, there is no sense of decency and feeling as regards mourning and I pity you with all my heart. I know what I suffered when I went to Eddy's christening – two years and a half after my loss and how I suffered! But how different to you! All surrounded me as before; no change in state. I had nothing of that awful kind to suffer. Besides which beloved Uncle Leopold led me. I am sure Henry will become softer and kinder still as time goes on and that even his views will change and enlarge. Only bear a little with him for he does love you very dearly. I hope for your sake and theirs that you will be able to pay them a visit and I hope you will be with poor Irène when the dreadful time [the birth of her first child] comes, as she has no mother and I cannot be with her. I venture to send you a bunch of heather and a wreath for the Friedenskirche as he loved the dear Highlands so much, most beloved Fritz. I love to wear the dear little bracelet constantly. His loss and your grief weighs more heavily on me even than the loss of my own children. He was such a support to us all. It has had such an effect on Bertie and on Louis too. He is much more serious and feels it dreadfully. I conclude that Sophie's marriage will not take place for some time, as both are so very young. I also send you some excellent oatcake and oatcake biscuits. . . .

From the Empress Frederick
BERLIN, OCTOBER 17, 1888

. . . I hardly dare think of last year, when he [Fritz] was doing so well and we were so full of hope, and all the former years when the 18th was so happily spent. There is an early

Communion tomorrow at the English Church and I am going there. The laying of the foundation stone of the mausoleum will be at two and at three there is a short service in the village church at Galn near Potsdam to which they have asked us. I plucked up courage yesterday to attend a sitting of our camerilla of aid for the sufferers from the inundations. A great deal has been done but I grieve to see that there is still a very great deal of distress. Of course there has been no harvest in the places where the water was out longest. The town of Berlin are going to hand over to me 575 hundred marks for charitable purposes in memory of our beloved Fritz. Some of the kind gentlemen from the town said they hoped I would look upon this as a silent protest against all that had been said and done to hurt and pain us (from certain quarters) since March last year. Of course they cannot proclaim it on the housetops, but they said they were ready to help on and support whatever Fritz would have liked. The town authorities here have always been so nice to us and also to me independently. I am much touched by this. All impartial people are quite shocked at Sir Morell's book having been confiscated. They feel how unfair it is to publish and authorize an attack and forbid the defence from being read. I knew that an unfriendly reception was being prepared for it, but I thought they would not be so stupid as to show the public that they feared the truth being known and were determined not to allow any version but that of Bergmann on the subject of our beloved Fritz's illness to be circulated. This is a perfectly despotic proceeding, worthy of St Petersburg. It will do Prince Bismarck and William no good. . . .

From the Empress Frederick
KÖNIGLICHES SCHLOSS, KIEL, MARCH 3, 1889

. . . I have again not ventured out of doors. Indeed I have been putting the layette into the cupboards and chests of drawers with Mrs Paterson. Everything has now arrived. Dearest Ninny [Irène] is very well, merry and cheerful. . . .

The harbour frozen over looks exactly like the Neva out of my window and the ships covered with snow and firmly wedged in the ice, a leaden sky over all, look more dismal and melancholy than I can say. I saw Henry and he was most kind and sympathetic. . . . Moretta misses all her kind English friends very much indeed, and is in low spirits. Still we are very thankful to be here quiet at Kiel and not at Berlin where I think I should break down altogether. The strain on my feelings would require almost superhuman strength to resist. I am so utterly alone. To live always with a gag on one's mouth is very difficult after thirty years of happy married life. Goodbye. . . . I sent you Stéphanie's letter.[25] How I pity her and yet I am sure she can find thousands to share her feelings and her thoughts. It is almost a blessing that she could not feel more deeply – what else would have been too bitter to bear.

AFTER THE MEYERLING TRAGEDY

From the Queen
WINDSOR CASTLE, MARCH 5, 1889

. . . I return you Stéphanie's somewhat strong [letter]. If she [his widow] loved him [Rudolph] very much, she could not write in that way. I have heard again that she did not take interest in what interested him and lived an independent [life] of her own, which is extremely wrong. . . . Uncle George was here last night, delighted with his journey [to Madrid, Gibraltar and Cannes] and in great spirits and made a great noise at dinner. . . . Lenchen leaves this evening. Poor Abby came to luncheon yesterday. He is miserable and says he hates the sight of a soldier and can't bear being on horseback and is to go into a cavalry regiment. A fine look out! I dread a failure. Louise starts on Saturday. . . . I always think I must give you my arm when I go out of the Dining Room [i.e. as she had done during the Empress Frederick's recent visit] and we miss you all very much. . . .

From the Queen

PAVILLON DE LA ROCHEFOUCAULD, BIARRITZ, MARCH 8, 1889

I have not written since Tuesday but I have telegraphed and can give you good accounts. We had an excellent crossing. . . . I as usual remained lying down below in my cabin and was quite well and read and worked. . . . We arrived at half past seven at Cherbourg, all the French Admirals there, a military band playing 'God save', and went on our way. The [railway] line is a very rough one but we slept well. . . . At Bordeaux the General commanding the district, who wore with pride his Crimean [War] medal, welcomed us and insisted on going the whole way with us to Biarritz where we arrived at 2.30. Then at the station there was a Guard of Honour and another military band, an escort, the préfet, the sousprefet, the English consul and his wife, the Spanish consul. . . . The comte de la Rochefoucauld received us at his home. . . . It is not a large house, nor is there much accommodation, but we are very comfortably lodged. . . . You see the sea and the Pyrenees from the house and there is a nice little garden. I have no time tonight to say much as the post goes. How strange is King Milan [of Servia]'s abdication. I cannot write much, but you should know that William is coming at the end of July in his yacht, with his ships, for a day or two to Osborne and *nowhere* else – more by messenger. . . .

From the Queen

PAVILLON DE LA ROCHEFOUCAULD, BIARRITZ, MARCH 9, 1889

I must write another line, for I have thought so much of you today. Oh, what a year of suffering and anxiety between hope and fear! Surely *then* that dear, dear, too precious life, and that reign, was not thought to be so short! Surely some months were hoped for! It is all too sad and no time can obliterate the feeling of bitter grief and longing that it should have been otherwise. God orders all for the best, we know, and some day we shall see why this terrible misfortune was permitted. Today has been beautiful and I wish you could have seen that marvellous sea with those towering waves and the strange rocks. . . . The air is delicious, so soft and light and the mimosas and camellias are in full blossom and primroses, violets, white and blue, and jonquils are all making such lovely nosegays. We wish we could send them to you. This afternoon we drove to Bayonne (only half an hour). It is a very curious old town, part of it very Spanish-looking. On our way back we drove for some way through fir woods like at Darmstadt and visited the curious convent of the Bernardines (sort of female Trappists) which is connected with a refuge or penitentiary which we had not time to visit today. It is most curious and in the woods. The Mère Supérieure Générale is a very pleasing, cheerful, nice looking person. We are very quiet and unmolested here.

From the Queen
PAVILLON DE LA ROCHEFOUCAULD, BIARRITZ,
MARCH 21, 1889

Thank God that all is so well over and that darling Irène is well and had a quick, easy time and has got, as the Highlanders say, 'a young son'. Would you not all of you rather have had a girl? And how strange that he should be born on poor Fritz Carl's birthday. However, we must all be very thankful that the dear child is doing well. I hope you are satisfied with the doctor and nurse . . . I fear she is inclined to coddle and keep people very backward, from what she told me herself, to keep them too long in bed. I thank you very much for your dear letter with the enclosures which I received quite safely yesterday and will write more about them by messenger. The answer [to the Queen's enquiry about an eligible *parti* for Victoria (Vicky or

Moretta)] you were asking about came yesterday. It was most kind but there is no hope there. I will send the letter. It is very disappointing as in every other respect it would be very desirable. We have had since yesterday evening frightful gales with tremendous showers of rain and hail and the sea is a magnificent sight – such towering waves and such a mass of seething foam with such a beautiful colour. I hope they will soon cease for it is not pleasant. I send you the copy of Affie's letter about the poor *Sultan* [foundered off Malta], written before she was finally lost. I shall be longing to hear all about dear Irène. . . .

From the Queen
WINDSOR CASTLE, APRIL 4, 1889

Charles of Sweden is I fear totally out of the question from what Helen wrote which in fact coincides a good deal with their letters. And I would not entirely refuse the other idea. He may have been, I believe was, very wild, but he is changed now and he certainly made Mia a very good husband, and they were devoted to each other and he is left with these poor little children all alone. I think Moretta would be more likely to be happy with someone a good deal older than herself and who had, like herself, loved someone before. I don't say I would have chosen him, but, what Princess Wied says so truly, the things one wishes most one seldom sees fulfilled and those one wishes least, often seem the best. We are in God's hands. . . .

AFTER THE DEATH OF THE QUEEN'S AUNT

From the Queen
WINDSOR CASTLE, APRIL 13, 1889

I just begin these lines before going to Kew for the last sad ceremony. I never was at any funeral (in England) nor at any

royal one, but at my own poor darling child's five years ago and
this is the only other one. And she [May, Dowager Duchess of
Cambridge, the Queen's aunt] is the last above me. Uncle
George [her son] and I are now the old ones, and we must feel
that. Few mothers live to their son's seventieth birthday, as she
did. Nothing but kind and loving words have been said of her by
all. Full of years and honours she is borne to her grave. We shall
be back before luncheon and then I will finish this. Many loving
thanks for your letter of the 9th. I can well understand how
dreadful that luncheon must have been. But that is inevitable
and I am glad you went. To see the wicked Great Man
[Bismarck] was worse; still, *that* even should be *wished* to show
respect. That all in the public are delighted to see you I do not
wonder at. I never told you how pleased I was at your
inheritance from the duchesse de Galliera being settled. How
much is it in English money, £.s.d? And I hear you have
likewise got some beautiful jewels. It is really very kind of her.

Later. The sad ceremony is over. We returned at half past one.
It was simple, not long and very impressive: just as at darling
Leopold's. I enclose a Ceremonial and the Service. The
church was very full. I was between poor Augusta (who looked
so crushed) and Mary [her daughters] with Alix and Beatrice
behind us, the only ones who had seats on chairs, quite close
to the coffin, which was placed facing the Altar, all the others
being in pews. There were quantities of beautiful wreaths.
Beatrice and I placed ours just after the second hymn when
the coffin was carried up three steps (a difficult task for the six
Guardsmen) and placed close to the Altar at the back of which
the mausoleum, containing the remains of Uncle Cambridge,
was and something had been taken out of the reredos so that
the coffin went a little down into it and slid gently down. They
sang beautifully. Poor Uncle George was very much upset.
Mary was also moved, but Augusta and George the most.
That last hymn ['Now the labourer's task is o'er', *Hymns
Ancient and Modern*, No. 467] is most beautiful. I was very
thankful to have been there with my poor cousins, the two
eldest my contemporaries, and it was a help to them.

From the Empress Frederick
SCHLOSS, HOMBURG, APRIL 15, 1889

... I went over today to Friedrichshof [her new house] where all is of course in great confusion but I liked the spot and the situation even more than I did before, though the day was cold and grey. If only Fritz had seen it! What a different feeling I should have! But you must come and see it, when it is finished and that will be such a comfort and such a pleasure to look forward to and a reason to try to make it as pretty as possible. The new roads are going to be a great success, I think, and the grounds in about a year's time will begin to look very nice. There is a great deal to do and as I am very fond of gardening, arranging and planning, it will be a lasting occupation. You ask about the duchesse de Galliera's bequest: she has left me five millions of francs and also some jewels which will be most welcome to me to arrange for my three girls. The words with which she left me these things are most touching and beautiful. I know that she was very fond of Fritz and of me and now that she has thought of leaving me this I feel doubly how much I should like to thank her. Of course I shall keep some jewels for myself, though I suppose I shall rarely wear any and certainly no coloured ones again. Her son, who as you know is very strange, wrote me a charming letter and has been extremely kind about the whole affair. . . . She little knew what a godsend her bequest would be to me as it enables me to make a comfortable and independent country home to end my days in, which I could not have done without any capital. All is so expensive nowadays, especially land and building. Labourers' wages are high in this part of Germany, which one can only rejoice at. There are some very poor villages near Kronberg where I hope to make myself of use. My stay at Berlin was very, very painful. All quarrels were avoided because I swallowed everything. My darling girls, seeing all going smoothly outwardly, do not know what I suffered and went through. . . .

From the Queen
WINDSOR CASTLE, APRIL 20, 1889

... I forgot answering something in one of your letters. You said B[ismarck] told you that Rudolph had had a dreadful scene with his father. I heard this from Lily [of Hanover] who had it from her sister who is very intimate with the imperial family and that it was quite true; that he had promised his father never to see Mlle Vetsera again and that when he broke his word he felt he never could show himself before his father again and shot himself. Prince Christian I think said the same. Drino and Ena are very flourishing and very amusing. He is getting more and more impudent. Poor Affie has had a very severe attack of Malta fever and was obliged to be taken to sea which at once lowered the temperature, but he is not well yet. I think he was greatly worried about the *Sultan*, and caught cold. Besides the Admiralty House there is unhealthy. He is on his way home. Louise and Lorne are coming tonight and go with me to Sandringham on Tuesday [23 April] where we stay till Saturday.

From the Queen
BUCKINGHAM PALACE, MAY 15, 1889

... Dear Tilla's death is very sad! A great link with the past gone! The last night she suffered dreadfully with her head, but then that passed away and she slept away, they could hardly know when. She was quite resigned and ready to go. Now poor Mr Blunt is also dead, who was Master of St Katherine's.[26] He died the day after dear Miss Hildyard [Tilla, former governess to the Queen's children]. They were great friends. I should indeed greatly like to have dear Vicky [Moretta], but she need not come before the 2nd or 3rd of June and can leave again on the 29th. She will not

86

Portrait of Queen Victoria by H. von Angeli, 1890

Portrait of Emperor Frederick III by Anton Weber, given to Queen Victoria, Christmas 1889, by the Empress Frederick and her children

have much gaiety this time, for she will see not a human being at Balmoral beyond ourselves and the week or so before at Windsor will also be pretty quiet. I think we may expect Beatrice's (untoward) event (which happens at a most unfortunate time) any moment from the 20th, but it might be before and *now*. *I* am ready as all my engagements till the last days of June are over. My favourite Spring visit to dear Scotland will I fear be very short. I hope for a fortnight but I would not leave Beatrice till a day or two after the fortnight when I have seen her move a little and sit in a chair. I am glad the Münsters are pleased at Sander's engagement. I am sorry to tell you that I was much disappointed by poor Mme San Martino's singing. I thought voice and execution both very indifferent. I am very sorry for her, poor thing, for I fear she will not get on. Another person I heard who told me he had played before you: Chevalier Obertheur, whose performance on the harp we all admired very much. Uncle Nemours and the Joinvilles came to luncheon and asked after you. I have been so often disturbed that I hardly know what I write and fear I must end. I send you today a photograph of dear Aunt Cambridge's room taken as she lay in her bed after her death, which I thought you would like, and two volumes of *Greville's Memoirs* with Lord Sydney's observations.[27] The others will follow later.

From the Queen
WINDSOR CASTLE, MAY 29, 1889

... I am so interrupted and overwhelmed with letters, visits, functions, etc. that I hardly know which way to turn. To continue about the 24th, at eleven we had a parade and Trooping the Colour by the Guardsmen in the Quadrangle which was a beautiful sight. I will send you a photograph of it. (I send you one of the Eton affair today). Then Bertie, Alix and their five children came for luncheon. Before dinner arrived Affie, Marie and little Beatrice who stopped till Monday [27 May], that is Marie and the child and Affie till yesterday. He is now at Portsmouth for an Inquiry about the *Sultan*. Yesterday evening Aunt Clém came and enquired much after you. And today I have the Monpensiers and the Chartres with Marguerite, their second daughter, who is just engaged to Philippe d'Orléans [her cousin]. . . . Darling Beatrice is on her sofa in her sitting room today and as well as possible, *unberufen*. The baby really is a very pretty child. . . . How well I understand the agonies the recollection of that wedding on the 24th must be to you. And how painful staying for the meeting with kind King Humbert! He went to the Friedenskirche. I hope to be able to hear and do something about the young Grand Duke Alexander [a possible *parti* for Moretta]. Both Marie E[dinburgh] and Marie L[einingen] would do anything to help you. Marie E[dinburgh] named another nice Grand Duke – Peter, the second son of the Grand Duke Nicholas. I must end now. *À propos* of poor Mme San Martino, I must say that Major Bigge, who heard her, had thought her singing very distressing and bad, poor thing. Thank the dear girls for their dear letters and lovely presents.

From the Empress Frederick
SCHLOSS, HOMBURG, MAY 30, 1889

. . . These lines I give my darling Moretta to take with her. I feel parting from her so much. . . . A Herr von Wedell accompanies Moretta. He is appointed as Kammerherr to me for six months, so that if he does not suit, it need not be a permanent appointment, but perhaps he will. He is almost a stranger to me, but a great friend of Marie Anna's. He has been staying for two months with her now. You would indeed make me most happy and do me the greatest favour, if you could induce Moretta not to be so foolish about her food. Her one craze is to be thin. She starves completely, touches no milk, no sugar, no bread, no sweets, no soup, no butter, nothing but a scrap of meat and apples which is not enough. She will ruin her health. She has a fine strong constitution. She goes to bed too late and takes almost too much exercise. I have begged and prayed, ordered, threatened, all to no effect. She is quite fantastical on the subject. Her pretty figure is quite spoilt from being too thin. If also you can persuade her to let Dr Reid vaccinate her. All the doctors say it ought to be done before going to Greece and even independently of that: from time to time one must be revaccinated. As for her prospects, should it fail with this young Grand Duke (which is possible, but of which I trust I may hear more from you), I hear much praise of this Prince of Schaumburg-Lippe (Adolf) – in a regiment in Berlin. He is nice and good looking, but of course, it is nothing as to position. Should it not be found possible for her to meet the young Russian which I still hope might be arranged, I am anxious for her to see this young Prince Adolf and this could be arranged when she comes back from England. I have also thought of the third Anhalt (Edward), a nice good young man with a nice fortune and not ill-looking, who would be sure to make a kind, nice husband and who has an amiable, cheerful disposition and is a favourite everywhere. I think the young Russian would be far more to her taste, whereas either of the two others I should feel she could be quite safe with from all I hear and I have enquired very carefully. If only she would make up her mind to consider the possibility and not reject the thought altogether, if other things fail. Please not to tell Moretta that I have written this.

From the Queen
BALMORAL CASTLE, JUNE 18, 1889

Most lovingly and tenderly do I think of you again on this most harrowing anniversary. A day never to be forgotten in history [because Waterloo was won that day] and a day when you lost the first of your dear children, now twenty-three years ago, and again a day last year when the earthly part of your precious and beloved husband, our darling, noble, excellent Fritz, was carried to its last resting place. . . . I don't think there need be any difficulty in sending a kind message to the Waldenses.[28] As regards the young Grand Duke and Moretta I fear there is no chance either, for he does not think of marrying for some time to come and no prospect is held out of it in the future. Now, dearest child, I think, it is a *Wink* [sign] that Russia is not to be, for this is the second failure. But I think we must go [no] further. You have had now *three direct* failures. Moretta has expressed a strong wish not to marry now and I own I think you should let it alone for the present. Let her see people, but pray don't force it on, for if she has no inclination, if she don't like anyone, it would never do. Send her again to us when you go to Greece for the wedding and she can join you later in Italy. But don't force or press her to marry for marrying's sake: that is dreadful. And I think it hardly right or dignified for you to go about trying to marry your daughter and getting refusals. I had something of that kind to go through with Louise and suffered and it was very painful. Do not, darling child, say you cannot forgive. Forget, no perhaps, but one must forgive. 'Forgive us our trespasses as we forgive them that trespass against us' is our constant prayer and our Saviour and Master taught us that. He prayed for His enemies once. Let me beg you not to say *that.* . . . Dear Moretta seems the better for being here and enjoys her rides and walks. . . .

From the Empress Frederick
SCHLOSS, HOMBURG, JUNE 29, 1889

. . . Let me wish you joy of Louise of Wales's engagement which doubtless will give you pleasure. We once spoke of the possibility at Windsor, if you remember and you seemed to think Bertie and Alix wished it and it might come about. Lord Fife (MacDuff) is very nice indeed and I am sure she will be very happy. Not having to leave England or be far away from her parents will be a great thing. I had to ask

Herbert Bismarck to dinner yesterday which was a bitter pill to me. I was as formal and stiff as possible. I could not avoid asking him, as I asked the other government officials here and he is an official person. If he had the slightest conscience, which he has not, he must have felt very uncomfortable. But these sort of people are brazen. By the time this reaches you, Moretta will have left you and I do not know how to thank you enough for all your kindness to her. Every one of her letters was overflowing with gratitude. The King of Greece is paying us a little visit. He goes away tomorrow. He is so lost at having parted with his daughter [Alexandra, on marriage to Grand Duke Paul], poor man. She was his constant companion. . . .

From the Queen
WINDSOR CASTLE, JULY 17, 1889

. . . It is all grievous and sad and if I do not say more about it all it is because I do not wish to add fuel to the flames. Willie is in dreadful hands, is not told what is right to do, though God knows his own heart and head ought to make him feel it. I have addressed to him to Friedrichskron[29] not to Potsdam and shall continue to do so. The changes and alterations are dreadful, such want of tact and taste. My uncle, William IV, did much the same – though of course a brother and a son is very different – still it shocked people very much. The Royal Lodge was pulled down, the uniforms in the army all changed, the naval uniform changed, the Windsor uniform[30] abolished and red collars given to the Pages. Of course this is nothing in comparison to what has happened now, but I only mention it as an example. The visit at Osborne is intensely painful and unpleasant but it cannot be avoided. Those horrible people I shall not speak [to] or only give 'Good Morning'. Liko and Beatrice think it would not be wise to go away. Bertie was here yesterday, not looking well and his leg had swollen veins. He is to go to Homburg as of course you know. This afternoon we have had a great treat. Albani and the two De Reszkes, a tenor and a bass, sang and so beautifully. I never heard anything, since Mario, so beautiful as the tenor, such powerful voices and such a fine quality. He sings Faust, Lohengrin and Romeo and the other brother, Mephistopheles, Faust and Marcel in *The Huguenots* [by Meyerbeer]. Baron Ferdinand de Rothschild dined here yesterday and spoke much of you. My visit to Waddesdon is put off to next year. . . .

From the Queen
OSBORNE, AUGUST 14, 1889

I have again lost time and cannot write as I would wish, but I will just once allude to the visit of William and the regiment. That both should be most painful to you I can well understand. But as regards the former you must remember that it was not the least for William's sake that he was so well received, though not more than any other great sovereign. It was as your and dear Fritz's son, my grandson and the sovereign of a great country with whom it is more than ever important we should be on friendly terms. This was what the visit meant and that the feeling was good and friendly between the Germans and English, I am sure, you can only rejoice at. It was your darling's and your aim. As regards the regiment, in former days such things were (foolishly) believed to be impossible and an offer was never made and very likely beloved Fritz would have offered it me as time went on, if God had spared his precious life. I thought dear Henry as Willie's only brother should have the Garter as also being twice over my grandchild [i.e. both by birth and marriage]. . . . I wrote to you yesterday about dear Bertie. Alicky arrived the day before yesterday looking like a rose.

From the Empress Frederick
SCHLOSS, HOMBURG, AUGUST 17, 1889

Today is our dear kind Grandmama's birthday. My
thoughts are especially with you. . . . Of course I am pleased
to think that the good understanding between England and
Germany has been displayed to the world. It was always
beloved Fritz's wish and my hope that the relations should
be as cordial as possible and the sympathy lasting between
our two countries in the interest of peace and the progress of
civilisation. [She comments on the irony of this friendship
being ascribed to those who had poured scorn on her for
being a too pro-English influence on Fritz.] I see no more
urgent reason for it now than during the last year or than
always. But this fitful, capricious policy has long shocked
me as you know. . . .

[Ps.] I have this moment received your dear letter of the
13th. . . . What I can do to watch over dear Bertie and
prevent his fatiguing himself I shall only be too happy to do.
I am unfortunately not in the same house with him. . . .

From the Queen
BALMORAL CASTLE, SEPTEMBER 3, 1889

. . . I am so glad you are going to Copenhagen as I know you
will be most lovingly received by the King and Queen and
all the family. Dear Alix telegraphs, 'My dear parents will
receive dearest Vicky as she deserves'. I have received a
letter from William today in which he says, 'With respect to
Count Hatzfeldt's affair, I had a long conversation with the
Chancellor. As soon as he heard from me that you would not
be opposed to the Count's remarriage with his [divorced]
wife [Helen Moulton, an American married at 17] under the
grave restriction of her not appearing in England, the
Chancellor immediately consented and waived all opposi-

tion. He declared that in this affair, solely your wishes would be followed and suggested that a little remark to Hatzfeldt or to our Government would suffice to set the affair going etc'. I am so glad that I have been able to do this for you and good Hatzfeldt himself. I should be glad that he and his children and Prince Radolin knew that I had done my best, speaking at once to Willie and again before he left and also in writing since and that I am very glad to have been so useful. It is so often so difficult to obtain what one wishes. These days are, indeed, memorable ones. We have fine weather and quite dry since we came and I only earnestly hope that it may be fine for the Gathering on Thursday which is to be at old Mar Lodge. Louise and MacDuff came here to lunch on Saturday and I had the pipers and all my keepers and ghillies out on the bridge and played them up to the door. They looked well and happy. In speaking of my visiting you, you say I never travel but in March, but this is not so. On account of Beatrice we went three week earlier this year, but else we always return at the end of April and sometimes the first days of May, so that that would do very well, when you can receive me. Many thanks for the white heather.

From the Queen
BALMORAL CASTLE, SEPTEMBER 10, 1889

I meant to write at length, but dear Bertie arrived and sat talking with me all the time, so that I have hardly a moment to do so. I am so glad that you let poor Hatzfeldt know that it was I who had obtained this answer, as it is the greatest pleasure to me to be of use, to help and cheer and to give pleasure, as you say in the letter which I got this morning of the 7th. What you quote from Goethe[31] is what dear Papa was always repeating and what he wrote in a book of mine. I can well understand what you feel about your dear little Sophie. It is I think such a strange thing that girls are to love [their homes] stronger [than boys do] and leave their happy

94

homes for what very often is no real happiness at all and the certain beginning of trials and sufferings and often very bad health. That is what I always feel and have felt and have seen verified in many cases. But in this case I think she is sure to have a happy home. I wish, indeed, Greece was not so far. I hope she and Tino will pay me a visit. . . . I am sure you must have felt parting from Bertie who is so very kind and grown so much softer and Lenchen who is very affectionate and good-hearted.

From the Empress Frederick
BERLIN, OCTOBER 15, 1889

Your dear *Verlobungstag*

The Emperor of Russia's visit passed off very well as far as I could judge. I gave a *familial souper* which he and William kept waiting for an hour and a half, so that, alas, the dishes were all spoilt. The roads were heavy and they had come home from shooting later than they expected. Yesterday I gave lunch to all the Captains who had come to Kiel with Admiral Baird. Sir Edward Malet brought them. Yesterday evening [dinner for the Tsar] was a terrible ordeal for me. The Schloss filled with guests and lit, all as in former years. . . . I thought the dear girls looked very nice: sweet Sophie and Mossy in their trains for the first time. How their dear Papa would have liked to have seen them! Dona had on all the jewels I wore for Henry's wedding. I had not seen them since. . . . We leave on the 19th early in the morning, shall be in Venice on the afternoon of the 20th and embark that evening. We are due at Athens on the 25th. Sophie will wear a white dress and bonnet and little cloak on arriving and I shall have to be in grey. For the wedding I shall also have to put on grey because they are so superstitious in Greece and think black an ill omen. [She returns to the dinner.] For poor Moretta it was intensely painful, walking behind Sophie all the while, but she bore it [loss of

precedence to Sophie because she was a prospective bride]
with a smiling countenance and great good humour. She
who had always been out with her Papa and me for four
years, of course, felt our new painful position of loneliness
much more than the others who had never been out at
all. . . .

From the Queen
BALMORAL CASTLE, OCTOBER 15, 1889

Let me thank you warmly for your dear letter of the 12th
and the beautiful and very like photographs of the fine
painting by Angeli of dear Sophie and Tino.[32] They are so
like and so well done. I shall send by the messenger, who
goes from England to Athens, on Thursday, eight old silver
baskets for bread or fruit which I would beg you to give Tino
from his future grandmama. I am afraid all these festivities
etc. must have been very trying for you, as I well know from
sad experience. That expecting he must come back, that
you must hear the footstep, see the door open and the
beloved one come in, I experienced. For years I fancied I
heard him coming along when any man's footstep was
heard. I send you in strictest confidence the account of
Count Hatzfeldt's interview with Sir E. Malet and the
latter's with that horrid creature, Herbert Bismarck. It will
be for Count Hatzfeldt to prevent the possibility of what I
suppose Herbert Bismarck wishes [i.e. to succeed him as
ambassador in London]. Pray let me have the letter back by
return messenger. We have fine weather and the colour of
the trees most beautiful. Today is my dear *Verlobungstag*, a
very happy day for me, though I did so dislike and dread the
thought of marrying. Next 10th of February would be our
goldene Hochzeit [golden wedding]. I remind you of it, as you
said you would like all to give me something in memory of
it, some little trifle to wear. . . .

From the Empress Frederick
ROYAL PALACE, ATHENS, OCTOBER 25, 1889

Now we have reached our journey's end and Sophie has held her *Eingang* [entry] in her new country [i.e. at Corinth]. We were all dressed at eight in the morning. A cloudless sky, like a fine summer's day, and a pleasant air! At ten we landed and were received at a tiny landing place by the King and Tino. There was a crowd of townspeople and country people. The Archbishop held a very long address to Sophie in a tiny railway station crammed full of people. After considerable waiting we got into the train and reached Kalamake [having crossed the Isthmus of Corinth] in a quarter of an hour and went on board the *Amphitrite* [to cross the sea of Saronicus]. It was very pleasant on board. We had luncheon with the King and arrived here at Athens at four, all the ships saluting. How pleased I was to see the dear British ships and how splendid they looked! Dear Olga, dear Bertie and Alix and the King and Queen of Denmark came on board. Sophie bore herself so nicely, and was gentle and quiet and composed. Endless presentations took place before we landed here. The way to the palace was crowded. The people made a good impression upon me. They look good-humoured and healthy, in short, comfortable, and behaved in a very orderly way. They gave Sophie a very enthusiastic reception. All went off very well. Here in the palace we went to a *Te Deum* directly in the little private chapel. It is the greatest comfort in the world that dear Bertie and Alix are here. The view out of my window is splendid – a strip of sea, a border of faint blue hills and in the foreground the Acropolis. The town is, of course, quite modern and not interesting and the landscape very bare, arid and sandy, but the King's garden is a perfect oasis and all the lines of the hills build up a most striking and interesting panorama, but certainly more eastern than European. They are all so kind and nice to my Sophie. . . .

From the Empress Frederick
ATHENS, NOVEMBER 16, 1889

. . . Our little tour to Epidaurus, Mytelene, Tireus and
Eleusis went off very well. I have asked Mr Rodd who was
with us to write to Sir Henry Ponsonby about it, so that you
may have a better account than I can give. It interested me
so much to see these places and see the vast heaps of ruins
from which one has been able to trace the ground plan of
these great fortified castles – Mytelene and Tireus supposed
to have been built 1000 BC, most likely described by Homer.
Schliemann, though no archaeologist, has certainly
rendered an immense service by discovering so much of
these remains and German and Greek scientists have followed up his researches and explained what has been found.
The tombs in the rocks are very curious indeed. The theatre
at Epidaurus is the best preserved one still in existence,
fifty-five rows of white marble stones as seats. I counted 101
steps up to the top. Of the temple of Asklepios [Esculapius]
nothing remains but broken fragments on the ground,
strewn far and wide, which have only lately been excavated
by the Greek government and the Greek Archaeological
Society. But some of the bits of capitals and columns and
benches and friezes are so lovely. The work is so exquisite
that one grieves over the destruction which has laid everything low and left not one stone upon another. It is quite
possible to reconstruct these edifices on paper from what is
left. Dr Dörffeld, who was with us, is wonderfully clever in
finding out the plan of the buildings. The country all around
is bleak and uninhabited, very mountainous in character,
but like one vast Scotch moor. I only wondered not to see
the game rise! The few peasants one meets now and then
driving a donkey or riding one are fine and picturesque. Or
else the only people one meets are the shepherds with their
flocks of sheep and goats that have the range of all the hills
accompanied by the dogs that are very like collies. Instead
of the kilt one sees the *fustanella*. I think the people one

meets so nice, civil and hearty and kind. I should much like to see more of them. The air was very fine, when not too cold, and we enjoyed walking. The sunsets are perfectly magnificent. As the hills are in part covered with low bushes, about a foot or two high, and heather and broken up grey stone, though without the fine bold shapes of granite, the setting sun throws a rose-coloured glow over all which is lovely. Nauplia has also a very pretty position. It is a squalid, wretched little town with a fortress on a very high rock behind it. I scrambled up the 960 steps to the top, where the state prisoners are kept. They looked so miserable, poor wretches, I could not help feeling very sorry for them, though they are criminals who have been very dangerous. The people at Nauplia were so kind and civil and received me so well! We put up in a small house belonging to a colonel of a regiment. It was so cold at night in my room that I wrapped myself in my Balmoral plaid and dressing gown in bed! The room felt like a cellar. Out of doors it was fine and pleasant, though the north wind was very cutting at times and one had to wrap up warm. All the higher hills of the Peloponese are covered with snow. . . . They say parts of Thessaly, Euboea, Sparta and the Peloponese have beautiful vegetation and that it is only Attica and Argolis, the two provinces I have seen, that are so devoid of water, vegetation and soil. Just around Nauplia the soil is cultivated and there are kitchen gardens. All the vegetables looked beautiful. There is also a narrow strip of marshland, but as it is not drained I should think it must make the place unhealthy and breed fevers. . . .

From the Queen
WINDSOR CASTLE, DECEMBER 16, 1889

I feel so shocked not to have written since the 7th, but my hands have been very full. So many Christmas presents to look after and many of the family in the house since the 13th to today. . . . Much, very much, I thought of you on the 14th and of the poor Princess Battenberg, who had none of her children with her but Marie Erbach yesterday. But I telegraphed to all but Sandro and Franzjos and got answers from all. You asked about the report of the death of Sandro's wife,[33] but you will have heard from the papers that the report was entirely untrue. How can people invent such things! She is to be confined [i.e. have her baby] this month and is not strong. . . . I am very glad that Naples is become so much wholesomer and trust that you will all keep well. It is to me even (I am no sightseer or lover of Roman or Greek history) incomprehensible that your girls do not care for Pompeii for it must be so curious and interesting to see. Anything so old and so highly preserved is always full of interest to me. I think you do quite right to wait to speak to Lord Dufferin about the Waldenses. But you can say that Lord Salisbury approved a message being sent. You will find the Dufferins very pleasant. . . . The music on the 14th was very fine and I send you the Order of the Service. . . .

From the Queen
OSBORNE, DECEMBER 27, 1889

A thousand, thousand thanks for your dear precious gift from you and all your children.[34] The picture is beautiful, very like and very well painted and just what I wished. The dear hands are so well done too. Many, many thanks to you all. Also many thanks for your dear letter of the 20th, received on Christmas Day. How beautiful and enjoyable Naples must be, though many people dislike living in the town and seeing the cruelty of the people to their poor animals so much. I mean to write again properly tomorrow but before closing my letter I must express my sorrow and sympathy at the shock you have had in receiving this letter of dear Fritz's with his last directions *now*. It is terrible [see pp. 5–6]. But I can't understand why he did not leave a duplicate with you. Our *Bescherung* was very nice, but we missed Liko and we thought of you and the dear girls and last year. . . .

From the Queen
OSBORNE, DECEMBER 28, 1889

... We are very busy preparing for the tableaux which we are going to have on the 7th, repeated on the 9th and there is also to be a little play on the 8th. Louise, Beatrice and Helen appear in the tableaux and the two sisters in the latter. You shall hear all about it. I may, however, say this. The tableaux will represent 1) King Ahaseurus and Queen Esther, in which my Indians take part, 2) Mary Queen of Scots taking leave of her attendants, 3) a Bedouin encampment, in which the Indians will again appear, 4) Queen Philippa interceding for the prisoners of Calais, and 5) Twelfth Night. The play is called *Little Toddlikins* and is very droll. I hope to see Mr Haggard tonight, who has just seen you, which will be very interesting to me. I am longing to hear if you are pleased with the picture. ...

From the Queen
OSBORNE, JANUARY 7, 1890

I direct this letter whither [Berlin] I grieve to think you will have to go, for it is a long and fatiguing journey and I am so afraid lest you should get the influenza. But you will take care and you are right to go. I am sure it [i.e. the death of the Empress Augusta] must have given you a shock – the illness was so sudden. I know you told me Dr Vollen thought her weaker. I wish he would write a *Bericht* [report] of her illness for me. Would you ask him? I cannot forget our long, long acquaintance – from 1845 – and till about eight or nine years ago great friendship. And her comparatively sudden death shocked me very much. She only telegraphed to me on Thursday or Friday to thank me for my New Year's letter and wrote to me quite lately. I am glad I saw her once more, in Berlin and at Charlottenburg. I got your dear letter of the

4th this morning. Of course it was written in utter ignorance of the poor Empress's illness even. It only began on Friday I think. . . . Of course all our tableaux and the little play have been postponed. I send you the copy of a letter from Leopold of Belgium about the fire which please send on to Lenchen and two from Arthur which please show to Marie Anna.

January 8. I finish today. I fear this hurried journey will remind you painfully of the one, on March 10, 1888. May God protect you and give you strength and courage to go through all that awaits you.

From the Empress Frederick
BERLIN, JANUARY 20, 1890

How very sad is the death of the poor Duke of Aosta! It will be a terrible shock to the King of Italy. The two brothers were so devoted to each other and such faithful friends. The King is such a kind-hearted man. I am sure he will be in despair. Poor Laetitia, left a widow so young with a tiny baby. How badly this year begins! . . . The Ladies tell me that she [i.e. the Empress Augusta] had intended giving soirées on the *Donnerstage* [Thursdays] again and different large dinners. Things I should not dream of doing any more. To me it is so inexplicable that she felt her only son's [Fritz's] death so little and would never speak of him but so much of her *Pflicht* [duty] to go on with everything just as it had been in the days of the Emperor William. On the whole we may say that her life closed in a merciful way for her. She could not have led the life of an invalid and she was already very helpless. But her mind and all her faculties were quite unimpaired. Her sight, her hearing never failed and her will remained iron to the last. It was a mercy too that Louise and Fritz of Baden [her sister and brother-in-law] were with her and that she had no anxiety or distress of mind at the last. She wished to live on, they all say, which is a sign that she did not suffer. This is all I could gather for you. The Empress's education, her opinions, and her ways belong to a generation which has passed away. She was always a marvel to me, for she was unlike all other people, except her own mother and her brother and sister, though she was far above the two latter. It is so sad to pass the empty palace . . . I feel terribly depressed and wretched, so many harrowing memories are brought up and so much wounds me. . . . Courage seems to fail and memory is such a torment under which one writhes. . . . You know all this, have gone through all this. . . . You have gone through the same. Forgive my troubling you with it. I have nobody to whom I can say it all or who can feel it with me. My little Sophie's room is like an empty cage. The little bird has flown and one has to do without one's pet, but she is happy. So I must not complain.

From the Queen
OSBORNE, JANUARY 29, 1890

. . . People will become more courageous and Uncle Ernest more and more discredited. It was too bad that that man who exposed him should have been punished. . . . The Empress Eugénie is here and three of the tableaux were repeated for her with the addition of one from *Faust* in which Beatrice looked lovely as Grätchen.

[Ps.] Could you not ask Louise [of Baden] to let me have the smallest trifle the Empress wore as a remembrance?

From the Empress Frederick
BERLIN, FEBRUARY 4, 1890

As you know your regiment of dragoons here celebrate their jubilee on the 23rd, I think, of this month. Did you think of giving them a souvenir of this festive occasion, perhaps something in silver for their mess? Of course, it need be nothing very large or costly. I was going to write to you about this last week. I heard that Charlotte said she had already asked you to do so. As one never knows whether what she says is quite correct I thought I would ask you whether it was the case, as, of course, it easily may have been, though I do not quite think it her business. Are you going to send Colonel Russell to represent you at the dinner or will Sir E. Malet? Excuse my asking you this indiscreet question.

From the Queen
OSBORNE, FEBRUARY 12, 1890

. . . I at once got a very handsome sort of vase or jug in silver with an inscription which goes today by messenger to Sir Edward Malet to present to the regiment. I hope you will like and approve it and I shall have my picture framed also for them by Angeli just the size of yours. Let me now thank you for the fine Prayer Book which you all have given me, which I value very much and which I will take to Windsor to use *myself* in the chapel there. Thanks to you I have Bible and Prayer Books here and at the mausoleum specially given me for them by you and I shall like to use this myself. The dear little picture of beloved Waldie, born that same day [i.e. on the Queen's wedding anniversary] gives me the greatest pleasure and shall be placed here. It is very like and the frame very pretty. My Household here gave me a lovely souvenir, a small enamel (in red) of my dear wedding picture framed in white heather with two sprigs of orange flowers in ormolu and the date. Dear Beatrice (my only child present) gave me a little golden basket full of delicious orange flowers and myrtle and I got many bouquets from my Ladies. Dear Liko returned that day at three after a beautiful passage, looking the picture of health, very brown and with a beard, which makes him look like Ludwig and Sandro, but I liked him better without it. How strange this act of Willie's is about the working classes[35] of which Prince

Bismarck disapproves as he told Sir E. Malet himself, saying he would probably retire soon altogether! It has made a great sensation here. . . . I believe (but I am not sure) that Irène and Henry are to be at Darmstadt at the beginning of March. I suppose they are afraid of Berlin at this time of year for the baby, but I wish you could have had them. He is a splendid boy I hear. Poor dear Lord Sydney still lingers with repeated little rallies, but gradually getting weaker. It is very sad. I believe this escapade of young Orléans is doing him and his family [no] good. . . .[36]

From the Queen
WINDSOR CASTLE, FEBRUARY 26, 1890

Your long and very interesting letter of the 19th, 21st and 22nd reached me on the 24th (the 42nd anniversary of the French Revolution [of 1848]). I thank you very much for it.[37] It touched me very much. I thank you very much for all you tell me. The visit of Bismarck and his admission must have been very curious. My Government intend meeting the proposal of William in a friendly spirit and accept the conference but with a reservation about the hours of labour for men which cannot be reformed and may be left to them. I mean we cannot tell them not to work beyond a certain number if they wish to work for more. . . . I send you today some platinotypes[38] from platino which have been brought to a great perfection by Elliot and Fry. . . . Bertie I thought very well, but he is much graver. The two girls are still rather weak from their influenza. The Government are very strong and have very large majorities which is a great thing. My poor Indians have been rather unfortunate lately. Yussuf Bey, the one who came at the end of October, fell with a tricycle which he is in the habit of using and broke his arm. Karim al Ali left me in October as he could not bear the climate. And my good excellent Abdul has been laid up for three days with what threatened to be a bad boil on his neck, but I am glad to say it is all subsiding and he is nearly well again. He is so useful to me that I was quite lost without him. Poor things, one must feel so much for them, away from all their belongings and dearest and nearest, and they are so touchingly gentle and patient that it is a pleasure to try and do anything for them. I went constantly up to Abdul, who lives just up the stairs. . . . On Tuesday next we go to town for a dreadful Drawing Room. It is so tiring for me to dress for it and I fear I shall not be able to stand at all hardly. My legs have been very troublesome this winter. I slipped just about two and a half months ago in my tub and saved myself from falling by catching hold of a sofa and in doing so I must have strained my sound left leg, though I was not aware of it at the time and since that, off and on, rheumatism got into it and makes me very lame. Just now it is worse again.

From the Empress Frederick
BERLIN, MARCH 10, 1890

The ceremony [of the 'inauguration' of the alteration to the old mausoleum to take the coffins and monuments of Emperor William I and Empress Augusta] yesterday was very painful to me. I had not the courage to drive through the garden of Charlottenburg and past the house, so I went round outside to the mausoleum. The chapel itself has been enlarged and, I think, completely spoiled. The proportions were just right for the monument of Frederick William III and Queen Louise. Now it has become a large square building in which the monuments completely disappear . . . and look quite insignificant. The candelabra are taken away and put against the walls. I think it the most unfortunate arrangement I ever saw. Under this large space, a square chapel, a fine large new vault has been arranged, well ventilated and lit, with square pillars and a niche with an altar, immediately under the one above. Closest to this altar are my parents-in-law's coffins, a little behind them, King Frederick William III's and Queen Louise's and, right and left, Prince Albert's of Prussia and Princess Leignitz's. This is very well done. You remember the smaller space at the top where you saw the Emperor William's coffin. This space is now empty and has the same skylight, filled with blue glass, as it used to have. In the upper chapel a monument will be erected to the Emperor William and the Empress Augusta, but they have not yet settled how. The mausoleum is now four times as large as the one at Potsdam [i.e. for Frederick III] will be. There was a so-called family dinner at the Schloss yesterday evening and one the night before. These occasions are the most trying of all for me and I feel most miserable amongst them all. There are so many things which make one feel so sore, that aggravate and wound one and rub one up the wrong way, that one would wish to run away and hide oneself and let one's life flow on in peace. . . . No one feels for one or grieves or understands what one is going through. So much is said and talked which one so completely disagrees with and yet it is best to keep one's opinion quite to oneself. . . .

From the Empress Frederick
SCHLOSS, HOMBURG, APRIL 23, 1890

. . . Yesterday the Empress of Austria took us by surprise and paid me a visit. She drew up in a dreadful droschke [a low four-wheeled hired carriage] and would not have our carriage to go back in. It was a terribly sad meeting. I saw her last at Norris Castle (1887). What have we both suffered and gone through since then! She was looking pretty well and unaltered, I thought. Her complexion a little weather-beaten, but her figure as young as ever. Valérie was with her. She stayed an hour and a half, but would not take a drop of tea or coffee. She talked a great deal to me and was as kind and amiable and natural as always. She invited me to come and stay with her next spring in the Lainzer Thiergarten, the house which the Emperor gave her. I will not trouble you with a long letter today as you will be only just arrived and no doubt tired and anxious to rest and have your things unpacked. Louise of Baden wrote to me asking whether I thought you would like to see her and saying she would much like to come. I think it would be very kind if you did ask her just for an hour and also allowed Anna to pay her respects. . . .

From the Queen
WINDSOR CASTLE, MAY 7, 1890

. . . I have sent off my letter to the Queen of Denmark and I hope to have an answer soon. I fear all hope of Alicky's marrying Eddy is at an end. She has written to tell him how it grieves her to pain him, but that she cannot marry him, much as she likes him as a cousin, that she knows she would not be happy with him and that he would not be happy with her and that he must not think of her. Victoria also wrote to him very kindly. It is a real sorrow to us and they have tried to persuade her, but she says that if she is forced she will do it but that she would be unhappy and he too. She shows great strength of character as all her family and all of us wish it and she refuses the greatest position there is. Angeli has arrived and has already drawn the picture in and it is so like.[39] I shall sit this afternoon. Yesterday evening Stanley came and dined here and afterwards gave us a short but most interesting lecture. You would have been greatly interested. Tomorrow I go to London and shall see Affie and Marie. On Friday is the Drawing Room and on Saturday we return here. On Monday dear Papa's statue will be *enthüllt* [unveiled on Smith's lawn, Windsor] but I have seen it up and it looks splendid and so like. . . .

From the Empress Frederick
SCHLOSS, HOMBURG, MAY 10, 1890

. . . I regret the present colonial policy in Germany and fear it will cost more than it is worth or than the country can afford. I was so glad Stanley was received at Windsor and thought his speech at the Albert Hall so interesting. . . .

From the Queen
WINDSOR CASTLE, MAY 15, 1890

I was so very sorry not to have been able to write to you by messenger yesterday, but our visit to Waddesdon took up the whole day. We left here at twelve and only came back at a quarter to eight. But everything went off extremely well and it is a most beautiful place. The position, view, approach are all beautiful and I think the style of the house – a real French château – so fine. The interior reminds one of Eu and St Cloud etc. and again bits of Cliveden. It was all very well and quietly managed. We lunched alone (we three) and Louise who went on there and helped in many ways. . . . I had my pony chaise there and went about the lovely grounds and even the orchid houses. Aylesbury was beautifully decorated. Baron Ferdinand asked a good deal after you. I here send you the Queen of Denmark's answer. It is great nonsense, but the Queen is wanting in good sense and in what is right, I have often seen. The unveiling of the statue was a very pretty sight. The sun came out and shone brightly and the whole ceremony (correctly put in the Court Circular) was very pretty and well done. The troops looked well. The dear statue is very fine and very like my darling one. I will send you a photograph but they are not very successful. . . .

From the Empress Frederick
SCHLOSS, HOMBURG, JUNE 3, 1890

Yesterday we spent the whole day going to Neuwied and back and paying a visit to the dear Princess of Wied at Segenhaus. I had not seen her since 1888. She was most kind and full of sympathy. She is so gifted and distinguished and good that I always enjoy being with her. Her son and Mavichje[?] were there and some friends, also Prince Adolf of Schaumburg Lippe who is in the hussars at Bonn, a young Countess Solms and a few other people. It poured all the time so the lovely place was not seen to advantage. The house is nothing particular, but the position and views are really beautiful. The Princess asked so much after you. She was so delighted with Helen's children. On Sunday Louis took us to Rengsdorf which interested me very much and is very picturesque. He has done up the old place very well indeed in the appropriate style. It was such a cold day. The potatoes, beans and peas in the plain have all been nipped and turned black by the frost. I hope it has not been so cold at Balmoral. It was just two years ago when we arrived at Friedrichskron from Charlottenburg and had to have fires lit. Oh, how every hour and minute of that time are before me: our last fortnight together on earth. I am pursued and tormented by recollections which are an agony. There are so many other painful things connected with that time one would be so thankful to be able to forget, but which one cannot. The impressions are too vivid and powerful and the indignation one felt then one feels now. I am therefore anxious to avoid being at Berlin on the 15th. I do not trust myself to be able to conceal and control all the bitterness I feel of which I am reminded when I am obliged to meet all those people. I should prefer to spend that day of pain here alone in peace and undisturbed where there is nothing to jar on one's feelings and one can sorrow in silence and unseen. Of course if the mausoleum [at Potsdam for Frederick III] had been finished, I should have gone and have taken arrangements into my own hands as much as possible and I think that my wishes would have been met to a certain degree and will be when the time comes which may be this autumn or winter.

From the Empress Frederick
SCHLOSS, HOMBURG, JUNE 12, 1890

... Now I have a piece of news to impart which is that yesterday the Prince of Schaumburg Lippe proposed to Vicky and she has accepted him. In her depression and discouragement, feeling that the happiness she had hoped for is not to be hers, she accepts this. I hope it is a wise step, but it made my heart ache to think it is not what she dreamt of. The Prince is the fourth son of the Prince of Bückeburg. His mother is a nice person, the sister of Helen's father and of the Duchess of Schulenburg. His eldest brother is married to Marie of Altenburg (daughter of Prince Newitz). The second is paralysed and the third lives at Metz. This one is an excellent, honest and straightforward creature who bears a high character in his regiment and is much respected. The Prince is serving in the hussars at Bonn. Perhaps´ Liko remembers him as he was in the same regiment. Vicky is quite willing to go and live with him at Bonn and then later perhaps he can leave the army if his father gives him a place. William wishes this marriage particularly. I have cried so much I feel quite ill. But I think the young man is thoroughly trustworthy and good and I am sure he will try to make her happy and that she will try her utmost to do her duty. Would you allow me to present him to you while we are in England? She has the very great wish that the family should know him. He has a nice and good expression in his face and very good health. He is the same age as William. This has all come about rather suddenly. Prince Adolf came here to see me. Then we saw him at the Princess of Wied's (she is his aunt *à la mode de Bretagne*). . . . He has seen very little of the world and has not travelled. I think it would do him an immense deal of good to go about a little. . . . I dare not think of parting with her as it will be dreadful and yet I am glad she should have a house of her own and someone to protect her in case I die, and I am also thankful to think she will not live very far off.

From the Queen
BALMORAL CASTLE, JUNE 14, 1890

You will easily believe how surprised and I must say, thankful, I was when I read the news in your dear letter of the 12th, received this morning. Strange to say I had a sort of notion that your letter might contain something and yet I don't know exactly why I should. You mentioned to me having seen Prince Adolf of Schaumburg Lippe at Princess Wied's and William had mentioned him to me so I thought and hoped something might come of it. Why should she not be very happy? Very likely what you wished might not have answered and any English marriage would never have been possible. He is Helen's first cousin. I think the father must be made to settle something on him, which I should think he would. As for rank and connections, I cannot see that you need complain. I am so very thankful that the dear child has at last found a good husband and I am sure she will be a good and affectionate and dutiful wife and that that restlessness will cease. I shall be delighted to make his acquaintance and think it quite right that he should know us all. His uncle married Alix's first cousin, sister to the Duchess of Nassau. . . . Can you send me a photograph of Prince Adolf that I may see what he looks like? It is a good thing that William likes the marriage as it will make it so much easier for you. I can but too well understand how it has agitated and upset you as there is nothing so horrid as a daughter's engagement and marriage and to go through it alone without one's husband is too dreadful. I hope you will be able to have them a great deal with you. I conclude you will leave her, and I trust Mossy too, with me as I hear from Mr Haggard that the heat in Greece is simply awful and that he has warned Count Seckendorff of it. It would be very bad for the girls. . . . I send you today Arthur's last and most interesting letters about Japan. When you and the girls have read them send them to Marie Anna and ask her to return them [as] she has done the others. . . .

From the Queen
OSBORNE, JULY 20, 1890

I write this to Athens or rather Tatoi, but I may try to catch you at Malta. What shall I say at this most unfortunate and yet fortunate event [the birth of Sophie's son on July 20] happening so soon? Though we must be most grateful for all going off so well so far, it is too distressing that you should after all be too late! . . . Having started so early and yet be ten or twelve days too late! It is unpardonable of Olga and Willy not to have been back. I long for details but can get none yet. But we know she is going on well. Poor darling, how she must have worried without you! Do tell me all you can when you get there. Don't pray mix the girls up in lying-in, unedifying and, for the future, alarming details. It must be a week at least too soon, for she won't have been married nine months till the 27th. Tonight or tomorrow we shall hope to hear from you. I have telegraphed Gibraltar. . . .

From the Empress Frederick
TATOI, AUGUST 1, 1890

I must begin by apologising that I did not write last night. I was too tired, too excited and too agitated and had such a business to hide all my tears from everyone that I am sure you will excuse me and not think it neglectful or lazy of me. The first thing whenever I arrive anywhere is to write to you, of course. And now my own beloved one is not there to whom to write, I feel more than ever the want of imparting to you all impressions be they bitter and painful or the reverse. It was indeed a moment to hold my child, my Sophie, once more in my arms. But, oh I was shocked at her appearance! Nothing but a little skeleton! . . . I trust she will pick up again in time. My sweet little grandchild is a little dear, very pretty . . . little George! Here in Greece they must call the children after the grandfather. It is a universal custom and they may only have one name! The christening will be here in the house in a few days. My Sophie was so pleased to see us. 'All my pleasure seems to come at once, now,' she said. She looked from Mossy to Vicky and to me. . . .

From the Queen
OSBORNE, AUGUST 22, 1890

. . . I do hope that there will be no difficulty in Sophie's coming to Germany for Vicky's marriage. It is strange that she should be so disinclined to make any little effort from day to day as I think one always is so anxious to do so. One word more, before continuing, on the subject of William's sending Olshausen: you say he [William] is only the brother, but he *is* the head of the family (that you cannot help) and as such had a perfect right, on hearing of the state of the case, to send an eminent doctor to enquire. I can, however, well understand how careful for dear Sophie's sake you must be not to appear to interfere. Still the mother has the right to do so, especially an Empress. . . . Beatrice is delighted with all she saw and, excepting at Oberammergau, was favoured by splendid weather. She was much pleased with the Passion Play and greatly pleased and interested with the splendid scenery and the marvellous castles and palaces of poor King Ludwig which she saw. . . .

From the Queen
GLASSALT SHIEL, LOCH MUICH, OCTOBER 17, 1890

. . . Beatrice and I with Emily Ampthill and Minnie Cochrane came here yesterday for luncheon in an awful storm of wind and rain (the worst day we have had at all this

season) but the dear little house was warm and comfortable and this morning, though slight showers may still come
on, is bright with little wind. We return after luncheon; for
I have my masseuse for my legs, an excellent woman, at
Balmoral and ought not to lose more than a day. But my
legs are better and imagine! I danced quadrilles the night
before last and twice before! We had a beautiful small
band of eight who play with an *entrain* like Strauss and
render all sorts of things, whom Fife has every year up at
Mar for a month nearly and they came to Balmoral on the
8th and stopped till yesterday, being billeted about in the
village, nice, quiet people who really play quite delight-
fully. . . .

From the Empress Frederick
BERLIN, OCTOBER 31, 1890

In answer to your telegram I write to say that the date of
the wedding . . . is . . . the 19th of November. . . . The
wedding will be in the afternoon; the civil marriage here in
the house, as I wish her to leave her home already married;
then comes the ceremony in the Schloss Capelle, but no
ceremonious *Tafel* [wedding breakfast] and no *Facheltanz*
[torchlight dance] as according to the strict old fashioned
notion. There are difficulties about rank and so on and on
account of Dona's state of health, it was wished to curtail
the ceremony as much as possible. There will also be no
Cour, for that reason and no ball, of course, as neither
Moretta nor I could have borne the thought of it. There
will be a gala opera on the 17th to which I, of course, will
not go and there is a large family dinner which I give on
the 18th and that is all. Adolf's parents come for the three
days and mostly all his relations. Our darling Sophie is to
arrive next week. . . .

From the Queen
BALMORAL CASTLE, NOVEMBER 15, 1890

I do not write much today but wish to say my thoughts and prayers will never leave you on the 19th which will be a terrible day for you, but your dear child will be in safe hands and she will not be far away from you. We shall be travelling on that day, but I mean D.V. on the 21st[40] to give a dinner in honour of the marriage to which Helen and Hatzfeldt and the gentlemen of the Embassy as well as the Salisburys are to be invited. . . . I had already read in the papers Stöcker's resignation with much pleasure. It is indeed curious that Vicky should be the innocent cause of this dreadful man's resignation. It is so nice that she is to wear your veil and lace, just as Victoria and Irène did their beloved mother's and Beatrice did mine. It is a nice idea I think. . . .

From the Empress Frederick
BERLIN, NOVEMBER 28, 1890

. . . I am greatly relieved to think that poor Louise Holstein's prospects will *not* be blighted. I think it would be a very nice marriage. Aribert [of Anhalt] is a nice and amiable young man and one may hope that it would be for both their happiness [married 1891, divorced 1900]. I wish indeed someone nice could be found for Tora, and do not at all despair of such being the case. My darling Moretta writes a little more cheerfully now, so that I trust she is getting over the parting and is beginning to take a less gloomy view of life. She says everyone has been most kind to her at Bückeburg and she telegraphed that she thought Detmold very pretty. The cold is intense here, really too miserable. One can hardly go out; 12 degrees Réamur below zero! and a north-east wind. It was so kind of Louischen and Arthur to come to stay here three days with me. I am afraid it is

neither very amusing nor very comfortable in my house. . . .
I saw Dr Douglas Powell twice and found him both very
clever and nice as far as I could judge. Koch's cure [for
tuberculosis] still, as you can imagine, excites the intensest
curiosity, excitement and interest and I am afraid that
people whose expectations have been unduly raised by the
tremendous noise in the press will be doomed to many a
disappointment.[41] There has, as yet, not been time to effect
a perfect cure, and no one can say with *certainty* that this can
be done. There is so much still to be studied and worked out
that it is wrong to form a hurried judgement one way or
another. The discovery is most important and most extraordinary, but whether it will be universally adopted as a
cure remains to be seen, and must be patiently waited for. I
was very glad that a difference between Mr Parnell and the
Gladstonites has arisen and shall watch the results with the
greatest interest. So many thanks for the charming photo of
yourself writing, which is so like and good. I sent your letter
to Moretta. She leaves tomorow for Frankfurt and then stays
a couple of days at Vienna on her way to Venice. . . .

From the Queen
WINDSOR CASTLE, NOVEMBER 29, 1890

. . . I hope you have heard from Moretta in a more cheerful
letter? Does a Lady go with her? If so, I hope a Gentleman
will also or it will else [not] be very *lustig* [jolly]. No Lady
would have been best. What maids has she got? . . . Here the
excitement is intense about Parnell and what the G.O.M.
will do. In Ireland the feeling is very strong against Parnell
on account of his proving himself such a liar and having
perjured himself. It is satisfactory to see wickedness punished even in this world. It is a just nemesis. . . . I have just
got a telegram from Moretta saying they are just starting.
The Christmas presents are an endless work. I must end to
get a little done before it is quite dark.

From the Empress Frederick
BERLIN, DECEMBER 19, 1890

Though I am sorry to say these lines will not reach you on the 14th yet they are to express what I feel ever and again when this day of woe, for you and for me, comes round and I think of those we have lost, of your bereavement and of the terrible time we passed through when they were torn from us. . . . Tomorrow I shall be at Potsdam in *our* mausoleum and our thoughts are sure to meet, and also to be at Darmstadt in the Rosenhöhe with our darling Alice. . . . I return Lord Rosebery's touching letter which shows how heartbroken he is [over the death of his wife]. Many thanks too for the paper about Greece which I return having read it with much interest. You say that for the first time I have written to you on a political matter since '88. It does indeed seem strange that now I am fifty I am completely cut off from the official world. Not a single official person ever comes near me! . . . But as a member of the thinking public, I do not stand alone and have many who care to exchange opinions with me. . . . It is impossible to lose one's interest in the affairs of this country and in the cause of peace and progress in the rest of the world. And when I go to Italy or to Greece, it is a pleasure to talk with King Umberto and with Willy of Greece. . . . With regard to Greece I should like to add one word. The most dangerous and ticklish question for peace in the East and the one that is always turning up again, is the Macedonian question. Both Bulgaria and Greece will never resign a claim to a portion of this country, and never be friends until this is once settled and arranged. Once Sandro had made a most excellent plan of how both could be contented in the event of this province being lost to Turkey. I often wonder whether England, Austria, Germany and Itlay could not try to arrange the Macedonian difficulty peaceably for these smaller Powers and thus do away with a dangerous apple of discord which may set the East in a blaze at any moment and give the Russians the much

The Crown Princess visiting Flete, Devon, in August 1887

Queen Victoria in travelling carriage, Grasse, April 1891.
(Photographer: F. Busin)

Queen Victoria's birthday table, 24 May 1891

The Munshi, Hafiz Abdul Karim
Siddiqui, 1892. (Photographers:
Elliott & Fry)

Silk programme for the Royal
Opera Company of Covent
Garden's performance of *L'Amico
Fritz* and *Cavalleria Rusticana* at
Windsor Castle on 15 July 1893

desired opportunity for interfering. I saw a friend of mine the other day, who is on the committee for the Anatolian Railways at Constantinople, and he told me he thought the Bulgarians the most promising of all the Balkan nationalities and thought the state was capable of greatly developing and having a very good future before it. It had made great strides and owed everything to Sandro. . . .

From the Queen
OSBORNE, DECEMBER 20, 1890

. . . No one can foretell what may happen but I don't think any German princes, like Abbat's son, are at all likely to be chosen [as husband for Queen Wilhelmina of Holland]. They (the country) dislike the Germans in Holland. There is but one voice as to Queen Emma's [her mother and Regent] excellence and good sense. The two gentlemen – Count Schemmel, Grand Maréchal de la Cour, and de Gervaux who had been with Queen Sophia – who came over to announce the accession of Queen Wilhelmina spoke in high terms of Queen Emma. . . . Today good and ever-to-be-regretted Sir E. Böhm will be laid to rest in St Paul's, where so many others are. He will rest near Landseer, Reynolds, Turner, etc. and many others are there besides, Wellington and Nelson. Poor Louise is going, a great trial for her, but it is right and nice of her to do so. . . .

From the Empress Frederick
SCHLOSS, KIEL, DECEMBER 29, 1890

. . . The landscape is a bit of scenery of Gastein and painted by Professor A. Hertel.[42] The little *Amour* was painted by Professor O. Kenille who did the head of Christ I gave you. I thought it so pretty that I hoped you might like it. Of course I have no letters yet from Greece. [I have had] a telegram from Brindisi to say that Moretta and Adolf left for Ismailia yesterday, so I hope they will arrive in four days. How nice your Christmas must have been at Osborne, with all the little families round you! ... I am also very sorry for poor Schliemann's death. I had only seen him so lately this summer. Here it is perfectly arctic. Thick sheets of ice on the [window] panes and the harbour half frozen over in spite of the waves and the north-east gale blowing. I hardly venture out at all. . . . But the Schloss is very comfortable, so one gets resigned to staying indoors. . . .

From the Queen
OSBORNE, DECEMBER 31, 1890

... Henry has written me most sensibly about the most unfortunate and uncalled for *row*.[43] But I hope and trust it will blow over, and that you are quite right to drop it, if possible. In a letter for New Year which William has written to me, he makes no mention whatever of what has happened. . . .

From the Queen
OSBORNE, JANUARY 24, 1891

How terrible, how awful is this death of dear young Baudouin [heir to the Belgian throne], 'the hope' of the country, the pride of his poor parents and the comfort of poor [King] Leopold who treated him as a son! I send you these telegraphic details from Lord Vivian and will send you any more I get. Attached as you are and, as you know, I am to our dear Belgian relations, you will share my true and deep sorrow for them. Good, excellent Marie Flanders, *what* a grief to her! The dear boy was clever and charming and just twenty-one. Oh, it is too grievous! Henriette was I believe as nearly gone as possible last week. The cold was very intense in Belgium too and I suppose perhaps in Baudouin's case attention was not paid at once to the symptoms. . . .

From the Empress Frederick
BERLIN, JANUARY 24, 1891

. . . I am so inexpressibly shocked and grieved as I know you will be at the death of poor dear young Baudouin, such a nice promising boy! . . . Many thanks for sending me the account from Athens. The state of things distresses me too much. It is most hard for poor Willy [King of Greece] – to see everything spoilt by this adventurer Delyannos and his followers! I only hope it will not last long and that Tricoupis may soon return. It is so easy to destroy the work of progress and the development of civilization in these countries and so difficult to build it up again. They had gained so much in the last few years in Greece under the other administration. . . .

From the Empress Frederick
BERLIN, JANUARY 30, 1891

. . . What a terribly sad day it must have been yesterday at Brussels! It is quite terrible to think of all the hopes and the promise now buried in the grave and the broken hearts that cannot heal as long as this life lasts! *You* know and *I* know *what* that is! One would so gladly have saved such sorrows and pain to one's friends. It will be a long while before poor little Albert can take the place of Baudouin, who was almost a son to Leopold. I had a few lines from poor Marie Flanders. She has an energetic disposition, and I am sure will bear her great affliction with courage. Just now poor Philippe's deafness must indeed be a great trial to him. I return the paper on Greece with many thanks. It is all quite true. Alas, neither England, Germany nor Italy are popular in Greece at this moment, only France. But the condition of popular feeling is very fluctuating and I think will change, if only care and attention are bestowed on oriental affairs. The King has no easy task. I hope the Delyannos cabinet will not last, or else they will make a dreadful hash of Greek politics. . . . You ask me whether I have been painting lately. I have not as much as unpacked my colours and canvases since October, having had no time, and then it has been usually pitch-dark here till 1 o'clock and then the days close in before four, so that it would have been impossible. The poor artists are always in despair here during the winter. It was dreadful for me to take off my black for the birthday [of William II] and christening [of his son, Joachim]. We have frost again but it is fine. Henry returns tonight from Brussels. I will certainly see about the lymph [of Dr Koch] for you, but I must name Dr Reid, or I should not be able to obtain it. It is not given except to known medical men and to hospitals. I think if you send it to Dr Tyler a condition ought to be made that it should only be used for patients in hospitals. Here it is not thought right or safe to be used in private practice. . . .

From the Queen
OSBORNE, FEBRUARY 11, 1891

I duly received on Monday your two dear letters of the 6th with the precious packet which I at once gave Dr Reid who is very grateful for it and will be most careful, and the pretty photograph of Princess Louise of Altenburg. . . . Our performances went off extremely well and were really excellent. We had it first on the 7th then on Monday the 9th and yesterday also – for the servants and people employed on the Estate. Our new building [at Osborne House] is going on rapidly and the Indian, Ram Singh from Lahore, who did the things for Arthur at Bagshot is here, making drawings for the Indian decorations of the rooms [mainly the Durbar room] which will be very pretty. He draws beautifully and will also make the models. . . . I was surprised at Crispi's fall, but it is well deserved. His arrogance and rudeness were intolerable. . . .

From the Queen
WINDSOR CASTLE, FEBRUARY 21, 1891

I have three letters to thank you for, two of the 17th received yesterday and one from Paris of yesterday. . . . You are doubtless going about everywhere with an activity and love of seeing things which you certainly have *not inherited from me.* I wonder if you will see the President, M Carnot, the Lyttons of course [you will see]. I hear Bertie is in a dreadful state and greatly alarmed at it all and that they think it will do good and that a stop will be put to that gambling in private houses. I am sorry General von der Goltz is not pleasant for I must ask him to dine on the Saturday as well as the Captain. I am not much looking forward to the launch as it will be fatiguing and cold-catching. The pleasure of seeing you and dear Mossy will be great. We are looking forward to Grasse and a quiet time there very much. Helen is going with her children to Cannes to the Villa Nevada. Louise told me you wish to have the picture of Missy painted by Millais and the boy playing on a pipe by Sir F. Leighton for your exhibition. I will try and write once more before you come here. The ship and all is ordered.

From the Empress Frederick
GERMAN EMBASSY, PARIS, FEBRUARY 22, 1891

. . . I get told here very often, *comme vous ressemblez à la Reine d'Angleterre,* and I always answer, *cela n'est pas flatteur pour ma mère. Je voudrais bien lui ressembler; ce qui la rapelle c'est mon deuil* [my mourning], *qui est hélas la même qu'elle porte depuis 29 ans.*

You say that I have not inherited from you the love of looking about at things . . . but I have a special reason. First of all, you always live amongst beautiful things. Therefore you do not feel the want so much *de vous meubler la tête* [to find furniture for your head] as I do who do not live in so interesting a *milieu*. Then, you never had the time or opportunity to make art a special study and, lastly, you can get everything arranged for you whereas I must direct the arrangements of my house myself and choose and collect every single thing and cannot leave it to other people. There are but few at Berlin who quite share and understand my taste, while in London and at Paris there are thousands and a great many in Italy. In Germany there are very few real amateurs and collectors. This taste is nearly confined to the artists and professors. But the interest has greatly developed in Germany the last twenty years and the exhibitions do a great deal of good. I will not bore you any longer with this subject. I am rather uncomfortable about Moretta and had a frantic telegram from Sophie yesterday saying Vicky and Adolf had stayed only a few hours and were rushing home. Vicky wanted to see me. Consequently all my last letters to Cairo and to Athens must have missed her and I now do not know where to write to, what she is going to do and what is the matter. Her house at Bonn is not ready, mine at Berlin is shut up and we are away. I sadly fear she wants to catch me before my journey to England for some reason or other and will find me gone. . . .

From the Queen
ON BOARD THE *VICTORIA AND ALBERT*, CHERBOURG
MARCH 23, 1891

Here we are after the most splendid passage I remember for many years. Perfectly smooth and the sky and sea a deep blue like the Mediterranean. We arrived at six. I was able to rest and read, take a Hindustani lesson and be on deck two hours. It is a great sorrow having to part from you after so short a stay [27 February to 8 April]. And I feel a great *Sehnsucht* [longing] to talk comfortably with my beloved child again as we have been doing. But you can really come over often for Homburg is so near. . . . I grudge your being in England another fortnight longer and we away. But it could not be helped. I require a little balmy air and rest, and must be home again at the end of April. If you send that sketch you did of Yussuf Bey to Irène to be sold for a charity, I should wish to buy it. Please arrange that.

From the Empress Frederick
SANDRINGHAM, NORFOLK, MARCH 29, 1891

. . . I had a letter from my darling Sophie in which she tells me that the ceremony of her reception into the Greek Church will take place on Saturday, before the Easter Sunday of their style. She does not say of what nature this ceremony is, and adds she means to write to William afterwards and tell him of the step she has taken. Please therefore say nothing about it except to Beatrice. I trust nothing more will be written or done to distress her, offend her family or annoy me, as it would really be terrible. Of course it gives me rather a pang to think of my child no longer belonging to our Church in which she was christened and confirmed and, of course, I think she will forego many an advantage and would rather the question had never arisen. Yet I cannot blame her or think it wrong and can only hope she will feel happy sharing her husband's faith and that in which her child is to be brought up, in the country which is now her home. . . .

From the Queen
GRAND HOTEL, GRASSE, APRIL 27, 1891

. . . I am glad you had Vicky's visit and that she should be so happy. She ought to have some rest before she begins *again*.

I feel greatly Henry's not having come to see you. It is careless, but you must be a little lenient with young people. It is not meant to be unkind, but it is thoughtless. I know how quite unintentionally on our part dear Grandmama used to be hurt when we did not tell her things or go to see her often enough. Henry is very affectionate and very devoted to you. I had a grateful letter from Olga [Queen of Greece] again saying she quite saw that I could not interfere [between William II and Sophie] and I hope all will go off well. . . . Louise and Beatrice have both been to see the Fragonards and say they are beautiful. . . . How grieved I am for dear, great, modest old Moltke![44] What a blessed end but what a loss to all! What a link broken with the past! I have ordered a laurel wreath to be placed from me. I hope an English General Officer may have time to get there. Poor Grand Duke Nicholas's[45] death is a release. We leave tomorrow at three, alas! I am very, very sorry to go from here as we all are. . . .

From the Queen
WINDSOR CASTLE, MAY 20, 1891

. . . I have consulted dear Bertie about this terribly distressing question about Sophie and he thinks, and I am disposed to agree with him, that Sophie should come to Homburg, but on no account alone but with Tino, not saying before they left Athens where they were going to – perhaps going to Brindisi and from thence to Paris incog. You have no official knowledge that William intends banishing his sister from Prussia and if she is accompanied by her husband, he will not dare to arrest the Crown Prince of Greece. Bertie is I know writing to you in the same sense. I think William would be very ill received here[46] if it was known that he wanted to banish his sister (which he really cannot, though he may refuse to see her or let her come to his house) and if he even gave up coming here of his own accord as he knows what we think, I should not be sorry. I had an answer evidently written in a fit of anger which I shall not answer. Alone Sophie ought certainly not to come, but with Tino, which makes the whole difference. Little Louise Fife is going on as well as possible. She was only ill five hours and it is a very nice plump baby I hear. Alix is quite delighted to be a Grandmama. Louis and Alicky arrived in London today and Victoria B[attenberg][47] comes there on Friday and they will D.V. arrive at Balmoral on the 23rd. . . . We start at 1.30 tomorrow as I have a great function at Derby on the way, where poor Lord Hartington cannot appear, having lost his only surviving brother, Lord Edward Cavendish. . . .

From the Queen
BALMORAL CASTLE, MAY 23, 1891

This is the eve of my dear old birthday. I have much to be grateful for in the affection of my children, grandchildren, relations and friends and my people, and in good health; but I have also many anxieties, not the least of which is my sorrow for all your cruel trials and anxieties which ought not to be. . . . The visit to Derby was a great success. The decorations were beautiful and very tasteful and the enthusiasm great though it was dull. There was no real rain to speak of. . . . Victoria B[attenberg] quite shares your feelings about Sophie's treatment. She had not heard of the last dreadful outburst till I told her. . . .

From the Queen
BALMORAL CASTLE, JUNE 15, 1891

My poor, darling Child, I must write to you today when my whole heart goes out to you in love and affectionate, deep sympathy for the loss, the world-wide misfortune which this day, three years ago, brought with it. More and more we all feel it and every day makes the misfortune more keenly felt, irrespective of the personal grief and loss to you, my poor child, and to me and all who loved and admired and respected darling Fritz. I do however rejoice to know you surrounded by Sophie and Tino, whom you love so much too, which is such a blessing, and dear Mossy and [Sophie's] baby. Perhaps Vicky will have come over too. . . .

From the Queen
WINDSOR CASTLE, JULY 1, 1891
Dear Alice's Wedding Day

. . . The christening of little Louise's child took place on Monday at 12 o'clock in the gloomy old Chapel Royal where I was married and you were married – thirty-three years [ago] and where I had not been for thirty-three years. I could see it before me. It is unalterd. You were not far wrong in the names. It is christened Alexandra (by which it will be called) Victoria Alberta Edwina Louise. Besides me, the Queen of Denmark, Bertie and Alix, Eddy and Victoria of Wales are sponsors. The Archbishop christened and I handed her to him, and Alix took her from him. It is a very pretty child; it cried rather. . . . Since I wrote this I have seen poor young Mrs Grimwood.[48] She is a most interesting young woman, very tall, pretty and graceful and told me a great deal of what she went through. [It] is really too dreadful and poor, poor thing, she never would, she said, have done it if she had not thought her husband was alive. She knew the Jabraj (or Senapati) very well and liked him and his brother very much and she thinks he never meant to kill the prisoners. She is quite lame, having twisted her ankle in falling when she was running for her life. . . . I am so sorry that Caprivi is not coming but he can't get away it seems. I wish you to know that I hinted to William not to bring that horrid Kessel as if he did, I would not speak to him, but I fear he will do so all the same. . . .

128

From the Queen
OSBORNE, JULY 22, 1891

. . . I will send you some views of the new wing and the rooms. From the sea and from all sides excepting from the court, it looks extremely well and then the general effect is very good. It is only where it joins the old house that I think it does not look quite well. . . .

From the Empress Frederick
SCHLOSS, HOMBURG, JULY 25, 1891

. . . By this time you must have seen the Prince of Naples, who I am sure was delighted to pay you a visit. . . . A friend is staying with me who has come straight from Bucharest, and tells me what I rather suspected, that this Mlle H. Vacaresco is rather scheming and intriguing and has Elisabeth quite in her pocket, who does not see through her, and has an *exalté* friendship and admiration for her. I believe she is neither young nor pretty, nor very lady-like or refined, and it is much doubted that Ferdinand [nephew and heir to King Carol] is in love with her at all. But he lives so secluded a life and has hardly seen other ladies, so he took up the idea and Elisabeth warmly interested herself in it. And it is now very awkward as the Vacaresco family are disliked in Roumania and party spirit runs so high that they do not want their future Queen to be from one of the families of the country. My friend says Ferdinand is very nice and good and behaves so well to the King and Queen and is as much liked there as they are capable of liking any foreigner. . . .

From the Queen
OSBORNE, JULY 29, 1891

. . . I fancy, though William's fall is not serious, that he is not able to move and is coming back early next week and has to abandon the rest of his trip. Irène heard it this evening from Seckendorff. . . . Dona is waiting to hear; I am giving her the yacht to go back in with her little boys [after the state visit to England]. In your letter of the 25th you speak of what you heard about Elisabeth of Roumania and this most unfortunate affair. Little Hélène Vacaresco is not at all handsome, is short, rather fat and not *distinguée* looking, but has fine, large oriental eyes, and beautiful teeth, with very marked eyebrows and black hair, but is very pleasant and clever and agreeable, speaking all languages, and was *commandée pour l'Académie Française* for her poetic works. She seemed devoted to Elisabeth and Elisabeth to her, but I never observed anything of this kind. On the contrary Hélène Vacaresco, who knew Emily Loch very well, was very anxious that Louise (Aribert) shoud marry Ferdinand and then afterwards Elisabeth wished for one of Affie's girls and this as last as last November. Therefore this is all new and I deeply deplore it, for I fear poor Elisabeth will be heartbroken if she loses her little poetess. But I hope Ferdinand will find a wife and then return. Why not the duchesse d'Aosta? . . .

From the Empress Frederick
SCHLOSS, HOMBURG, JULY 31, 1891

Many thanks . . . for the photo of the new wing. I cannot quite judge of the effect, though I quite understand now how it is connected with the house. It was, of course, not easy to do and this must have been the most useful and comfortable way of tacking it on. For more beauty, I should have said, it would have almost looked better to repeat a bit of the open colonnade on the other side, so as to have left the middle free and untouched. . . . From the lawn it looks very well and I have no doubt it is a great convenience to have this extra room. I suppose you use Beatrice's former sitting room as a little tea room. I am puzzled to think how the dinner reaches the large dining room from the kitchen?

From the Empress Frederick
SCHLOSS, HOMBURG, SEPTEMBER 2, 1891

. . . I am again going to ask a favour, and this time it is a big one. You know I have a collection of medals of which I am not a little proud, but I have not your coronation medal (though I have often seen it, it is small), nor your wedding medal, if one was made, nor the medal of the Exhibition of 1851. I should be so glad if I could have them. Perhaps you have some duplicates somewhere that you do not want, either in bronze or in silver?

From the Queen
BALMORAL CASTLE, SEPTEMBER 7, 1891

Louise arrived here on Wednesday and on Thursday we went to see the Gathering which was at Invercauld, close under Craig Cluny and the day was beautiful till when we went away. . . . We had a theatrical performance on Friday when D'Oyly Carte's Opera Company from the Savoy, being at Aberdeen (one of the travelling companies) I sent for them and they performed *The Mikado*, which I had never seen, very well. Actually there were forty people in one or two scenes at once on the stage. . . . I had a very unhappy letter from poor Princess Wied, in great distress about poor Elisabeth [her daughter]. Charles [King Carol, her husband] of Roumania has gone to Venice. You will be losing

Bertie tomorrow. Next week he comes here for a few days. Liko returns today from his three weeks' yachting and visiting tour. . . . You shall have the medals you wish. Papa did not take so very much interest in the medals and they have never been regularly arranged at Windsor, but they are at Osborne. I however always send medals to the so-called collection at Windsor. The other one is at the Swiss Cottage [at Osborne].

From the Queen
BALMORAL CASTLE, SEPTEMBER 19, 1891

. . . We had a great treat last night which gave us great pleasure. Albani most kindly sang on the little stage *en caractère* and most exquisitely and acted so beautifully. There were three items from [Gounod's] *Faust*, the Jewel Song and Bösig von Thade, the last scene from [Verdi's] *Otello*, which is very beautiful and very affecting and the mad scene from *Lucia* [di Lammermoor]. Her singing was marvellously beautiful and she acts so well. She surpassed herself. Between, we had some fine instrumental playing. . . .

From the Queen
BALMORAL CASTLE, SEPTEMBER 22, 1891

. . . That speech of William's was really dreadful.[49] Bertie was very indignant. It is inconceivable. Can Caprivi or someone not prevent such things and altogether beg him not to make so many speeches? Neither his dear Father nor Grandfather were given to making speeches. He quite forgets that the Kings of Bavaria and Saxony and the Grand Dukes of Baden and Hesse, and I think others, were made so by Napoléon and which none are ashamed to claim. Say what you will, Napoléon was a great man and a great soldier. I had meant to write about Crete and Greece but leave that to another day. . . .

From the Empress Frederick
SCHLOSS, HOMBURG, OCTOBER 10, 1891

Many most loving thanks for your dear letter by messenger and also for the medals, which it is so very kind of you to have sent me, and which are so valuable to me for my collection. I put them into the case at once and trust to show you some day how I have arranged them. I am delighted to hear dear Beatrice is going on so well. Her baby seems to be as fine as Ena was. She was splendid. I saw dear Victoria yesterday who came over from Darmstadt to say goodbye, and I thought her looking well. My darling Moretta went back to Bonn yesterday. I felt the parting from her so much and wish I could think her as well and strong as she always was and ought to be. Today William comes here for lunch, as he has to pass Frankfurt on his way from Stuttgart, he could hardly avoid it. To the accident of the poor king of Württemberg's death, his first visit to me is due. I was quite aghast when Eulenburg telegraphed that he brings six gentlemen and thirteen servants! . . . It is really not very civil and into the bargain Kessel, who I declared should never set his foot in my house! To have him thus forced upon me is not being treated with respect. I shall cut him completely. . . . I wish today were over. . . .

From the Queen
BALMORAL CASTLE, OCTOBER 23, 1891

Many thanks for your dear letter of the 19th from Innsbruck of whose beautiful position I have a lively recollection. I can well imagine how sad and depressed you were on that dear 18th, but that the beautiful mountains did you good as they always do me. I wish you could just see the view from my window this morning – the brilliant sunshine, purple hills, golden birches, interspersed with some perfectly green beeches, red rowans and dark fir trees. I love November and you know how well this is expressed in Byron's poem: 'He who first saw the Highlands' swelling blue. . . .'[50]

From the Queen
GLASSALT SHEIL, LOCH MUICH, NOVEMBER 12, 1891

Having come here with May and Dolly [Adolphus] Teck, as well as Beatrice and Liko, to show the place to the two former and have just finished luncheon, I write a few lines before taking a little walk which I hope, when not too cold or damp or windy, to take again daily . . . . We have had two very successful performances of which I send you the programme. They were extremely well acted. Mary Hughes acts quite beautifully, like a professional actress. *Barbara* is a touching piece without much plot. Colonel Collins is admirable in the comic piece and Major Waller also and Ethel [Cadogan] acted excellently as well as General Dennehy, who was very good as the old Dr Timmerman. . . . We have seen a good deal of May and Dolly Teck during their ten days visit here and I cannot say enough good of them. May is a particularly nice girl, so quiet and yet cheerful and so very carefully brought up and so sensible. She is grown very pretty. Dolly is also a charming boy, so amiable and with such nice manners. . . . I hope you will delay your return to Berlin as long as you can. I am sorry you have all that annoyance about Kessel who certainly should not be where he is. . . .[51]

From the Queen
WINDSOR CASTLE, NOVEMBER 26, 1891

I am glad that my presents are what you wished for

November 27. Here I was interrupted and stopped so I go on today. We had really a very great treat yesterday in hearing Mascagni's opera *La Cavalleria Rusticana*, a perfect gem, and a simple, truthful, very sad story, most dramatically composed and acted. I am sure you would delight in the music. It is so original, so very effective and the rendering of the story so beautiful. It is quite affecting and I felt nearly crying during parts of it. The instrumentation is very fine and there is an intermezzo which is perfectly exquisite. You should get Mossy to play it. It is published. . . .

From the Empress Frederick
BERLIN, DECEMBER 5, 1891

. . . I do not think the state of things very satisfactory here. . . . There is great poverty, and the middle classes have lost a good deal of money, and very little business is done. There is just a great confidence in Caprivi's honesty and steadiness and moderation, but Miquel (who is very untrustworthy) does his best to undermine him. I do not think he will succeed! The principal cause of uneasiness and insecurity as to foreign affairs is the fear that Mr Gladstone will have 'a turn' again before long and that the Russians and French will take this opportunity of making war. . . . William is not at all popular. Every question has been taken up and then dropped again and a deal of irritation caused and nothing of consequence done. . . . Some time ago, if you remember, M. George de Bunsen begged me to ask you whether he might have leave to publish a selection of letters from beloved Papa's correspondence with his father, and you said he might if all were first submitted to [you] and I was to look over them first. All these letters are in your possession! After old Chevalier de Bunsen's death, Ernest de Bunsen (his rather absurd eldest son) returned them all to dear Papa. Do you think you could send me some of them to look at, and show George de Bunsen? I promised I would ask you. Perhaps Muther or Sir Theodore Martin would only send what there is no harm in publishing, if the papers are looked through at Windsor. . . .

From the Queen
WINDSOR CASTLE, DECEMBER 6, 1891

. . . Since [yesterday] the great event of Eddy's engagement with May Teck has taken place. People here are delighted and certainly she is a dear, good and clever girl, very carefully brought up, unselfish and unfrivolous in her tastes. She will be a great help to him. She is very fond of Germany too and is very *cosmopolitan*. I must say that I think it is far preferable than *eine kleine deutsche Prinzessin* [a little German princess] with no knowledge of anything beyond small German courts etc. It would never do for Eddy. What Mary will do without May, I cannot think, for she was her right hand. I can well understand that many things must make you very sore, but many are *really unavoidable*. . . . Tonight we have Prince Napoléon here. He has dropped the Victor. He is very good-looking with a fine presence and pleasing. We met him at Farnborough Hill at the Empress's [Eugénie] yesterday where we lunched. On coming home I found Eddy who came himself to announce the news of his engagement to me. . . .

From the Queen
OSBORNE, DECEMBER 28, 1891

. . . I think you will wish to hear from me about poor Christian. Thank God, he is going on as well and as quickly as possible. An excellent night, he slept nine hours, no pain whatsoever, but the poor eye, to *my* horror and to our general distress for there is nothing so terrible I think as that, had to be removed yesterday. It is most extraordinary for he was very far off. The bird was killed and yet the *whole* charge lodged in his left eye and he has got shots in the forehead above the other eye and on the side of his chin! It is the greatest mercy in the world it was no worse which it very easily might have been. The distressing part of it all is however that poor Arthur did it! His despair and distress were terrible and Louischen's too. I shall never forget his asking to see me just as I was getting ready for luncheon and coming in, with perspiration standing in his poor dear face and Louischen in tears and telling me there had been an accident out shooting: 'I shot Christian' and I said I hoped nothing serious and he replied: 'I am afraid it is. It is in the eye'. . . . But the blemish is very sad and for poor darling Arthur and poor Louischen it is a *lifelong* painful reminder. It has upset me dreadfully and my dislike to and fear of shooting will only increase. The other eye is quite safe and well. I have told you all and you shall have a telegram daily till he is quite recovered. . . . I am delighted about the old ruin of Kronberg being given you and that it gives you pleasure. William wrote it to me that he had got this *surprise* for you which he hoped would please you. He wrote to me after he had seen Friedrichshof how immensely he admired it and the taste with which you had done everything.

From the Empress Frederick
BERLIN, JANUARY 1, 1892

Let me wish you with all my heart every blessing for the New Year and kiss your dear hand in all duty and tenderest affection. . . . So many thanks for your dear letter yesterday giving me a full account of poor dear Christian's horrid accident, and what you all must have gone through! I feel just as you do about shooting and have a perfect horror and dread of it. . . . The accounts of the sufferings in Russia are something too fearful and grievous. Those unfortunate people! And it would seem as if the Government were totally unable to cope with the distress [famine and cholera] which is so far spread and the winter not half over! It really makes one's heart ache to read the accounts and to hear what people say who come from Russia.

From the Queen
OSBORNE, JANUARY 11, 1892

. . . There really has been so much of one kind and another ending on Saturday evening with the dressed rehearsal (before dinner) from before 6 till after 8 of our tableaux for tonight and tomorrow night, which will be most successful. *Think*: my three daughters, a son, a daughter-in-law, two sons-in-law, three granddaughters and two grandsons all appear in them. I will let you hear all about them after they are over and send you a programme. . . . And now a new trouble has fallen upon us. Poor Eddy has got influenza which has developed into inflammation of the left and a little of the right lung. The temperature was very high on Saturday but has diminished. . . . Is it not terrible? Poor Bertie and Alix are very sorely tried with the last year. I own I think it very likely that the wedding will have to be put off. . . .

AFTER THE DEATH OF THE DUKE OF CLARENCE

From the Queen
OSBORNE, JANUARY 16, 1892

. . . The last sad ceremony[52] is to be at Windsor, just like dear Leopold's. I shall naturally go there, and think I may be of some use to poor dear Bertie. . . .

From the Queen
OSBORNE, FEBRUARY 10, 1892

... Alas, dear Bertie and Alix and their dear children left us yesterday morning. Their visit did them good and quieted them. ... As regards the letters from Bunsen to dear Papa, they are none of them kept separately but all bound into the papers on Germany and it will take time to find them out and copy them, but Mr Muther will make a point of going to look at them and see what can be done. ...

AFTER THE ILLNESS OF LOUIS OF HESSE DARMSTADT, WIDOWER OF
PRINCESS ALICE

From the Queen
WINDSOR CASTLE, MARCH 5, 1892

... Oh, what sad news from Darmstadt! Are we never to be out of trouble and sorrow? Since Georgie's illness everything goes wrong. Dear, dear Louis,[53] so beloved by us all, so adored by his children, a real son to me, to think of him paralysed and helpless. He certainly gave one the fear and dread from his appearance of late that such a thing might happen and this deranged state of the action of the heart was very uncomfortable. Poor dear Irène, how distressed she will be. I can think of nothing else. ...

AFTER THE DEATH OF LOUIS OF HESSE DARMSTADT

From the Queen
WINDSOR CASTLE, MARCH 15, 1892

... I feel, not ill, but broken-hearted, crushed, bewildered and unable to realize, away from the scene as I am, the dreadful reality. Never again! Those dreadful words, how often have I had to repeat them! Dear old Darmstadt, and the nice palais, the charming drives, dear Louis taking me wherever he thought I would enjoy it, driving with me or driving himself with his four horses which was his great amusement and the nice little dinners etc. . . . *all*, was such a pleasure. . . .

March 16. I finish this today, having just returned from Frogmore. . . . I am so glad you are going to Darmstadt. . . . How I would have wished to be there to pay the loving respect and affection towards my beloved Louis. I feel weary and crushed, but not ill. I pray so earnestly for dear Ernie, that God may guide him aright. Tell him not to make sudden changes – to leave the old people in their places till he sees what will be best. I hope dear Alicky will be more than ever with me now, for she has no dear father to look after and nothing to make it *unbequem* [uncomfortable] for her as poor dear Eddy is gone.[54] I am so sorry you cannot go to Greece. Will you not come to us in June when we return from Scotland or come in May and go with us to Scotland? I hope you can manage it. I send this to Darmstadt. Tomorrow at a quarter to eleven we have a memorial service here. . . .

From the Empress Frederick
NEUES PALAIS, DARMSTADT, MARCH 18, 1892

. . . I shall not fail to speak to dear Ernie in the sense you write. I trust and hope he will go on carefully and gently and feel his way by degrees. He is in no way trained or prepared for his work and has no experience but enough sense to see that there is no occasion for changes and that he cannot do better for the present than keep everything as it is. . . . Dear little Alfred, or rather young Alfred, is not well, a little intestinal trouble I fancy though not a real peritonitis. . . .

From the Queen
COSTEBELLE, HYÈRES, APRIL 6, 1892

. . . You ask which place I like best: Biarritz, Grasse, Aix or this. The first named is not a nice or pretty place, very bleak and barren with a constant high wind and no vegetation. The sea is very grand to see in a storm and there are many interesting recollections of the wars of the Visigoths but I would never care to go there again. Aix is beautiful and quite in the mountains but the vegetation is not very southern, no orange trees or palms or stone pines and it is often very cold at the end of March and very backward. Therefore I don't so readily go there. The two first times, in '85 and '87, it was wonderfully fine. Grasse is beautiful, grander and wilder than this and not so hot, but there are not so many drives as here, nor is the vegetation quite so fine, though very nearly. *This* is much more private and quiet and very pleasant, only the heat is terrible just now, but I hear it is the same everywhere – England included, quite unusual so early in the year. . . .

From the Queen
BALMORAL CASTLE, MAY 21, 1892

. . . Regarding Aunt Elizabeth, the Landgravin, I think August might help [you to do] it [i.e. to write a memoir of her]. She did a great deal of good at Homburg to which she was much attached, but she was not so 'very good', for she was very hasty and *remuante* [restless], very fond of politics, *pas facile à vivre* [not easy to live with] and a great trial to poor Aunt Adelaide when she came on her many months' visits and interfered and meddled and took possession of the King [William IV]. . . .

From the Empress Frederick
SCHLOSS, HOMBURG, JUNE 7, 1892

Yesterday darling Bertie and Georgie came here and spent the day. I cannot say what I felt on seeing his dear face again on which sorrow has left its shadow and its lines. How willingly I would be the only one of the family to bear the load of grief and pain if it could be spared to the others, but each, alas, must have their trials and cares and we can only draw closer together in love and sympathy and help one another along. Dear Bertie had a bad cold, but I think the air here and the walk he took – and a glass of champagne – did him good. Dear Georgie was looking very well, I thought. But, oh, to see them both and feel that dear Eddy is gone, that kind gentle boy, it is too sad! Bertie tried to be cheerful and I did not find him bitter; he seemed to take an interest in everything as of old. We took a little stroll in the Curgarten and he looked at Fritz's monument. After luncheon he drove over to Friedrichshof with me and looked round the house and grounds. We drove back through the woods in time for him to catch the 7 o'clock train. Sophie and Tino are coming today. . . .[55]

From the Queen
BALMORAL CASTLE, JUNE 14, 1892

. . . I got this morning a very kind, confidential letter from the Princess of Wied about her poor dear daughter [Elisabeth of Roumania] who is now entirely under her sole care and she seems already a little better. The doctor seems to have managed her badly. The *Verlobung* [engagement] of Ferdinand [to Affie's daughter, Missy] has given her a shock but she is not ill-disposed towards poor little Missy. I think dear Georgie [of Wales] so nice, sensible and truly right-minded and so anxious to improve himself. Ferdinand of

Bulgaria has been extremely well received in England and is thought very clever and sensible, and so he is, and he is *gemütlich* [pleasant], clinging much to old family affections and memories. He reminds me of his father, his mother, very much of Amélie and even of Uncle Leopold while in his walk he is like Louis Philippe and Montpensier. . . . Our elections will begin in a fortnight or less. The result is very uncertain, but the chances are in favour of the Government now which they were not. If the unscrupulous Opposition come in, though I think it is very uncertain, whether they could form one [i.e. a government], they could only stay in a very short time and could not do any real mischief, though the effect would be deplorable abroad. . . .

From the Empress Frederick
SCHLOSS, HOMBURG, JUNE 20, 1892

This is your accession day and I send my loving and respectful congratulations. I must now tell you of the event which took place yesterday evening at Philipsruhe and which I was unable to telegraph as we were obliged to inform William and ask for his personal consent before announcing it to anyone. Mossy is engaged to young Frederick Charles (Fischy) of Hesse [Kassel]. He asked a month ago, but she could not make up her mind. Now she has accepted him and I think she is very happy and contented and it is a great relief to her to have decided. He loves her devotedly and is really a very nice boy, so steady and quiet though rather timid and delicate looking. He is intelligent and cultivated with a taste for learning and art and writes charming poetry. I am so sorry that you do not know him. He is not rich and does not possess a place of his own, but he is quite comfortably off and I hope will be independent. You can imagine how upset and agitated I am, though very thankful to think my own precious darling will be happy – though I shall now be left quite alone. I dare not think of giving her up; it will be so very hard. Anna and

Elizabeth[56] are in ecstasies and Tino and Sophie much pleased. What they will say at Berlin, I do not know. Please excuse these hurried lines. The young man is gone to Berlin and I have written to William.

From the Queen
WINDSOR CASTLE, JUNE 22, 1892

This is a surprise! You never gave me the slightest hint of such a thing being likely though I knew you liked him. I hope and believe it is what you wish, but *I* think Mossy ought not to have left you so soon at any rate. I agree with the Mohammedans that duty towards one's parents goes before every other, but that is not taught as a part of religion in Europe. As Fischy has no place of his own, could they not chiefly live with you? You ought to make conditions and I am sure the Landgravin [of Hesse Kassel] who is so devoted to you would do all she could to help. For *you* to be quite alone will never do. . . . What you say about Ferdinand of Bulgaria and Sandro I quite agree in. They are totally different. But I think Ferdinand does his best and speaks most properly of his predecessor. But Sandro is still immensely popular there. As regard the elections, I don't think anyone now thinks Mr Gladstone will have a large majority as some did some months ago. There has been a great change during the last five weeks and Mr Gladstone has made many blunders since and stated things which are not true and put forward the Home Rule as the *one thing* to be carried which the English don't care for and which could not pass through parliament. I hope things will remain as they are as these changes give so much trouble and do such incalculable mischief. The prorogation and dissolution will be on Tuesday, 28th, but the elections won't begin till the following Monday [4 July]. No one can tell what the result will be, but the press is much against Mr Gladstone. The feeling amongst the loyal Irish is very strong. Ireland has recovered its quiet and prosperity so wonderfully that it is

very wicked to try and upset everything again. I am longing
to hear more about the *Verlobung* [engagement]. Why did you
not give me a little hint of its possiblity? Mossy had a
malheureuse passion [unfortunate passion] for Max of Baden
which was not returned, was not it so?

From the Empress Frederick
SCHLOSS, HOMBURG, JULY 15, 1892

. . . I am watching the elections with as much interest and
anxiety as you are. It almost seems certain that Mr Gladstone will have a majority, but his régime cannot be of very
long duration, nor will he be able to carry his extremist
measures, I fancy. Yesterday Ferdinand [of Bulgaria]'s visit
went off very well and we had some talk together on various
subjects. He spoke so nicely of Sandro, which I did not think
more than right, but which one was glad to hear. Tino and
he had never met before and I think it was a good thing that
they did meet as the feeling between the two Governments
[of Greece and Bulgaria] is none of the best and it is so
important that these states should stand by each other and
not be torn asunder by jealousies, distrust and conflicting
interests and aspirations which ill feeling is purposely
fomented and kept up by Russia. Of course politics were not
touched upon by the two young men. . . .

From the Empress Frederick
SCHLOSS, HOMBURG, AUGUST 5, 1892

. . . I am very glad to hear you say you like Hatzfeldt. If there
is a change of government, he will be very valuable as with
his tact and cleverness and *savoir faire*, his experience and
perfect temper, he is sure to get on with anyone and he is so
earnestly anxious that all rubs between the two countries be
avoided and the best understanding kept up. He is our best

diplomat. Fritz always thought of him as minister of foreign affairs. . . . As for Prince Bismarck, he is exactly what he always was, and behaves exactly as was to be expected. I am not the least astonished . . . I am afraid the descriptions of Friedrichshof will make you think it a great deal more than it is. It is nothing in the least wonderful, but there are so few neat and comfortable and well built modern houses in Germany in pretty situations that perhaps this one may appear exceptional. We have neither the plants nor the grass that will grow in dear England. Friedrichshof is not nearly as striking as Jugenheim or Seeheim as to position or immediate surroundings, but much easier to get at, as there are no steep roads and it is on a plateau and very open. Of course I shall not be able to put up one half of the people I can accommodate here *tant bien que mal* [somehow] in this old rambling house. Still I know there will be nothing that is downright ugly or common or out of proportion and taste. Friedrichshof is a country house and not a *Schloss* [castle] according to German ideas, though it has a bit of a tower and a terrace. It is more comfortable and compact than Babelsberg or Reinhardtsbrunn, but about that size and with that amount of accommodation, as many rooms as Bagshot I should think. We are expecting Aleck today – Fischy's brother. . . .

From the Queen
OSBORNE, AUGUST 20, 1892

. . . On Thursday – the day these horrid new people [i.e the Liberal Government] came – [there was] a terrible thunderstorm in which they left. You say that Mr Gladstone is very loyal towards me and so in a certain way he is. But it is quite idle to attempt to have any influence with him. He listens to no one and won't hear any contradition in discussion. He is really half crazy, half silly and it is better not to provoke discussion. But it is awful to have such a man at the head. Please God, he will have to give up soon. The late one was the best Government of the century. I felt so safe. Lord Rosebery is very low and thinks he can do very little, but I cheered and encouraged him and I know he wishes to follow Lord Salisbury and says that the O.M. [old man, i.e Gladstone] won't interfere the least with him. I was anxious to tell you this as I hope and think Egypt will be safe [i.e. continue in British occupation]. . . .

From the Empress Frederick
SCHLOSS, HOMBURG, SEPTEMBER 21, 1892

. . . We leave this evening for a little trip to the lake of Como and perhaps to Venice, before going to Berlin, so as to give a little rest to my throat before we settle in town. I have not travelled under an incog. name the two last times. Fischy goes with us and Mossy is looking forward to the trip very much. I should have liked to have stayed here for another month but there were difficulties. Dear Georgie came over from Heidelberg[57] to see us yesterday, looking very well and getting on with his German I think. He planted a tree in my garden. . . . Mr Labouchere told a friend of his here that as soon as parliament met he would begin a campaign against Mr Gladstone. What a man!

From the Queen
BALMORAL CASTLE, OCTOBER 1, 1892

. . . I suppose you will be away about five or six weeks at least. I hope you will have fine weather and enjoy it. It is very nice having Fischy with you as he is full of taste for art and nature which poor Adolf is not and your great favourite, Tino, also not, I believe. . . . Poor dear Arthur sprained his knee again last Saturday [out stalking] and is unable to walk out of doors and can't enjoy his holiday which is very hard, but it is improving. I have been riding within the last ten days and it does me good and I have been walking again a little out of doors. I am sure it will get better with patience. My Aix masseuse is coming in a fortnight. I have to see a person I particularly dislike and cannot respect and to have whom here after his dreadful speeches is a great trial, viz: Sir William Harcourt.[58] He is terrible-looking now, but it was said I had better see him as he was very amenable to any attention paid him. But I hate it. He only stops till the 6th. Lord Spencer was very nice. Forgive this stupid disjointed letter. Lenchen is enchanted with Baden which certainly is a charming place and now very quiet.

From the Empress Frederick
HOTEL BELLEVUE, CADENABBIA, OCTOBER 7, 1892

... You are so good and kind to think of my sorrow at parting with my sweet Mossy, my Benjamin. Indeed, no one knows what a wrench it is to me, nor how utterly forlorn I shall feel, for, as you say so truly, in our positions we are, and must be, so isolated. It is like a nightmare to me, when I think that *vie de famille* [family life] is to be over for me and that for the first time in my life I am to be alone. You can realise what that means. Still it would not be right or fair to Mossy and Fischy if I were in any way to infringe their liberty and independence and I am the last to wish to put a drag or restraint on them. *Our* young bright days were so spoilt often by the thraldom in which we lived. I should be sorry indeed not to add what I can to my children's happiness. I think they will always love to come back when they can. . . . There are some charming girls I know who I am always glad to have with me for a little and I think I can get them. . . Time never hangs heavy on my hands. I have so much to do and to think of. It is the presence and companionship of a much loved being which one will miss so cruelly. . . .

From the Queen
BALMORAL CASTLE, OCTOBER 15, 1892

These lines will I trust reach you on the dear 18th which must still be a bright day though so different. You will like to spend it at your favourite Venice which I wonder if I shall ever see. . . . I hope you read the account of the funeral of our great poet [Tennyson] whom I am sure you mourn. I send you here a copy of his very last poems which are very fine and were sung at his funeral.[59] 'Crossing the Bar' was also sung and purposely set to music by Dr Bridge of St Paul's. I received a touching and beautiful letter from his son (a very amiable nice man who really only lived for his father) which I know will interest you and I had it copied for you. The Government are beginning badly in Ireland. The present Lord Chancellor is here now and a particularly amiable and agreeable man.

From the Empress Frederick
HOTEL TRENTO, TRENT, NOVEMBER 9, 1892

. . . Each time I leave Italy I feel more and more how little I really know about Art History. It is a vast study. . . . Did you read the last interview Prince Bismarck has had?[60] He never loses an opportunity of having a hit at Caprivi which can do the latter or the Government no sort of harm; the only mischief that Prince Bismarck's speeches may make is that his blind admirers think they must take their cue from him and at the present moment it will swell the ranks of those who are distressed and dissatisfied at the enormous demand for money to increase the army. It is only the true sensible liberals (the only party in Germany who have any principle or any political commonsense) who can see through all this and to whom what Bismarck thinks or says is utterly indifferent. I consider this party the only really conservative force there is, as they are opposed to all socialism, to all antisemitism and protectionism on principle. They are what our Whigs were. Alas, William neither knows them or understands them. In his eyes they are simply 'radicals' and without as much as perceiving it he has gone many a step towards socialism. . . .

From the Queen
WINDSOR CASTLE, NOVEMBER 30, 1892

. . . I am glad you like my answer to the G.O.M.'s essay[61] – so full of self-deception. Your *Auffassung* [interpretation] seems to me quite correct. *He* it is who has done all he could to set class against class and to produce the cry, if there be any, for home rule in Ireland and Wales, and *he* only. I saw him on Friday and thought him become slow of app-rehension and very deaf and the expression in his eyes and face generally, unseeing[?]. It is very difficult [to know] what to talk of, as Ireland is impossible and I was particu-larly warned by Lord Rosebery (who is my support and very open towards and much devoted to me) not to mention Uganda,[62] so that one's political conversation was vey restricted, but we talked of other things. It is really a form, and a form merely, seeing a Prime Minister with whom one is on such terms. He is [over] 80 and looks like 65. The whole thing seems to me most disjointed and insecure. Their own followers, as well as some of the ministers, say they will be out in May and some say in March. They will never pass a Home Rule Bill even through the House of Commons. The Irish are all divided. Some of my new Household (nice people) are most anxious not to be con-sidered as followers of Mr Gladstone in everything and many not in Home Rule. I fear this Army Bill in Germany will not pass and may cause great difficulties.

From the Empress Frederick
BERLIN, DECEMBER 2, 1892

. . . [Ps.] I envy you having three men of science as Lords-in-Waiting. That has hardly been since the days of Queen Elizabeth, I fancy?

From the Empress Frederick
BERLIN, DECEMBER 7, 1892

. . . There is so much poverty and distress here this year and so much dissatisfaction and uneasiness. Everyone seems depressed. The new taxes, which are preparing, I think a very great pity. All works of art are to be taxed. In a country as poor in art as we are here, it is a death blow to all endeavours to stimulate artistic production of any kind. People are so heavily taxed already that they will do anything to avoid paying another shilling. What will become of the artists, are students and art schools? I own it makes me feel frantic. . . . This new army expense swallows up everything. . . .

From the Queen
WINDSOR CASTLE, DECEMBER 7, 1892

. . . Lord Acton is very agreeable and pleasant, but I should never have thought he was so learned and scientific as he is light in hand and agreeable upon all topics. He spends his day in the Library which he is delighted with. He wants to rewrite something he said. Little old Lord Playfair, of course, is intensely scientific but a very nice person and so attached to dear Papa (in whose Household he was) and to Bertie who recommended him to me. Who is the third scientific Lord [-in-Waiting] you mention? This reminds me

that George Bunsen has never returned dear Papa's letters
and surely he must have done with them now. Could you
tell him that I want them back? You never told me that
Adolf's father was so ill till now you say he is 'a little better'.
When did he fall ill and how is the poor son? I am afraid that
Fischy's brother will be a trouble. He is certainly much to be
pitied but he is inamiable. I am so sorry that Bertie cannot
go to Berlin for Mossy's wedding but it would not do if he
refused to go to one [Marie's at Sigmaringen] and went to
the other [Margaret's at Berlin]. The Roumanians and
Charles were so anxious he should come to Germany, but it
could not be so close to that terribly sad anniversary [of
Albert Victor, the Duke of Clarence's death on 14 January];
every day from the 8th being full of such dreadfully sad
recollections. Poor May was here with her parents yesteday,
looking well and very pretty. I, like you, cannot share
Morier's enthusiasm for the marriage of Missy, so young as
she is too. But the child is devoted to Ferdinand and he to
her. Lord Acton knows him very well and likes him. . . .

From the Empress Frederick
BERLIN, JANUARY 7, 1893

. . . I am afraid the situation here is not at all satisfactory.
The generals and the military authorities are perfectly
convinced that the Army Reform is absolutely necessary for
our safety! I quite believe what they say and wish with all
my heart they could obtain what they want. Alas, the
Government have gone to work in the most awkward way.
Instead of slowly trying to prepare public opinion (especially convincing the [Reichstag] deputies) they come upon
the nation with this immense demand of money at a time
when all the sad consequences of the Bismarck régime are
most felt. The depression of trade and the unsatisfactory
state of agriculture, the ever-increasing, now almost
crushing burden of taxation, also William's great unpopu-
larity and the general discontent, make this bill so distaste-

ful to the people that I fear there is no chance of its being passed. A dissolution would make things worse and Caprivi's resignation would be a misfortune. This is all very sad and I often feel very anxious. In these four years the monarchical principle has suffered very much. . . . I wish with all my heart I could help him [i.e. William] but his whole education as regards politics *serait à refaire* [would have to be done again] – a totally different set of people ought to have access – things be explained thoroughly from the right point of view. . . .

From the Queen
OSBORNE, JANUARY 11, 1893

Many affectionate thanks for your two dear letters which give an anxious picture of the future. These matters may turn out better than you fear. But it is a great anxiety. Here also, there will be trouble, but not in the country. The people are so essentially loyal. I did not like to say anything to you, before I knew, for fear there should be a disappointment which I am happy to say I hear will not be the case. I wrote to dear Moretta to say how much I wished she would come here with you, with or without Adolf, and that if he could not come at first, he could perhaps come later and fetch her and that I felt sure he would grant this to please me who, excepting for an hour at Darmstadt [have not seen here] since she married. And I got her answer to say that it could all be managed if you would bring her. Now I need not doubt that you will be delighted to bring the dear child, and that you will not have to come alone. Adolf could fetch her later. It will be a great additional pleasure to us. Yesterday poor little Missy was married – the irrevocable step taken 'for better, for worse'. I ought not to tell you now, who have this so soon before you, what I feel about a daughter's marrying, but to me there is something so dreadful, so repulsive in that one has to give one's beloved and innocent child, whom one has watched over and guarded from the breath of anything indelicate [and that she] should be given over to a man, a stranger to a great extent, body and soul to do with what he likes. No experience in [life (?)] will ever help me over that, especially when the mother is a widow. . . . I am sending you today all my gifts for Mossy as well as a silver dish for Fischy. You will give them when you think right. I hope you will like them and the comb [a jewelled comb, sent earlier]. I enclose the list of them. . . .

From the Queen
OSBORNE, JANUARY 23, 1893

I enclose a letter for Mossy and a ring which I hope she will often wear. My thoughts will be much with you on that dear day, your own wedding day, which is very present to my mind. How bright all was then! All you say about the marriage of a daughter shows that we agree, only I think you are fonder of the *Verhältnis* [relationship] with your sons-in-law than I can ever be. I hope and trust that the day will be bright and fine. I shall give a large dinner on the day and have asked Count Hatzfeldt and Count Metternich (exclusive of more) to dine here. They [i.e. her Household] are all much occupied with the rehearsal of a play which is to be acted on Thursday and Saturday and which is a very ambitious undertaking. It is *She Stoops to Conquer* by Goldsmith. Louise and Beatrice and Maggie, Fritz and Arthur Ponsonby [i.e. three Ponsonby children], Major Bigge and Colonel Collins act in it the principal parts. I hope things are coming right about Egypt. . . .

From the Queen
VILLA PALMIERI, FLORENCE, MARCH 29, 1893

. . . I send you today a small Easter offering from Florence which I hope may be useful for your house. It is carved here. I am thinking with sorrow that I can only write once or twice more to you to your old home before you leave England. Your dear letters are a great pleasure to me. . . . Yesterday we went to the Palazzo Pitti and I saw some of the glorious pictures there, but I would only see some, intending to go again. I was rolled about in a long chair which I had sent on by Mustafa. They are in very good order. . . . But how splendid the Rafaels are, the portraits as well as the Holy Family, and the Titians, Andrea del Sarto, Tintorettos etc. We went a little in the beautiful Boboli gardens afterwards and the town with the Duomo looked beautiful in the evening light and the bells were all ringing for Vespers. We came back by the Ponte Vecchio which I delight in. . . .

From the Empress Frederick
BUCKINGHAM PALACE, MARCH 29, 1893

. . . I went into Westminster Abbey yesterday evening when it was quite empty and spent some time amongst the tombs – deeply deploring that some little repairs are not made to keep the principal tombs a little bit in order. Queen Elizabeth is still without her sceptre and the forefinger of her left hand and poor Mary Queen of Scots, after having lost her head in her lifetime, now is represented on her tomb with both her fore and little fingers missing (which might so easily be replaced) and the Scotch lion at her feet is still without his forepaws and sword. I wish you would take pity on our poor ancestor and give her pretty small hands back their fingers. . . . It is an irony that Queen Elizabeth, who in her life held her sceptre with a firm hand, should not be allowed to carry it on her tomb. . . .

From the Empress Frederick
BUCKINGHAM PALACE, APRIL 1, 1893

So many most loving thanks for . . . the charming pair of bellows. How kind of you to think of me and to remember that I was looking for some in London. . . . I am indeed so glad to think that you enjoy dear Florence and have also been to see the pictures. Yes, they are indeed lovely and to me like friends. I wish I could have shown you what are my special favourites. It amuses me and flatters me so much that you remembered me when you saw the bright, new gilding. It is a barbarous way of treating works of art. I hope you will never allow them at Windsor or in Buckingham Palace to regild the frames round old pictures nor to regild the splendid old French gilt bronzes in which the china is set or on the cabinets, tables and pieces of furniture. It is grievous to see it and would make French connoisseurs' hair stand on end. . . . It must make you proud to think what collections you yourself possess. Here in the tiny room between my sittingroom and the poor Emperor Napoléon's bedroom there hangs over the door one of the most beautiful Titians in existence.[63] In preservation, colours and tone it belongs to the very best works of art, and is immensely valuable. Angeli always raves about it. In that little room no one can see it. Could it not go into the Gallery – also the Perugino and Mabuse in that room and the lovely Francia I missed so much in Papa's sittingroom. They would be so much more and better seen and are such important pictures. Almost any modern pictures would do in that tiny room. . . . I went yesterday to visit Miss Florence Nightingale and found her in bed with a bad cough, but looking extremely well and quite unchanged in face. The heaps of papers, boxes, books everywhere in her rooms bore testimony to the work she still does. I had an interesting conversation with her. . . . She is very unhappy about the Nurses' Register and the Charter and hopes it may not pass the Privy Council.[64] She spoke so nicely of dear Lenchen, and for *her* sake too she wished and hoped and prayed that nothing might be done to lower her prestige. Miss N. is afraid that . . . it will deteriorate nursing and nurses in more than one way, and she puts forward other grave objections, which I have always seen. . . .

From the Queen
VILLA PALMIERI, APRIL 21, 1893

. . . We went on Wednesday to a very curious old place, San Gimignano, about twenty-five miles from here, which we went to see by rail and by road. It is very celebrated for retaining its mediaeval character, its extraordinary old towers and walls and was the scene of sieges and fights. It dates in part from the twelfth century. We left the railway at a little place called Poggi Bonsi and anything like the enthusiastic welcome I received there and at San Gimignano from a peasant population I can't describe. It is really quite touching. I am glad Charlotte told you how much I admired and enjoyed the country and places. I think William's journey and visit [to Rome] unasked and with such a suite [of sixty-seven persons] quite a mistake and uncalled for. Altogether poor people, this visit *will* be awful, with such a number of people, to entertain. Yesterday there was a most successful *Fantasmagoria luminosa* which we again witnessed from the Riccardi Palace. It was a most curious sight; not torches, but objects represented by lamps; animals, butterflies, vegetables, insects, all represented in coloured lamps carried by soldiers, 1,200 in number, with bands. It was really a very pretty sight. The night was beautiful and so warm. The nightingales sing all night and a good deal in the daytime. The garden here is full of them. I am so sorry your house will not be fit for you for so long which is a great pity. The sickness from which Mossy is suffering seems to me to leave no doubt in my mind as to the *reason* for it. Poor thing, I pity her so much. It is really too dreadful to have the first year of one's married life and happiness spoilt by discomfort and misery. I have a most lively recollection of what it was before you were born – the sort of fuss and precautions of all kinds and sorts, displaying everything and being batted about and worried to death of which I think with perfect horror. In addition to which I was furious and indignant at being in that position. . . .

From the Queen
WINDSOR CASTLE, MAY 7, 1893

... You never answered my telegram about Georgie's engagement [to May Teck] which I am surprised at and I have no letter to answer. On Wednesday evening on coming home after seven I received a telegram from Georgie informing me of the event and asking for my consent, which I naturally gave very readily. On Thursday he came to see me and told me all about it. They had met on Tuesday at dinner at White Lodge and then they went over to Sheen next day without Mary [i.e. her mother] who was not well, and Georgie took a walk with her in the garden and it was settled. He seems contented and happy. I shall see him again tomorrow and also, in the afternoon, Mary and May and on Tuesday they are to dine with me. The wedding will be at the end of the next month or beginning of July. More I cannot say at present. Poor dear Alix feels satisfied and knows it must be, but it tried her very much. She will not be back before the 18th or 19th, if then. The country are delighted. I saw yesterday my Indian escort which thanks to the stinginess of the India Office and Government is composed of only eight men. Several of them are splendid men, all cavalry. They will ride in the procession on Wednesday [i.e. at the opening of the Imperial Institute of South Kensington]. What do you say to the rejection of the Army Bill and to the dissolution of the Reichstag? I fear it is serious. ... Fraulein Swoboda and her brother are both here and doing lovely things. The former has done an admirable sketch of Liko.

From the Empress Frederick
COTTAGE, FRIEDRICHSHOF, MAY 16, 1893

... About the pictures at Buckingham Palace. I am almost afraid at so great a distance to say now exactly the places I think they would look best in, as one ought to be on the spot. The beautiful Titian I fancied ought to go in the Picture Gallery, just over or under the lovely landscape by the same great master,[65] to the right of the door leading on to the staircase. The Franceso Bigio – an altarpiece in the same room at present – also wants more space and a longer wall. (Or may be it is a Perugino; at this moment I do not quite recollect.) Would you perhaps wait with placing them until I have the pleasure, perhaps next year, of paying you another visit. . . . I am longing to put up my things here . . . but it will take a couple of months before the furnishing can begin.

From the Empress Frederick
COTTAGE, FRIEDRICHSHOF, MAY 24, 1893

. . . I love to remember its [i.e. the Queen's birthday's] brightness and happiness in the dear days, long past – our excitement as children, the bouquets chiefly of lilies-of-the-valley and pink geraniums, the wreath round your birthday table of violet field orchis, at dear Osborne; you always with a pretty, new gown, normally a muslin, white or coloured; dear Papa with a summer light waistcoat – so long – arranging everything for you; we all in new frocks to our great delight, a great trouble to the maids because we were too impatient to have our sashes tied and pinned properly, and our hair carefully plaited; no lessons; a band at luncheon and lovely flowers on the table; and dear Grandmama looking so beaming and happy. I remember it all so well! Alas, the remembrance of 1888 and Henry's wedding . . . and it was by far the prettiest wedding we ever had. . . .

From the Empress Frederick
COTTAGE, FRIEDRICHSHOF, MAY 27, 1893

. . . It interested me so much to hear about the reception at the Imperial Institute.[66] But really it was not quite the right thing to hiss and boo poor Mr Gladstone who was Bertie's guest, though the Home Rule Bill deserves any amount of 'groans'. I wonder what impression it made on him, as he is so accustomed to ovations etc. I am very busy all day, looking after the house and the garden. I often wonder whether you would really like it. I think you dislike all that looks in any way mediaeval in look and colours and sadly I fear you will not approve, nor think it modern enough. Yet the house is really very light and the windows are very large. . . . There is a great deal of oak panelling and I am afraid you do not like that and think it gloomy. . . .

From the Empress Frederick
TATOI, JULY 7, 1893

. . . [Ps.] You tell me you had a French company to act some French plays before you and I cannot help calling your attention to the fact that Madame Eleanora Duse is, I believe, still in London. Her acting is by all competent critics pronounced to be perfect in its way and those who have seen her have been greatly struck and delighted. I have, of course, never seen her on the stage, but I heard so much about her, and she is a very nice respectable as well as amiable person, and Countess Wolkenstein brought her to me and she was presented. I thought her very pleasing, very simple, quiet and modest, and not the least like an actress. It interested me very much to make her acquaintance. I do so wish you could have seen her. The Queen of Spain has been very kind to her and at Venice she goes out into society. I thought you might like to know her.

From the Queen
WINDSOR CASTLE, JULY 13, 1893

. . . I am feeling tired as I have many people to see and dinners etc. We stop here till the 20th to enable Beatrice to go to the Opera. I fear I cannot manage to hear Mme Duse, besides which I should not understand her at all, I fear, but I will enquire. We shall have the *Cavalleria* performed here on Saturday with Calvé who is the greatest actress almost there is, as well as a splendid singer with Mascagni himself to lead and one act of the *L'Amico Fritz* is to be given before. I can quite enter into your feelings about the Army Bill which it seems will pass. In the House of Commons here things are going from bad to worse – almost fighting there last night.

From the Queen
OSBORNE, AUGUST 5, 1893

. . . I write a few lines to congratulate you on the birth of your eleventh grandchild and ninth grandson [Sophie's second son]. I am so thankful to have such good reports and trust she had not too severe a time, and that she is not very weak and that you are satisfied with the doctors and nurses. This has been a very gay week: Cowes crowded with people. Dear Georgie and May had a very pretty and hearty reception on Monday, 31st – arches, flags, nine hundred schoolchildren, soldiers from Trinity Pier almost up the hill to the Lodge and our tenants inside the grounds. The evening was bright and fine. I cannot say how much pleased I am, as we all are, with dear May . . . I really feel quite happy about the dear young ménage, whom may God bless and protect. . . . William won my cup. I think him looking well and less stout. [Ps.] I enclose a letter from the Dean of Westminster.[67]

AFTER PRINCE ALFRED'S ACCESSION AT COBURG

From the Empress Frederick
SCHLOSS, HOMBURG, SEPTEMBER 2, 1893

. . . I am sure dearest Alfred will make an excellent Duke.[68] If he will only observe the constitution of his country, as an

Englishman would, and not copy the tricks played at Berlin with the constitution, he will secure the respect and confidence of all the best German elements and in due time become a support to the right-minded people and an example to William. . . .

From the Queen
BALMORAL CASTLE, OCTOBER 12, 1893

. . . Louise is quite delighted with your house. I will send you a copy of what she says. Few people have studied art as you have and are so strict as to what should be or not. I am afraid I cannot aspire to such knowledge for I am much more easily satisfied and like to have my favourite pictures, my portraits and views, all about me. I am not very fond of electric light everywhere which Beatrice is. I dislike it in my room. It is a failure in the corridor at Windsor and either hurts one's eyes or is too dark. In the Durbar Room at Osborne it is a great success. You have not told me how to answer Marie about poor Elisabeth. I am sure it would not do for her to return till all illusions are gone. But I hope that she will quite trust her excellent mother. But I know Elisabeth and many others disliked Roggenbach and the rather peculiar position he had in Princess Wied's household.[69] Many people think that he was not discreet about dear Fritz's affairs. . . .

From the Empress Frederick
SCHLOSS, HOMBURG, OCTOBER 17, 1893

First let me congratulate you on the birth of Missy's little boy. . . . Perhaps if you were to say [in answer to Marie of Edinburgh] no doubt poor Elisabeth had been under very bad influence and her kindness taken advantage of, but that you fancied her eyes had already been opened a great deal and that you hoped in time she would be able to return and that the King would be able to watch over her. . . .

From the Queen
WINDSOR CASTLE, NOVEMBER 22, 1893

. . . Oh dear! I knew how you would mourn our beloved great Sandro [died November 17, 1893] – that dear splendid hero, so infamously persecuted and treated! But it is an immense *Genugtuung* [atonement] that the feeling of regret and admiration for him should be so universal, and the love and affection and admiration of the Bulgarians so great. They claim his dear remains to rest them at Sofia which I think is so fine, so touching. Ferdinand has behaved with the greatest kindness and respect for him. Did you know that he was godfather to the little girl and the Archduchess Marie Thérèse was godmother? His poor wife, not hardly recovered from her confinement, is quite broken-hearted for they were devoted to each other and it is so terrible for her. . . .

From the Queen
WINDSOR CASTLE, DECEMBER 9, 1893

. . . I don't think I told you of the two Indian ladies who are here now, and who are, I believe, the first Mohammedan purdah ladies who ever came over and kept and keep their custom of complete seclusion and of being entirely covered when they go out, except for holes for their eyes. They are the wife of my Munshi [lit. language teacher] and his mother. The former is pretty with beautiful eyes and wears a small ring always in her left nostril, but besides that in full dress a ring through her nose. She was beautifully dressed with green and red and blue gauzes spangled with gold, very gracefully draped over head and body. She wears long petticoats, but her mother, like some Hindu ladies I have seen, wears tight-fitting satin or silk trousers and her shawl and sari only to her knees. It looks like a man. They were shy and frightened the first, but not the second time. They are living at the formerly called 'Couper Cottage'[70] at Frogmore. The good Munshi, Abdul Karim, is very happy to have them here. . . .

From the Empress Frederick
BERLIN, JANUARY 27, 1894

. . . Yesterday all went off well. Prince Bismarck had even more of a reception on the part of the Court than was needful, but it was not quite an easy matter. He came to see me and I thought him unaltered! To save him the staircase I saw him downstairs, and it happened to be the very room in which I had not seen him since the morning in May 1887 when he came to ask me not to allow Bergmann to perform the operation on my darling Fritz's throat which was in contemplation. I reminded him of it, and he said 'those are past times', and added *'wie liebenwürdig und grossartig war doch der Herr in seiner ganzen Krankheit'* [how lovable and noble he was throughout his illness]. The interview only lasted about eight minutes and then he drove off again.

From the Queen
VILLA FABBRICOTTI, FLORENCE, MARCH 28, 1894

. . . I am very anxious about affairs at home. Lord Rosebery has pleased nobody, and has gone as far as Mr Gladstone with the further disadvantage that he has not any conviction in what he says. It is a great pity and I regret he should be prime minister, for as foreign minister he could restrain the others which he cannot or will not do now. But things cannot go on so. There must be a crisis and a dissolution [of parliament]. . . .

From the Queen
VILLA FABBRICOTTI, FLORENCE, APRIL 11, 1894

... These two last days have been much cut up and taken up by the King and Queen [of Italy]'s visit. They arrived yesterday morning early. After waiting and waiting without ever being able to find out when they would come and the hours were changed and changed and up to the last, one did not know if the Queen were coming or not, they arrived quite early yesterday as I said before. At three they came here to see us, with the poor little Prince of Naples (who is terrified before his father) and the duc d'Aosta. Then at half past five we returned the visit and [I] had to be rolled along the room, the distance being very great, which made me very shy. Today we lunched there *en famille* at one o'clock and the Ladies and Gentlemen were presented afterwards. They leave tonight after giving a great dinner. The Queen asked very much after you. ... I hope you will spend a very happy day with dear Vicky and Mossy at Rumpenheim. ...

From the Empress Frederick
FRIEDRICHSHOF, APRIL 14, 1894

... After much difficulty, at last, two little medals were found at Berlin, but unfortunately not in gold, only in silver. They are no more the fashion, no more required, our day is gone past, our portraits, medals, chiffres etc. only to be found in museums, and are made no more. It is a fact which it is not particularly cheerful for me to realise, but it is so. ... I will bring the two humble little medals with me to Coburg. ...

From the Empress Frederick
FRIEDRICHSHOF, APRIL 24, 1894

It seems like a dream that I am back here again and the days at Coburg already past! I cannot say how pleased and thankful I was to see you . . . I carried away the satisfactory impression that I have not only seen Ernie and Ducky happy, but also Alix and Nicky and this will be a comforting thought to you tomorrow on dear Alice's birthday, as it will be to me.[71] I arrived here yesterday forenoon and was very tired before the evening came; there was so much to look after. It is despairing that William's visit [30 April–1 May] takes place so soon, when the place is not half ready and it gives so much trouble and people have to hurry through their work which will then not be good and have to be done again afterwards which is an extra expense. If he only had come alone with two Gentlemen, but he brings eighteen people! I assure you it is a great *corvée* to know how to put them up in rooms that are not quite finished yet.

From the Queen
BALMORAL CASTLE, MAY 26, 1894

. . . Imagine my getting four hundred telegrams and forty-three letters on the 24th and some still coming in!] . . . I am so grieved that you found Sophie and Tino pale and tired. You must speak to the King of Denmark about Sophie and I can write to the King of Greece asking him to prolong their leave, that they may come and see me and you should have a consultation of doctors and then they must frighten the King. Strange to say, on my birthday it was quite like a fine June day and we were able to take our tea out some way beyond Invercauld. In the evening we had some charming tableaux arranged by Mr Yorke of which I send you a programme. Let Vicky (Moretta) see it and do tell her that

Duse acted on the same small stage which was put up for her (Moretta) five years ago in the same room. The illustrations of Kingsley's *Three Fishers* which Beatrice sang was extremely effective. The three keepers were the men and the girls were also from here. Dr Profeit's girl, who was too young, only appeared once. Liko and Drino as Hubert and Prince Arthur were very pretty. The Indian scene was also very striking and the first with Laura and Sapho very pretty. . . . The visit to Manchester was one of the most wonderful demonstrations of enthusiastic loyalty and real affection I can remember excepting Liverpool. The streets were beautifully and tastefully decorated. There were over a million of people out. It was dull and a little rainy, but it cleared later. The ship was the most trying, as it was so drafty and I think my poor left leg has suffered from it.

From the Empress Frederick
FRIEDRICHSHOF, JUNE 21, 1894

. . . Sophie and Tino have had to give up going to England to their immense regret. . . . I fear they leave for Greece on the 9th of July. I think the German Government are quite wrong about the Congo and that they are making themselves odious for no reason. It is too absurd to suspect England of falseness and treachery – that is not in our line. I always was strongly against German colonies in Africa. They are of no use to Germany, only an expense and a trouble. They do not understand in Germany how to manage or govern them, and it only makes the Germans quarrelsome and pretentious and always on the *qui vive*. In short, it seems to me very unnecessary to embark on any such adventures. Fritz always thought so. Prince Bismarck used to be strongly opposed to these colonial enterprises and then suddenly took them up. One of his friends (I think it was General von Schweinitz) expressed his surprise at this change and Bismarck answered, 'I too think Germany would be better off without this colonial policy, but I must have it as a means of stirring up German indignation against England whenever I want it, because the Crown Prince (Fritz) will be too prone to form a friendship with England, and I must be able to keep him in check by German patriotism. I want England's co-operation often, but I will not have the influence of British ideas in Germany: constitutionalism and liberalism to which the Crown Prince is given. I must also have the means of bringing England to terms when I want her support. Therefore I must stimulate German colonial enthusiasm.' . . . William's one idea is to have a navy which shall be larger and stronger than the British navy. . . . [In a postscript she asks the Queen not to tell Rosebery of Bismarck's remarks.]

From the Queen
WINDSOR CASTLE, JUNE 27, 1894

. . . You rejoice as I do, indeed, and as the whole nation does, to the most wonderful degree, at the birth of dear Georgie's boy.[72] It is a great pleasure and satisfaction but not such a marvel, for if Alicky had not refused Eddy in '89 I might have had a [great] grandchild four years ago already. As it is, however, it is true that it has never happened in this country that there should be three direct heirs as well as the sovereign alive. I went over yesterday with Beatrice, Nicky, Alicky and Marie L[einingen] to see May and the baby, who is a very fine strong boy, a pretty child. May I did not see, as it was rather too soon and the doctor specially wished she should be kept very quiet, but she is perfectly well. . . . The newspapers have charmingly written articles. But oh, what a frightful contrast is this horrible assassination of poor Monsieur Carnot! The two events seem almost parallel and the contrast too awful. It is like the murder of Henri Quatre [in 1610]. They ought not to have allowed the people to crowd round the carriage. It is very unsafe. It is too shocking. He was a good man, and one feels so much for her. I fear it will mean bad feeling between France and Italy.

Who, I wonder, will they elect? Dear Nicky is very amiable and quite at home with us. . . .

From the Queen
WINDSOR CASTLE, JULY 9, 1894

. . . We had a treat on Friday evening. First Gounod's pretty opera of *Philémon et Baucis* in which Plançon sang so splendidly – he has a voice like Forini's with a far better method – and then Massenet's new short and most thrilling tragical opera of *La Navarraise* in which Calvé is too splendid, singing and acting are marvellous and she is so handsome even in the common poor black dress she wore. How you would admire her! She is so handsome! A Spanish tenor, Alvarez, and Plançon again sang extremely well in it too. . . . The christening [of David, the future Edward VIII] is this day week at the White Lodge.

From the Empress Frederick
FRIEDRICHSHOF, AUGUST 28, 1894

. . . I am still very unhappy about this Greek finance business, and the attitude of the German Government which has spoilt and *embrouillé* [confused] matters still more. . . . Our excellent German consul at Athens came to see me and is certainly most clear-sighted and impartial, but was dreadfully distressed at the position the German Foreign Office had taken up and thought it very imprudent and ill-judged. But this is only *entre nous*, please. . . .

From the Queen
BALMORAL CASTLE, SEPTEMBER 25, 1894

. . . I telegraphed to Charles and Elisabeth as well as to the Princess of Wied my congratulations on Elisabeth's happy return [to Roumania] and I had very happy answers from *all*. I do hope and pray all may go on well and that Charles will look after her. Christle arrived yesterday and in the evening we had a beautiful theatrical performance by Bier-baum [so spelt] Tree and his wife and company.[73] He is of Dutch descent, educated in Germany, then came to England. He took to the stage and is a wonderful actor. . . .

From the Empress Frederick
FRIEDRICHSHOF, SEPTEMBER 28, 1894

. . . I am very glad you enjoyed the play acted by Mr Beerbohm Tree and his company. . . . We had Baron Ferdinand Rothschild here for a day and showed him about. He is an excellent gardener and good botanist and has a good deal of artistic knowledge and taste, so that it was very agreeable to show him what has been done. His sister's place is twenty minutes from my door. . . . It is a very charming place, even now before it is quite finished.

From the Queen
BALMORAL CASTLE, OCTOBER 14, 1894

. . . Dear Henry and Irène left us to our mutual regret on the 10th. It was a very dear, happy visit and Henry could only come on the 6th. You will I hope think them looking well. Irène walked so much and well. And Henry proved himself a very good (and always very careful) shot. Affairs continue serious in China, but a general understanding of that war would be a great thing. . . .[74] Missy's baby arrived a fortnight before they expected it, but not too soon really. Marie [her mother] arrives there [in Bucharest] tomorrow. . . .

From the Empress Frederick
RUMPENHEIM, OCTOBER 21, 1894

When I wrote to you yesterday morning at seven I had no idea that three-quarters of an hour later, I should receive two telegrams, one sent at 4 a.m. that Mossy was taken ill and the other that a second little boy was born. I rushed off by road as there was no train at that hour and arrived here in two hours. I found all well. . . . The doctors gave her no chloroform. . . . Fischy and Mossy are delighted that it is a second boy and so am I as Fischy and his brother are the only two in the family. Aunt Cambridge was the last baby born in this house – 1797, I believe. Mossy is far more comfortable and quiet here than last year in the Savigny Strasse at Frankfurt in Anna's little house. . . . This is your twenty-first great grandchild and my thirteenth grandchild. I have eleven grandsons and two granddaughters.

From the Queen
BALMORAL CASTLE, OCTOBER 30, 1894

. . . I am engaged in writing a strong letter to Lord Rosebery on his outrageous proceeding with the House of Lords. You will hardly believe it when I tell you that I was never told of this till forty-eight hours before he made that violent speech! That the House of Lords should perhaps be reformed all sides admit, but to hold such language and to wish to rouse the country against the House and to agitate when there is no excitement is wrong in the extreme. The sense of the country should be taken first. I am disappointed and shocked at Lord Rosebery but he is pushed on by the others. I mean his followers. Another beautiful frosty day! I am delighted Mossy is on the sofa. What a difference to last time! Missy is walking about and Minnie is going to Livadia.

From the Empress Frederick
RUMPENHEIM, OCTOBER 31, 1894

All is going on well here. Mossy is kept very quiet. Her nerves are none of the strongest as you know and as she is very sensitive by nature, it is well to keep her as calm as possible. She is looking very well and not fatigued with being on the sofa. Caprivi's resignation will have surprised you. It is in many ways much to be regretted. Chlodwig Hohenlohe is the best successor he could have under the present circumstances but I fear too shaky and feeble in health to stand the work and the strain for long. I have my doubts whether dear Hermann's appointment to the Stadthaltership of Alsace Lorraine[75] will be a good one, fond as I am of him. However, it is difficult to judge. The so-called war against the 'subversive elements' of society, which is the very vague and somewhat dangerous programme William has taken up seems to me a mistake. One cannot frame and proclaim such a policy, though one cannot be watchful and careful and prudent enough in trying to prevent mischief and the growth of socialism, but the measures which ought to be adopted seem to me of a very different kind. . . .

AFTER THE DEATH OF TSAR ALEXANDER III

From the Queen
BALMORAL CASTLE, NOVEMBER 5, 1894

. . . What a horrible tragedy this is! And what a position for these dear young people [Alicky and Nicky]. God help them! And now I hear that poor little Alicky goes with them to St Petersburg and that the wedding is to take place soon after the funeral. I am quite miserable not to see my darling child again before, here. *Where* shall I *ever* see her again? I hear Minnie [widow of the Tsar] is calm but broken-hearted and that she means to travel back with the Russians. What a journey! I am so thankful that Mossy is well and have no doubt that keeping her very quiet is the great thing. . . . I can't understand Hermann's being made Stadthalter. He is not clever enough and not very conciliating, I should think. . . .

From the Queen
WINDSOR CASTLE, NOVEMBER 25, 1894

. . . I hope the christening went off well and that the baby was good. Is it not curious that Beatrice's second child was also christened on the first birthday of the eldest one? The *surprise visit* was certainly rather overpowering and inconvenient but as you say it was certainly kindly meant. Tomorrow morning poor dear Alicky's fate will be sealed.[76] No two people were ever more devoted as she and he are and that is the *one* consolation I have, for otherwise the dangers and responsibilities fill me with anxiety and I shall constantly be thinking of them with anxiety. God will protect them. I daily pray for them. I give a large dinner in the evening [of Alicky's wedding day, 26 November]. . . .

From the Empress Frederick
BERLIN, DECEMBER 8, 1894

So many thanks for . . . the kind interest you take in the fire. Alfred's servant did not know that two or three rooms off there was a telephone and also bells all over the house – or in two minutes everyone might have been roused. I shall have it written up outside the door so that guests can see directly how they can get at the housekeeper, porter and castellan. I was very thankful Alfred was there, and not some nervous or helpless lady who might have lost her head, though often women are very calm and cool-headed in danger. Is it not terrible about these poor Armenians? . . . I wonder pressure is not put on Turkey by other Powers. There has been a little row directly in the new Reichstag. The Socialists refused to get up when three cheers for the Emperor were asked for. . . .

[Ps.] I forgot to say how very sorry I am that poor Mr Barber is dead. I thought him such a charming clever artist; he would have got on so well. His works were already much appreciated and would have been more and more so. . . .

From the Queen
OSBORNE, DECEMBER 25, 1894

. . . Thank you so much for the lovely painting by Professor Lutteroth. It is so like the lovely scenery of the Riviera which D.V. I hope to see again early next spring. Christmas was rather sad this year from the many who are gone since then [i.e. last Christmas] and whose families are mourning. The heads of the House and I myself feel [it]. And it is rather sad to be rolled about in the *Bescherung* and with glasses to look at everything near and far. It is sad. I have suffered a good deal since our return to Windsor, which I am sure was most unwholesome, with my legs. The weather here is muggy, damp and foggy and for two days without a single blink of sun. I think Ferdinand behaving very unwisely. He is said not to be at all popular. It must have been very peaceful at the Friedenskirche though sad to go alone. You will surely go again before Moretta leaves you. Caprivi's departure is much to be regretted. . . .

From the Queen
OSBORNE, JANUARY 2, 1895

. . . Our tableaux went off extremely well and were really very pretty. I send you the programme. They are repeated again tonight. . . . I have reason to know that the Unionists will side with the Conservatives under Lord Salisbury but this better be kept secret at present. A crisis is not very far off and indeed the conduct of the Government causes great indignation. To try and tamper with the constitution is really wicked. . . .

From the Empress Frederick
BERLIN, JANUARY 4, 1895

. . . I must say I am horrified when I read of what Ferdinand is doing in Bulgaria. It seems that he is dying to be recognised by Russia [and the other Powers] and thinks he can attain Russia's favour by all these concessions to the Russophil party which concessions seem as dangerous to me as they are undignified and will not buy Russia's good graces one bit, while they will do Bulgaria harm. The Russian expedition to Abyssinia I also regret.[77] I will certainly not say a word about the Unionists being ready to go with the Conservatives; but of course I do not wonder [at it]. It would be a most fortunate thing for the Conservatives; they have so few really eminent men in their party. . . .

From the Empress Frederick
BERLIN, JANUARY 25, 1895

. . . The news from Greece were rather startling and made me feel a little anxious. Tino could not have acted otherwise than he did and simply did his duty. His troops were ordered out without his knowledge – or wishes – so he went out and fetched them back and I was glad the King supported him as he did. Tricoupis only wanted a glorious sortie for himself to be able to resign, throwing all the blame on the royal family. . . .

From the Queen
OSBORNE, JANUARY 27, 1895

It is pleasant to think that in a fortnight I shall have the happiness, D.V., of seeing you again. . . . Poor Sir Henry[78] is a little improved but it is terribly slow. . . . Regarding duels[79] I cannot quite agree with you. I think them at the German universities abominable. But I do think that the sense of honour and especially in any cases concerning women has fallen considerably where duels no longer exist. There is no longer any chivalry. . . . Lord Randolph Churchill's death is a misfortune, but a melancholy ending to a life which had promised better things. He was only forty-five. His poor mother who idolised him is in despair and quite broken-hearted.

From the Queen
DARMSTADT, ALTES PALAIS, APRIL 27, 1895

I must write a line to thank you again for all your kindness to me yesterday and to tell you how much I enjoyed my visit to your beautiful and comfortable house which I so greatly admired. It was all so nicely arranged and I got back quite easily after seven. I wish also to say how much I liked Fischy and how glad I am that you should have so amiable and nice a son-in-law. Dr Reid has gone off and will arrive at one. If the Munshi is able to go tomorrow you will kindly remember that he is my Indian secretary and considered as a gentleman in my suite and that, as you kindly proposed, Herr Walter would show him about and especially let him see the charming house. He can take no meat and only a little milk and fruit could be offered him. If Herr von Reischach should happen to be at home, perhaps he would just see him for a minute. I hope I am not troublesome? . . .

Once more let me say what pleasure it gave me to visit you and see your beautiful house.

From the Empress Frederick
FRIEDRICHSHOF, MAY 4, 1895

. . . I think England's attitude with regard to Japan a very wise and judicious one and I am sure the Japanese will never forget it and it will be very useful. The other Powers can after all not effect much and will not hinder the Japanese from carrying out the greater part of their intentions. The German and Russian press display a good deal of jealousy of England just now but I think one can afford to let that pass quietly. To my mind the German Government are making a great mistake.

[Ps.] Vicky and Adolf make their solemn entry into Detmold today. They will remain there for the present.[80]

From the Empress Frederick
FRIEDRICHSHOF, MAY 8, 1895

. . . I am very glad the visit of the Queens of the Netherlands went off so well; I should much like to see them. I have the greatest respect for Queen Emma [Regent for her daughter]. . . . The young Queen [Wilhelmina] must be a charming and interesting girl. . . . Yesterday I saw old General Stosch. You know what a clever and shrewd old man he is and how he interests himself as much as ever in politics. His opinion is that Germany and England would do well to further Russia's wishes in China as much as possible, so that Russia may have to devote all her energies, time and money to coping with China; then she will be fully occupied and leave Europe alone, and leave India alone. This is an argument I have heard at different times. . . . I am rather inclined to think the opposite course would be the best. . . . [She recommends an article by Herr von Brandt and *La Race Jaune* by Maxime du Camp.] Perhaps Beatrice and Liko would read both these things for you and mark some passages. . . .

From the Queen
WINDSOR CASTLE, MAY 15, 1895

. . . I am terribly worried and bothered about the question of Commander-in-Chief, not as to its retention for that must and always will be, but as to Uncle George's resigning and as to the immediate successor and I am worried and bothered to death about it all.[81]

From the Queen
WINDSOR CASTLE, JULY 1, 1895

. . . I have been so bothered and busy and troubled. . . . Your dear children's short visit was a great pleasure but far too short. Dear Sophie looked delicate but very sweet and has such a pretty manner. Tino was quite charming, so simple and unaffected and so sensible. He is grown very handsome and reminds me of his mother and the Russian family. He has got that fine line of feature which comes from the Empress Catherine and which the Emperor Nicholas and the Grand Duchess Mary and the late Queen Olga had. . . . The change of Government was not a source of such satisfaction as perhaps it might have been for I lose some people I was very fond of and who were very able. Lord Spencer, Mr Campbell Bannerman and Mr Fowler were terrible losses, not to speak of Lord Carrington and Lord Breadalbane who cannot be replaced. And *personally* I am very fond of Lord Rosebery and prefer him [in] certain [respects] to Lord Salisbury. He is so much attached to me personally. . . .

From the Empress Frederick
FRIEDRICHSHOF, JULY 20, 1895

This murder of poor Stambuloff is a very shocking thing and very hard for Ferdinand. The German papers are down upon him in the severest manner, even too harsh I should think! Still, if he were wise he would rush back to Sofia, have a strict enquiry made and the murderers brought to justice even though they may be in the pay of the Russian Panslavist community. . . . I own the state of the East seems very uncomfortable just now. The horrors that have been committed in Armenia and the lukewarmness and half-heartedness of the Great Powers in obliging the Sultan to stop them; the signs of rising in Macedonia are also very disquieting. . . . If the Slav population, Bulgarians, try to shake off the Turkish yoke, now, you may be sure that all the Greek population in Epirus, Thessaly and Crete will do the same, and no Government can keep them quiet as for generations it has been their aim and they have dreamt and thought of nothing else. Least of all has the Greek Government the power to keep it down though it may make every effort to do so. Then we should have the East in a blaze. And the Great Powers of Europe are not of one mind. . . . Do you know that some years ago Prince Lobanoff elaborated a scheme for 'putting Bulgaria in order again' (in the Russian sense, i.e. regaining it for Russia). I am afraid now he is in office he will think the time come to carry it out! Does Lord Salisbury know this? . . . When one has a granddaughter in Russia, one in Greece and one in Roumania, one can but feel more than disquiet at the thought of a conflagration being so near [she writes 'one' to avoid the familiarity of 'you']. . . .

From the Queen
OSBORNE, JULY 24, 1895

. . . This murder of Stambuloff is monstrous, too horrible for words. I have had some details from Sir A. Nicolson. It appears that an attack appeared in one of the Government newspapers almost pointing to his murder a day or two before. Sir A. Nicolson, my chargé d'affaires, saw poor Stambuloff a few minutes before he was murdered in the Club. He went in a new carriage (not his own) and the street is broad and it was fine and bright! The only person who was arrested was Stambuloff's servant who ran after the assassins! He begged to be allowed to go to Carlsbad as he was very ill and it was refused by Ferdinand! All you say is very interesting. Affairs in the East are not at all satisfactory. I will tell Lord Salisbury what you say about Lobanoff. The elections are wonderful. The [Conservative] Government have gained upwards of seventy seats. Four of the late [Liberal] cabinet and three of the Household were turned out. . . .

From the Queen
OSBORNE, AUGUST 11, 1895

. . . I had a letter from Beatrice . . . from Friedrichshof which she was again admiring so much. You will be glad to hear that the British Museum bought Nelson's Ms and that several other people bought other valuable relics which, being given to the nation, have gone to Greenwich. I hope, therefore, that the most have been saved for the country. There is a curious teaset made for him which I took tea [out] of at Cumberland Lodge when Lord Bridport was there and they have been selling the large cups for £25 a piece and a cream jug for £35 and smaller cups for £15, one of which I bought as a recollection. William left last night, much pleased with his visit[82] and in excellent spirits, but he does not think Dona well: her nerves are in such a bad state. I fear poor Hatzfeldt is very unwell. Feo Gleichen has done a really beautiful bust of Calvé for me, life size, also two little statuettes of her as Carmen. . . .

From the Queen
BALMORAL CASTLE, SEPTEMBER 10, 1895

. . . I share your feeling about the speech [of William II on the fifteenth anniversary of Sedan]. These speeches are made at the wrong moment and to the wrong people. . . .

From the Queen
BALMORAL CASTLE, OCTOBER 6, 1895

. . . I am so provoked at Adolf hurrying off Moretta before the time (far too short as that was) that she agreed to stay. If one of my sons-in-law was to behave in that way I should be furious and protest. A daughter has her duties to her mother, who has no child living with her and is a widow. It is too bad and selfish. I hope the visit to Detmold will make a little up for this. . . . .The news from Constantinople are very serious and the Armenians are behaving so badly and wildly that it will render it still more difficult to help them. . . .

From the Empress Frederick
FRIEDRICHSHOF, OCTOBER 16, 1895

. . . I really do not know how I shall get through that ceremony on the 18th [the birthday of Frederick III and the unveiling of a statue to him on the site of the battle of Wörth]. I shrink so from all that is show and ostentation and which forces one into public when one's feelings seem so sacred that one cannot bear to be amongst a quantity of people, some most well-meaning and others who have behaved so ill and now make a show of loyalty, the hypocrisy of which makes me sick. . . . I deeply regret a new most ill-judged telegram of William. . . . I tremble at tactless and unfortunate speeches being made at Wörth and that I have to be present and listen.

From the Queen
BALMORAL CASTLE, OCTOBER 22, 1895

. . . I can well understand all your feelings of pain and sorrow expressed in your letter of the 16th as well as all your emotions on the 18th before and during the ceremony. I am sorry dear old Baden, which I liked so much and which I should like to see once again, is so much built up. I liked it so much! My dear little house I was very fond of too.[83] I find it no advantage to have a place of my own abroad as it either ties me to go there, or I have the necessary expense of keeping it up without going there. I have just sold the little property I bought at Aix-les-Bains six years ago. The *real* south would be a real temptation, but that also would not do on account of the distance. . . .

From the Queen
BALMORAL CASTLE, OCTOBER 27, 1895

. . . The scenery [at Trent] must be splendid. I should of course like to see it, but the journey would be too long, the drives too steep and March and April are not the time for a very mountainous country. I must own I like *shops* and foreign towns. They amuse me. . . .

Queen Victoria in her pony carriage, with Beatrice, Princess Henry of
Battenberg, and attended by Francis Clark, watching the sports of her
servants at Balmoral, 31 September 1893

The Glassalt Shiel, Loch Muick, 1895

The arrival of Tsar Nicholas II and Tsarina Alexandra Feodorovna of Russia at Balmoral, 22 September 1896. (Water-colour by A. Forestier)

The Empress Frederick with her family at Friedrichshof, 24 May 1900

From the Empress Frederick
HOTEL TRENTO, TRENT, NOVEMBER 14, 1895

... I am so glad Carlos's visit went off well and that he made a pleasing impression on you. He must have enjoyed himself very much, as he so seldom leaves Portugal. The news from Turkey are indeed most sad and disquieting. It is a great blessing that all the Powers wish to act together at present, but how conflicting are the interests! The present sort of rule in Turkey is terrible and consequently it will always be left to chance whether there are risings in the different provinces or not. The Eastern Question crops up again and again, and though all is done to keep it quiet and smooth matters down, the measures are only palliatives and some day it will have to be tackled. It will need a great and wise statesman to content all the many claims and interests contained in this question. I suppose Constantinople will have to be a free port some day and Macedonia parted between Greece and Bulgaria. Uncle Leopold would not go to Greece [in 1830][84] unless the greater part of Macedonia belonged to it as he said the position would be untenable without.... As for Crete, it will never be quiet unless united to Greece. There, they are not anxious for changes, but popular opinion is very strong and if the Turkish rule in Europe is at an end of course they will not rest until those of their own race and religion are united to them, which after all is but natural. ...

From the Queen
WINDSOR CASTLE, NOVEMBER 25, 1895

Ernie's and Ducky's birthdays

... Since I wrote our dear excellent Sir Henry [Ponsonby] has been taken and his spirit [freed] from the bondage of a poor suffering body. But though he was totally lost to me since that sad 7th of January, I feel the actual fact of his being really gone, very deeply. I miss him sadly and more as time goes on. The work is as smoothly done, but it is his advising, his authority and his great kindness to all which makes the loss so grievous. All the servants mourn him so deeply; all wish to go to the funeral and some of each department will go. Arthur represents me. Liko cannot go, for he is so busy with preparations for his departure for Ashanti. A great trial for me! Dear Sir Henry is by no one more deeply mourned than by my good Munshi. He says he has lost his 'second father', that his 'right arm is gone'. He was so kind, so friendly, giving advice when asked, above all prejudice and narrowness which, alas, is not the case with everyone. Dear Sir Henry is to rest at Whippingham[85] and by my particular desire carried on a gun-carriage and some of the Grenadier Guards will carry him into the Church and to the grave. By her [Lady Ponsonby's] and my wish a band will attend the procession and play Chopin's and Rachmaninoff's marches. A great number of my Gentlemen will go. A special train takes them there and the *Alberta* takes them across and they come back the same evening. The Bishop of Winchester (Davidson from Rochester) performs the service. I send you the account of dear Sir Henry's last hours and death. . . .

[Ps.] It was very sad that dear Sir Henry should just die on your birthday.

From the Queen
OSBORNE, DECEMBER 22, 1895

. . . What you say about the birth of the dear little boy [the future George VI] is very true. I send a copy of dear Georgie's letter. . . . It is a great pleasure to me that he is to be called Albert, but in fact, he could hardly have been called by any other name [since he was born on the anniversary of the Prince Consort's death]. I think you will like to hear about Mary Ponsonby whom I went to see on Thursday morning and found very calm and much softened. . . . On Tuesday morning Beatrice and I went to the churchyard and visited the grave of our dear and valued friend [Sir Henry Ponsonby]. . . .

From the Empress Frederick
KAISER FRIEDRICH PALAIS, DECEMBER 25, 1895

First let me offer my most affectionate Christmas wishes . . . then let me express tender thanks for all the lovely gifts I found from you around our table last night. The lovely watercolours . . . the beautiful new book *Marvels of Westminster Abbey* and the pretty vases . . . all gave me so much pleasure. Charlotte, Bernhard and Feo were also delighted with their things. . . . We were a party of five ladies and three gentlemen. . . .

[Ps.] I thought it might interest you to hear that I have seen General Goltz (i.e. von der Goltz Pasha) who left Constantinople ten days ago. . . . He told me that 50,000 people had been massacred, that the Sultan had known all about it beforehand and that the massacres at Zestan, which would take place immediately, would be even far worse! . . . Goltz Pasha does not think the Sultan's rule in any way endangered, as nobody seems likely to interfere with him. . . .

From the Queen
OSBORNE, DECEMBER 26, 1895

Many loving thanks for your lovely presents. The little vase is lovely and the large collection of views of your beautiful house are delightful to have and beautifully done. Many, many thanks for them. Our Christmas *Bescherung* was rather sad but still went off cheerfully enough. The children are so grown that only two could play with toys. . . . Dear Mary P[onsonby] was sitting for more than an hour with me and quite herself and able to talk of other things. But she feels the going from here very much. . . .

AFTER THE KRUGER TELEGRAM

From the Empress Frederick
JANUARY 4, 1896

. . . Since I wrote this morning I saw Prince Hohenlohe who lunched with me. I slightly touched on the question of the Transvaal and I asked whether a certain telegram[86] I mentioned this morning was to be rejoiced at? He answered that it certainly was in accordance with German public feeling at this moment, from which answer I gather that the telegram was approved. Prince Hohenlohe who is so cautious, so gentle and courteous did not say much on the subject but told me he had seen a great deal of President Kruger's Secretary of State, a Dr Leyds, and the latter had made a most excellent impression on him. Evidently this Dr Leyds has influenced the German Government a good deal and most likely German public opinion. . . .

From the Empress Frederick
KAISER FRIEDRICH PALAIS, BERLIN, JANUARY 11, 1896

. . . I am sure you must be worried to death with all this business. For two days the German press seemed to be a little quieter. They had exhausted their venom and had nothing more to say. Now they are at it again. I trust this new fury will also soon spend itself. The less the English press retaliates the better. When they see that we can also hold our own, they will respect us but also cool down. How miserable it all is! . . . If only this does not prevent my journey to England. If all calms down I should leave here on the 8th of February. I could not get away before, having many engagements. This state of excitement cannot last, but if I were to go home [i.e. to England] at the moment they are in such a mood here it might make mischief, i.e. mischief would be made for me, and I should not like to be the cause of any unpleasantness. Perhaps you would have me in the autumn instead? . . .

AFTER PRINCE HENRY WAS REPORTED ILL IN ASHANTI

From the Queen
OSBORNE, JANUARY 15, 1896

I meant to write on Saturday or Sunday but that evening, though we knew he was improving, we were so anxious about Liko[87] that I delayed writing and then the cable got damaged and we heard nothing whatever from Sunday night till yesterday after 6 p.m. The suspense was dreadful, but darling Beatrice behaved wonderfully, so calm and courageous, doing everything as usual and she has been rewarded. We heard this morning that he was out of danger, had reached Mansu and had slept in his hammock on the way. It has been since Friday, when we first heard of his having fever, and especially since Sunday such a terrible time of anxiety. God has watched over him and please God, he will return safe to us in a short time. Loving thanks for your dear letter of the 11th. There is no reason whatever to prevent your coming when you propose to do so and your putting off your coming would only have a bad effect. I send you the copy of William's letter to me and my answer which you can keep. My answer is what Lord Salisbury advised and I also asked him about your coming and he answered just what I told you. Our weather has improved. . . . Mr Chamberlain behaves admirably, so firmly and very strong in upholding the Empire and *giving up nothing*. I must now end for today rejoicing to see you soon, only regretting you come so late.

From the Queen
OSBORNE, JANUARY 23, 1896

. . . Our grief, and our misery is untold! We are not ill, but we feel that the sun is gone out of our lives with beloved, noble Liko! Darling Beatrice is quite admirable, so patient, so resigned, so courageous and calm but broken-hearted. She adored him; never were two people ever happier. He was so beloved and such marvellous and touching sympathy is shown. . . . We expect the dear earthly remains about the 3rd and he will be laid in the mausoleum [at Frogmore], though whether permanently or that he will be brought here later on is not decided. I fear you will not see Osborne this time as I shall of course go to Windsor for this terrible event and not return here and I intend to go abroad sooner as I long for and require sun and Beatrice does too.

[Ps.] I feel as though I was living through the December and January of '61–'62. It wrings my heart to see my darling child's grief. Though she is very calm [and] she can cry quite naturally. We had some prayers read this morning which did her good. Arthur's presence was and is invaluable, and he was like an angel of goodness to her and to me.

From the Queen
WINDSOR CASTLE, MARCH 4, 1896

. . . The state of affairs in Armenia is indeed awful though it is improving, but we can do nothing. We can't send an army there, they do not belong to us and the other Powers won't now move. Since I wrote to you I saw – yesterday – Dr Taylor who managed the whole of the medical department in the Ashanti expedition and admirably. He says, as Christle does, that the climate broke Liko down, depressed him and he could not fight against it. . . . Sir F. Scott whom I have just seen and who commanded the expedition which was most successful, thought his spirits were very good. He was Sir F. Scott's military secretary and he said he helped him so much, was very intelligent and an excellent soldier, that he was immensely popular amongst officers and men, who would do anything for him, and that the shock was terrible among the whole force when the news of his death came. . . . He was a worthy brother of dear Sandro, but had a more determined character than Sandro. . . .

From the Queen
GRAND HOTEL DE CIMIEZ, NICE, APRIL 14, 1896

This is a sad day for us – my poor darling Beatrice's birthday. But thank God she has got through it better than I expected. But she says her grief is telling on her more. 'I feel such a widow' she said this morning . . . when she came to my bedside. The present of [the] picture and miniatures of darling Liko pleased her. Fortunately he was not here last year, so there are no harrowing recollections as there will be at Windsor. Many thanks for your dear letter received yesterday. You don't mention the dreadful duel and poor Herr von Schrader's death. It is terrible. I hope you will telegraph the hour of your arrival as, being Sunday, we must arrange our [movements] accordingly. . . . Christle and Franzjos who have been here with us the whole time, leave on the 17th. Looking so much forward to seeing you . . .

From the Empress Frederick
ON BOARD AUSTRIAN LLOYD STEAMER *VORWÄRTS*,
AT SEA BETWEEN BRINDISI AND TRIESTE,
JUNE 7, 1896

I left Athens the day before yesterday, and I cannot say what a pang the parting from my child gave me. I did so hate to leave her before she was on her feet and about again. . . . But it could not be helped. Thank God however the swelling of the leg has greatly diminished, only the foot is still rather swelled, but the limb must be kept up and bandaged for some time yet. She might ease it if she would use a crutch, but this she will not do! She has been so good and so patient, never murmuring or complaining though it was really a great hindrance. I hope Tino will be here tomorrow or the day after. Baby Ellena [Sophie's third child] is getting on very well and promises to be as pretty as little Alexander. . . . I feel leaving my little grandsons so much – the eldest [George] so sensible and well behaved. He and I lunched en tête à tête all the time since his papa left and he seems such a nice little companion and besides reminded me of my Waldie so much, not in face but in ways and disposition – though he is a little more timid than Waldie was who really was afraid of nothing. It is very funny being here on this ship with so many people and so much merchandise but they (the Lloyd people) have been most amiable and have tried to make me as comfortable as possible. The cargo of lambskins and goatskins (not pre-pared) smells very horrid and I fear my boxes and clothes will be very nasty for some time. . . . When I left the thought of Crete was uppermost in everyone's mind. The situation is a very sad and painful one. Of course I heard most from foreigners and not from Greeks who are very cautious and reticent about it. Public opinion was much divided as to the course the Greek Government had taken. Many thought that Greece has lost her opportunity for *ever*, as she sent *no* ships to protect *her* subjects at such a terrible moment whilst other Powers did! The Cretans themselves are furious with the Greeks and say they have abandoned them in the hour of need and changed and left them at the mercy of the enemy!! This is really very hard. There were three Greek iron-clads lying in Phalesan Harbour quite ready to go with their steam up – provisions on board for a fortnight, ammunition and all, and waiting for orders. In order to please the Great Powers and to show how litle the Greek Government wishes to encourage a rising in the Island the ships were not sent!! Of course the newspapers abused the Government, while it was really a sacrifice on their part which is very hard to take. . . . Bulgaria was freed the other day – the rest of Greece was freed 60 years ago. Italy has been liberated from a far less cruel monster. Why should not a movement be favoured of saving these wretched people from a dominion which is really quite dreadful. . . . You know I have plenty of sympathy for the Mohammedans but the Turkish Government, as masters over Christian populations are really impossible. . . . I will not say that the Russians behaved much better at Khiva or that their rule is good, but at any rate they do not persecute the Christians – though they behave ill enough to the poor Jews. . . . Tomorrow I shall be at Trieste. . . .

From the Queen
BALMORAL CASTLE, JUNE 20, 1896

Fifty-nine years since I received these heavy burdens [and] thorny crown and tomorrow is the anniversary, the ninth already, of the Jubilee and of the brilliant procession. Three of the Princes and three dear sons-in-law present then are gone! . . .[88] I am glad you have good accounts of dear Sophie. . . . There has been such a frightful shipwreck off Ushant of one of Sir D. Currie's fine boats [the *Drummond Castle*], coming from the Cape, one of which has experienced an accident before, and everyone perished but three. It is terrible. . . . I believe that the Cretan affair will be settled without massacres as all the Powers are agreed. We had Sir Vincent Caillard here on Friday, a clever, agreeable man, to have, I thought, and who is the head of the Ottoman Bank and sees the Sultan often and knows him well. He is of French origin but is English himself – Sir Vincent *Caillard* – and he told us a great deal about the Sultan who is monogamous. Sir F. Grenfell is here, having come to tell us about Moscow (he having gone with Arthur [to the coronation of Nicholas II] there). He was formerly Sirdar to the Khedive and gained the victory of Tokar. I am so sorry dear Vicky stopped so short a time.

From the Queen
WINDSOR CASTLE, JULY 6, 1896

... Dear Beatrice arrived safely after a rough passage but was not ill. She seems to have derived real benefit from her cure at Kissingen and the *Nachkur* at Oberhof. Affie ... will also go to Kissingen. I did not think him looking well.... He is rather out of spirits. I am expecting dear Lily [of Hanover] today. It is Victoria of Wales's birthday and the wedding day of Louise and Arthur and George and May. The little children of the latter are staying here as they feel the heat so much in London and the eldest was not very well. May is going with her mother (who I fear is not at all well) to St Mortiz. Forgive my crooked, untidy writing, but I [am] on the sofa and rather in the dark on account of the sunblinds.... The wedding [of the Prince of Wales's daughter, Maud, to Carl, later King Haakon of Sweden] is definitely fixed for Wednesday the 22nd and the private chapel at Buckingham Palace. I have promised to be present but only at the ceremony and not at the breakfast. I shall return here the same evening. The bridesmaids are to be Victoria of Wales, Carl's two sisters, Tora, Daisy and Patsy, little Alice Albany and little Alix Duff....

From the Empress Frederick
FRIEDRICHSHOF, JULY 29, 1896

... How well I can imagine what it must be there daily and hourly to miss dear Liko and look in vain for his familiar figure – so young and handsome and apparently strong and well – in the surroundings it was wont to be! How I know what that is, to live with constant silence and a blank and empty space by one's side in every room and on every path one treads. One cannot realise it or get accustomed to it. . . . Thank God that good and great men have sown seeds of things indestructible by their influence and example – by the history of their lives – they have left their mark on the world and their deeds do live after them. So it was with beloved Papa whose career on earth was so short and I think with my beloved Fritz it is so also, in another way. I have a feeling that no life is lived in vain. . . .

From the Queen
OSBORNE, AUGUST 19, 1896

. . . I am glad to say that Beatrice even remembers her [the Queen's mother] quite well. She was so fond of you all, had such a loving tender heart. It is from her that the *Mitgefühl* [capacity to sympathize] many of us possess comes and causes people to love us and sympathise with us. I am informed that Tino and Sophie are with you. I am very glad, as they said they must be back on the 19th. A terrible accident happened during the Portsmouth Regatta during the racing. A poor little yacht belonging to a Baron Radowsky or Galitz, who I hear has often been here before, was run into and demasted by William's yacht, the *Meteor*, and the unfortunate owner was killed by the mast falling on him. It is very awful. It was a terrible sight, I hear from an eye-witness. . . .

From the Empress Frederick
FRIEDRICHSHOF, AUGUST 29, 1896

Most loving thanks for . . . the photograph of yourself and little Edward of York, David as they call him. It is a touching group and I am so glad to possess it. . . . What a

business this is about Zanzibar! The German newspapers
are not pleasant reading. This is a fresh opportunity for the
most bitter, unjust and violent attacks on England. It makes
me so savage that sometimes I cannot finish reading the
articles; they are so unfair and sneering and nasty. I am glad
to see that most other European Powers are coming round
to Lord Salisbury's view with regard to Crete. . . .

[Ps.] You say I am so particular about photographs. Perhaps
I am, but as I admire my dear Mama and want others to see
her as I see her, I feel vexed when a portrait does not do her
justice or when there is a little fault in the arrangement
which spoils the picture or the likeness. Most photographers are not artistic and are so occupied with the
technical part of their work that they overlook many an
artistic consideration. There is no reason why a photo
should not be a good portrait *and* a work of art to be quite
successful and satisfactory.

From the Empress Frederick
FRIEDRICHSHOF, SEPTEMBER 19, 1896

. . . I fear things in Constantinople are very anxious still.
The cruelties and atrocities make one's hair stand on end!
Still I wish Mr Gladstone would not have meetings etc. It
makes Lord Salisbury's very difficult task still more so.
Crete thank God is in a better state. The Greeks will never
forget England's kindness and I hear their gratitude is great.
What they feel towards other Powers I had rather not say;
after all it is but too natural. I consider the Austrian prime
minister [Badeni] a misfortune. He is a man of a most
inferior turn of mind and few abilities, quite the wrong man
in the wrong place. . . .

From the Queen
BALMORAL CASTLE, SEPTEMBER 26, 1896

I have no dear letter to answer but I write to tell you how well the visit [of Tsar and Tsarina] is going off. They arrived by torchlight which was very pretty and there were bonfires and an escort of Scots Greys and the wet day held up at that moment. Dear Nicky and Alicky are quite unspoilt and unchanged and as dear and simple as ever and as kind as ever. He is looking rather thin and pale and careworn, but sweet Alicky is in great beauty and very blooming. The baby is magnificent, bigger than she and Ella ever were, and a lovely, lively [great] grandchild. They have pleasant people with them, Mlle Vassiltchikoff, Count Woronzoff-Dashkoff, Prince Galitzine (who was with them in '94) and Count Benckendorff. . . . Our quiet occupation of Dongola is an immense success and it took place on the day[89] of which the people make so much but which *I* do not wish to celebrate till my *sixty* years are full D.V. But I have received the most enormous number of telegrams from all ranks of my subjects and Lorne has written the accompanying very pretty lines. I feel and will say publicly that all these blessings are owing to dear Papa's guidance and tuition.

From the Empress Frederick
FRIEDRICHSHOF, OCTOBER 3, 1896

Today Nicky and Alicky will be leaving Balmoral. I trust they will have a good passage and the visit to Paris, which I almost regret, will go off well. I think it excellent that Nicky and Lord Salisbury had conversations together and I only hope no counter-current in Russia will destroy the effect of the visit to England and of Lord Salisbury's words. Oh if only my beloved Fritz were alive, how easy it would be to improve so much and how thoroughly Germany could be trusted and depended on. What an honest, straightforward liberal and prudent policy would have been followed. No fits and starts and incoherencies and inconsistencies and fantastic speeches and telegrams right and left, and expressions and demonstrations of approval or disapproval on all occasions! ... Germany is disliked and distrusted, which might quite well have been avoided and here an Anglophobia rages in the disgusting press and in large sections of the public.... It is artificial and could be dispelled if the Colonial Party and Prince Bismarck's admirers did not keep it up.... I am sure William means all for the best and wishes to act for the best but his self-reliance and self-confidence and his want of discrimination are his misfortune....

From the Queen
BALMORAL CASTLE, OCTOBER 6, 1896

... I write just to say that apart from their being so dear and simple and unchanged, I think the charming visit will have done great good. I had a very frank conversation with dear Nicky who I think very good and very thoughtful.... I quite agree in what you say about Willie and Germany. It is too true. In great haste ...

From the Empress Frederick
RUMPENHEIM, NOVEMBER 27, 1896

The news has just come that dear Irène has a little boy. I am indeed glad and thankful. How Fritz and her dear parents would have rejoiced! I congratulate you on the birth of this little great-grandchild. Of course I have no details as yet but trust all has gone well. Mossy and the twins [born on 8 November] are doing quite well. They do not think it advisable for her to put her feet down yet. Fischy [who was ill with rheumatic fever] is just the same and not allowed out of bed yet. . . . Thank you for your kind enquiries about poor dear General von Loë. I had a long account today, alas no better. . . . Poor dear man, I am so unhappy about it all as he is one of our best and truest friends.

From the Empress Frederick
RUMPENHEIM, DECEMBER 17, 1896

. . . You say Rumpenheim is not a place for the winter. No doubt it has its disadvantages in the winter, but when Mossy married, the place was so arranged to be heated throughout with hot water pipes and the house is very warm; there are stoves in some rooms besides and fireplaces in others, also double windows towards the north, so that one is very well protected. The rooms are many of them very small and very easily and quickly warmed. The disadvantage is the ferry and the difficulty of getting out and the long distance one has to drive round before one gets to Frankfurt. . . . No doubt as soon as Fischy is well again a change of air will be most necessary. To go south to Italy, without my taking them with me, would be rather too great an expense. . . . Torquay would also be too expensive I fear, or that would be very good, or Ventnor?

From the Empress Frederick
SCHLOSS, KIEL,[90] CHRISTMAS DAY, DECEMBER 25, 1896

So many wishes and blessings for today. I well know what a sad Christmas it must be for you, and I feel so much for you and Beatrice for her sorrow must naturally be yours. Let me thank you now most tenderly for all the beautiful gifts you have so kindly sent and which I found on the table under the Christmas tree: the pretty views of dear Osborne terrace with the bright geraniums, the lustre of staghorn with the ancient figure I was so anxious to have and which will look so well in the old Schloss at Kronberg. . . . The books you so kindly sent I am delighted with, also with the beautiful things you sent Henry, Irène, Charlotte and Feo for which they are all very grateful. We ate the woodcock pie and mincemeat and decorated the rooms with the dear English holly and mistletoe, most thankful to you for having sent it.

From the Queen
OSBORNE, JANUARY 3, 1897

. . . I was so grieved about Fischy, this long illness of two months is very distressing and very trying. Ought not some fresh advice to be obtained? This intermittent fever makes one anxious about the heart. Poor dear Mossy! What a sad time for her!

January 4. I could not finish last night so I do so today. . . . I have just taken leave of dear Arthur and Louischen. It is such a comfort and help to have him in the house. The loss of a male relative is severely felt. Dear Liko was such a help. It was very civil and kind of William to send the cardinal over to good Sir J. Millais's funeral. Would you wish to come over in the yacht or rather in one of the large quick packets? I must end this stupid letter to save the messenger.

From the Empress Frederick
KAISER FRIEDRICH PALAIS, BERLIN, JANUARY 16, 1897

. . . [Ps.] In a letter I received from Sophie I find the following passage which I simply repeat in the hopes that Lord Salisbury and you may find a means of preventing what would be horrible. I have of course no right to speak about it, but if one can do any good by not being silent, it is better to speak. *Here* I should not dare to do so, but perhaps you would tell Lord Salisbury. He is wise and will perhaps find a way of warding off a misfortune which may assume greater dimensions than we can foresee. Sophie says:– 'I am dying to go to Grandmama's Jubilee but there will be many things to prevent it. I fear fighting in Macedonia and Crete; there is no possibility or hope of preventing people here; they were *poussés à bout* [exasperated]; they make their preparations secretly. Do not speak about it in general. It will be known soon enough. This is, alas, the result of the Powers doing nothing decided enough and letting matters drift.' You can imagine how this torments me. The Sultan is an impossible creature and does not keep a single promise.

From the Empress Frederick
[IN ENGLAND,] FEBRUARY 19, 1897[91]

I thought you might like to see what Sophie says in the letter I received last night. How one longs for this nightmare to be removed and to be able to sleep and breathe again.

Extract, Athens, February 18, 1897 Things look very black everywhere, it seems to me the danger is imminent and cannot be averted. If not in Crete, there will be fresh trouble in Macedonia, I am sure. Here people are sanguine we shall have Crete. If the Powers could only see for once that the only way of preventing an insurrection in Macedonia is by letting us have Crete! The insurrection in Macedonia has long been preparing and may break out any day. Nothing can prevent it. The people's exasperation against the Turks and hatred of them has grown too strong. This was sure to come, sooner or later, now nothing can keep it down. The Powers might have helped some time ago, but they did not, and the small states, despairing of any other means, will try to help themselves. Of course it is mad and dangerous to run such risks, especially for us, but people are desperate. I think with fright and horror of the future. It makes one mad to think of all the misery that may yet come. Even if the Powers do not give us Crete, they must know that never,

never will the Cretans rest or the island have peace until they are Greek. The keeping of all the refugees from Crete here is a terrible expense. A Committee of Ladies has been formed and we are trying to do what we can. *End of Extract*

This is a specimen of what is thought at Athens and though no doubt the Powers do not think it worth their while to enquire or to think about what is thought in so small and insignificant a country, yet England has always had humaneness and [been] more large-hearted in this respect and has considered the claims and the situation of the weak and would perhaps not willingly see a country that has made much progress in the last thirty years, though it still has much to learn, annihilated by the Turk, as no doubt the German Government of today would. . . .

From the Empress Frederick
[IN ENGLAND] FEBRUARY 25, 1897

I return these papers with many thanks for allowing me to see them. It is indeed most sad of course. Palliades [English affairs] are in wiser and better hands than those of outsiders [Germany] but for my part I much regret the decision about Crete. It may be unavoidable, but it will not prevent war or further difficulties. I see that the British Government could not do otherwise as it has to go with the other Powers, but I do not think the solution a good one, especially as the Turkish troops are to remain after the Greek troops have left. I fear that will be the stumbling block. We must wait and see and hope for the best. Greece is in an *impasse* and unless some friendly hand is extended to show her a way out, she will be a prey to those who would willingly see her annihilated. However, who knows, perhaps some fortunate chance may present itself. I only fear that she will wish to save her honour and will think it hopelessly compromised. Still I should think she has done all she could, and to have to submit, to give way, to superior force is most humiliating but not dishonourable. I am so ashamed and annoyed to be unwell just now, but hope to be nearly all right tomorrow. Kissing your dear hand I remain . . .

From the Queen
EXCELSIOR HOTEL REGINA, CIMIEZ, MARCH 19, 1897

. . . The news will I fear not cheer you. It becomes more and more difficult. The Powers press for the blockade of Volo and I fear if we don't join (and we are very unwilling to do so) the concert will be broken up.

March 20. . . . I fear Volo will have to be blockaded and that this may stop any further reinforcements being sent. Greece can really not defy all Europe. If their ships are foolish enough to fire on any of ours as they did on the Austrians, we must return it and sink them in spite of all our wishes not to do so. I cannot say how distressed I am for you and poor Alix who is gone to Denmark [to the King and Queen, her parents and also the parents of the King of Greece] which is best for her as Bertie is not in England. She is looking very well but poor Affie very much the reverse of it. Sir J. Reid thinks his state an anxious one. His nervous system is quite broken down and I fear he is again very imprudent. . . .

From the Queen
EXCELSIOR HOTEL REGINA, CIMIEZ, MARCH 31, 1897

. . . As regards public affairs, I do feel so deeply for you, poor darling child, and for darling Sophie and all. We are doing what we can but it is very difficult. You will I am sure [be] greatly surprised to hear Franzjos was engaged the night before last to the Princess Anna of Montenegro, a charming girl who is quite determined to marry him and is devoted to him. We are all most pleased as it is in every way a good match, being a near connection with Italy and also

Russia.[92] The Prince of Montenegro arrived yesterday and I saw him today. He is a great man.

AFTER THE DECLARATION OF WAR BETWEEN TURKEY AND GREECE
OVER CRETE

From the Empress Frederick
SCHLOSS FRIEDRICHSHOF, APRIL 18, 1897

I have just heard that Turkey has declared war and seven Greek columns crossed the Turkish frontier. My alarm and anxiety know no bounds. So far away! Without much news, without anyone who understands one's feeling and sympathises with one, it is dreadful. What Tino and Sophie are going through makes one quite miserable and I cannot help them or be with them and share their troubles and dangers and perhaps make myself of a little use! That is so hard! Greece and the King were much in the position of a man whose home is set fire to and, the doors all being locked, he has to jump out of the window even at the risk of breaking his neck. They seem to have tried their utmost to prevent war. Delyannos's speech clearly showed it and Tino liberated the Turkish prisoners taken by the irregulars and sent them home. What my feelings are when I read of the encouragement given to Turkey by Germany and the German officers in the Turkish Army, you can imagine. The Three Emperors are all agreed and on the wrong tack and it grieves me bitterly to think that dear England is so bound and so tied down that she cannot act as she would wish. Alas, William's personal hatred to Greece and enmity to the King and whole royal family is well known everywhere and does not improve matters. The Turks are a fearful foe, not for Russians or European troops, but for the Greeks. They are like wild beasts in their cruelty. There is not a Greek who has not some record in his family, that has been handed down from generation to generation, of this awful cruelty suffered at their hands. There will be no more sleep for me now for days. Sophie is at Volo, the darling children at Athens. Oh, if Fritz had been spared all this would never have happened! Germany would have mediated and appeased and England could have gone hand in hand with her. . . .

From the Queen
EXCELSIOR HOTEL REGINA, CIMIEZ, APRIL 24, 1897

I hardly know how to write to you, my whole heart bleeds for you! Oh! If only the 'Powers' (who are useless and worse than useless) had acted with us, this terrible war would have ceased. Yesterday everything seemed in favour of the Greeks and today we hear of a great defeat. I cannot say how I feel or how my heart bleeds for our darling Sophie and you as well. And to think of William's shameful behaviour, for he it is who has urged this on! People in England and in France are very angry at him. . . . I am so distressed, darling child, about you. It is so terrible and I often think the Jubilee will never come off. . . .

From the Queen
BUCKINGHAM PALACE, MAY 11, 1897

. . . The Drawing Room is a very full one. I stayed an hour but it is still going on. At the Drawing Room I heard from Lord Salisbury that: 'I hear mediation has begun'. . . . And yesterday Alix (who was very tired but very calm) told me she had just got a telegram from her father [King Christian IX of Denmark, also the father of Willy of Greece] saying that he had just heard from Nicky saying he was taking measures to bring about a mediation. The *one* [and] only Power who tried to stand out against this is (alas) Germany. It is too dreadful. There are no end of difficulties and dangers about the Jubilee. . . . Since I began the above I

---

have a number of telegrams, all satisfactory as to mediation being accepted and facilities given for the Greek ships to bring away the Greek troops – thank God!

From the Queen
BALMORAL CASTLE, JUNE 14, 1897

... My thoughts are truly sympathising with you. Already nine years [since Fritz's death] and I fear next week will be a great trial to you. So many dear and sad remembrances will crowd in upon you. Today is dear Sophie's birthday, also a day of harrowing recollections. All [at the Diamond Jubilee on 22 June] will in many ways be different to 1887. . . . I sent an extract of what you said to Lord Salisbury, but I really think that the negotiations are going on and that the dangers you apprehend are not so great. A garrison for Crete is proposed and, I believe, agreed upon by all the Powers – a success. Turkey may be obstinate, but I hope this will be overcome. . . .

From the Empress Frederick
ON BOARD THE *VICTORIA AND ALBERT*, FLUSHING, JULY 3, 1897

... I am so thankful I witnessed the ceremonies of your Jubilee and left you looking so well, in spite of being tired which indeed you must be. It was a never-to-be-forgotten time – enthusiasm and loyalty for you in the very air, and all went off so well, and was so well organised, and on the whole the weather was most favourable. Your guests were all delighted, I am sure, and went away with grateful hearts. Your servants all worked like slaves and with untiring zeal and good humour and you must indeed feel proud and relieved; for it must have been a most difficult task for your Court and Household. No accidents to mar the recollection of the festive scenes and splendid pageants! One must indeed congratulate you. All the blessings called down on your dear head seemed to take a tangible form and a spirit of affection and kindliness, peace and goodwill was abroad. The dear ones gone, whom we missed so cruelly, would have rejoiced with us, and in our thoughts and hearts they were always present. Yesterday afternoon's ceremony [review of colonial troops at Windsor] was most interesting I am sure. And I am indeed sorry not to have witnessed it. Let me thank you once more for having allowed us to come over in the dear yacht and return in her which we appreciate so much. . . .

From the Queen
WINDSOR CASTLE, JULY 12, 1897

I am so very sorry for dear Moretta and Adolf. I do wish they had never gone there.[93] Why do they not stay some little time with you? Affairs I hope do look better. Austria and Russia have answered Turkey urgently advising her to yield to the wishes of the united Powers and to make peace as quickly as possible or else the consequences might be very serious. . . .

From the Empress Frederick
FRIEDRICHSHOF, JULY 28, 1897

. . . Peace seems to me almost concluded now? But how ever is Greece to find four million of pounds to pay to the Turks? The Turks have never paid their war indemnity to Russia, how can they expect [that] a so much poorer and smaller country can pay them so enormous a sum? The Turk seems to ignore the liberation of Crete and expect to send a Governor there, keep their troops and all. This I trust will never be allowed by the Powers. It would really be too shameful. I hear William has invited Grumbkov Pasha to the manoeuvres. How unnecessary that is and how it must offend the poor King and Tino! Even Count Eulenburg could not understand that being done. I forgot to tell you that on the day of your Jubilee the whole of the town of Homburg was beautifully decorated, covered with flags etc., which I thought so nice of the people. . . .

From the Queen
OSBORNE, AUGUST 5, 1897

The visit of the King of Siam prevented my writing to you by yesterday's messenger. He is very intelligent and speaks quite fairly, *mais cherche ses mots* [but he searches for his words] and speaks very low. He is very kind and civil and is easily pleased. But I could hardly help laughing when he said to me 'Your Majesty has a very nice *little* house here'. Today I saw the Empress Eugénie who, as you know, has been to Athens and seen Olga and darling Sophie who, she said, did not *look* ill and who she spoke of in the highest terms, her anxiety, her devotion. You would have been pleased to hear her. Poor Willy too she spoke kindly of. She is here in her yacht. . . .

From the Queen
OSBORNE, AUGUST 18, 1897

. . . The bad feeling between England and Germany is indeed a great distress and anguish to me – as to you and to many – but I trust this will pass away gradually if William will not keep it up by speeches and colonial follies. The peace is again rendered difficult by him which is incredible. These railings you have so often spoken of have something to do with it doubtless. I am sending for you the photograph I think Vicky wished for and for you one I had done of myself in the exact dress I wore on the 22nd. I am having it photogravured so that I can then send it to some of the family and a few other friends who were not there. . . .

[Ps.] As my presents are going to be shown and described (excepting the jewellery), will you tell me exactly where the beautiful Chresopias paperweight came from? Please to telegraph it as we are anxious to get it done.

From the Queen
BALMORAL CASTLE, SEPTEMBER 11, 1897

. . . I heard today from Lord Salisbury that he thought the peace would be signed in a few days, which is very encouraging. The success in the Soudan is very satisfactory and was done very quietly. General Kitchener allows no news correspondents to go with him. Uncle George has returned, much pleased at his reception being over. He said the entertainments and standing about were somewhat fatiguing but he had come back quite well. The feeling of loyalty and duty towards me in India at the renewal of hostility of the [north-west] border tribes is very gratifying and wonderful. George and May have been wonderfully well received in Ireland. And now goodnight.

From the Empress Frederick
FRIEDRICHSHOF, OCTOBER 9, 1897

. . . Is the red enamel cross with your cipher in gold and the dark blue bow you gave me to wear, also given to ladies and princesses, not English, who are connected with hospital work during a war? I fancied you had initiated the order for such who had helped the Red Cross Societies or done independent work for the sick and wounded. If so, would it be opportune for you to send this cross (you gave me some years back) to Olga and to Sophie? William has just sent Sophie a little red cross to be added to her Louisen Order (not a separate decoration, so it would not look uncivil towards Olga). Whereas, if it should be possible or admissible, etc., to send such a decoration to Sophie, it would not do to omit Olga, who has done just as much. You know they nursed Turks also in their hospitals. But of course I am ignorant of the rules and regulations attached to the order you gave me, perhaps it was only for nurses and for us your daughter and daughters-in-law. Pray excuse my asking this question. . . . I have just received your telegram in answer to my letter in which I alluded to reports emanating from Strelitz. Should we be told anything more I will tell you. I only hope we shall not.

From the Queen
BALMORAL CASTLE, OCTOBER 15, 1897
My engagement day

. . . I really must scold that you continue to speak of something dreadful which if true would render the whole Strelitz and Anhalt family wretched for ever and then refuse to say anything, but you write in the same strain in every letter! You should never have said anything if you could not say what is supposed. I shall now try (without mentioning your name) to [find] out from other sources, as it is too unpleasant to have such mysterious hints[94] thrown out, without saying what it is! I am enquiring about the Red Cross which I should be very pleased to give to Olga and Sophie if it is possible. . . . In India I hope there may soon be peace on the frontier after one more fight, but saving officers. I should much like to have a photograph of Feo's intended. I am sure you are right and that it is better so. Though it is not a brilliant match, I think it wrong of the Duke to put it off so long. . . .

From the Empress Frederick
HOTEL TRENTO, TRENT, NOVEMBER 10, 1897

... Affairs in Greece are still very serious and Germany does all she can to support whatever Turkey puts forward to the detriment of Greece. The sufferings of all the poor refugees are terrible; it seems without proper shelter; food and clothes wanting. It is too sad. The news from India seems more reassuring and the military operations successful, alas, not without the sacrifice of many a life. England has her hands full indeed, but I hope and trust with every prospect of satisfactory results in all her enterprises. I do not know whether Alfred is in England now, but I heard he was to be there this month. I trust you will find him better, he has suffered so much this year, I hear, from that dreadful gouty eczema which is very painful and trying. Henry and Irène have been in Rumpenheim for a day and night, but will soon return to Kiel. Charlotte and Bernhard are back at Breslau and Vicky is at Bonn, still in the hotel as her house is not ready yet, though they are hastening on the work and hope to inhabit part of it before Christmas. She misses Detmold terribly which is no wonder. Have you heard how Tora is getting on in Russia? I am sure she is enjoying herself greatly, seeing so much that is new. I am so glad for her that she went.

From the Queen
WINDSOR CASTLE, DECEMBER 6, 1897

... I had also a later letter from dear Henry [who had a naval posting to Chinese waters] proposing to come to see me on the 19th at Osborne to take leave. ... Of the other dreadful story I will also write as there are some things I want really to know the truth of. We are going to hear Grieg and his wife play and sing his beautiful composition this evening. Some three weeks ago we heard Mde Chaminde play her charming compositions which she did beautifully. . . . Thank God, peace [between Greece and Turkey] was signed the day before yesterday.

From the Queen
OSBORNE, DECEMBER 20, 1897

. . . Louischen should not be told [of the Mecklenburg–Strelitz affair], but she knows all and she said her mother wrote to say they could not hold up their heads. It is a most deplorable thing and most immoral. I think [things] have been universally mismanaged. . . . Henry . . . will sail this morning. He seemed to feel much having parted with you all. But, alas, these speeches at Kiel [of William II]. How unfortunate and I must say absurd![95] Henry is so unlike him [i.e. William II]. . . . I think it monstrous that they send the unfortunate girl's child away.

From the Queen
OSBORNE, JANUARY 19, 1898

. . . I fear Germany, or William, is again giving [the Greeks] difficulties about Crete. I send you three letters from Sir T. Martin which speak for themselves. As he knows so many of the editors I asked him if he could not do something to prevent these constant attacks on Germany and William saying a dignified silence on our part would be far better and these are his answers which I think very satisfactory. Please return them, but keep copies if you wish. Affie left yesterday for Venice *en route* for Egypt. He is I fear as bad as ever and will not give up beer and wine entirely as the doctor says he ought and never takes any exercise. It is so distressing. I fear waters cannot do any good if he won't observe these principles. . . .

From the Queen
OSBORNE, FEBRUARY 9, 1898

... Affairs continue anxious but I believe will get right. It seems China said to Russia what she said to us, viz: that we threatened her if she accepted a Russian loan and we arm! Crete remains unsettled. I hope the journey to Jerusalem of William and Dona may fall through. It would be such a bad time for going. What may not happen before May! The little poem which is for my accession is very pretty and I return the letter with many thanks.... Tomorrow is the fifty-eighth anniversary of my dear wedding day and I shall miss you.

From the Queen
WINDSOR CASTLE, FEBRUARY 28, 1898

... How much startled you must have been to hear of this awful attempt on poor Willie of Greece and what a merciful, miraculous escape he and Mary had. It is one of the worst attempts I ever heard of. But it has brought out great loyalty and attachment to the King and his family and will really do good, as they escaped. But [such an attempt] leaves always a painful sensation and want of confidence. Sophie telegraphs this evening that the assassins were caught this morning. Poor Olga, how painful for her! We are in anxiety and distress about dear Aunt Clémentine who suddenly got worse last night and this evening Philip telegraphs ... [a message in German that she was dying]. It grieves me beyond measure as I loved her and our friendship dates from 1843, over fifty-five years. Tora arrived this morning having only left Petersburg on Saturday evening. Alicky is progressing rather slowly. All went off well in London....

From the Empress Frederick
PALAIS SCHAUMBURG, BONN, APRIL 5, 1898

I see by the papers that you have been on board the *Surprise* to see poor dear Alfred and I am so thankful to hear he is really better and that the operation has been successful. Bertie thought him better than he expected. My thoughts will be so much with you for the Confirmation of dear little Alice of Albany which will be very touching in *that* chapel [i.e. the memorial chapel to Prince Leopold at Cannes]. The weather is still very cold and uncertain and spring very backward. Vicky's house [at Bonn] is charming. So cheerful and comfortable, so prettily arranged in such good taste. She has taken a great deal of trouble with it, and certainly with great success. It is not large and the garden is not so either, but they have some nice trees and grass and the lovely Rhine before them with the Siebengebirge. A beautiful new drive and quay is being arranged along the banks of the Rhine and steps from Vicky's garden lead down to it. The town is growing and also improving very much and a large bridge [is] being built across the Rhine which was so much wanted as till now there were only ferries. This house was only a little villa belonging to a merchant. . . . Now it has been transformed into a nice small English country house. . . . They had the same architect who built Friedrichshof [the Frenchman, Hippolyte-Alexandre-Gabriel Destailleur]. . . .

From the Queen
EXCELSIOR HOTEL REGINA, CIMIEZ, APRIL 26, 1898

This moment I got your letter announcing the arrival of your Greek children and grandchildren, which must indeed be a great joy to you after all they suffered. . . . Tomorrow, alas, dear Marie Erbach leaves us. I am so very fond of her who is so dear, sensible and good. Yesterday I saw the young Queen of the Netherlands, such a charming girl, so simple, dignified and pretty with a sweet expression and lovely complexion and pretty figure. She reminds me of myself from her extremely youthful appearance. Her excellent mother [Queen Emma] came with her, so pleasant, simple and *sympathique*. . . .

From the Queen
WINDSOR CASTLE, MAY 8, 1898

Darling Irène and the little boys arrived safely at a quarter to eleven after a rather rough passage. She is looking very well and seems so strong. I thought Toddy[96] looking well and seeming so. He is very happy with Leopold and they are quite a match, Leopold being just a little taller. The baby is a very fine child but very cross at present. . . . This Spanish war distresses me very much and surely I think ought to be stopped. No doubt Cuba was dreadfully governed, but that does not excuse America and the principle is dreadful. They might as well say we governed Ireland badly and they ought to take possession of it and free it. . . .

From the Empress Frederick
FRIEDRICHSHOF, MAY 13, 1898

. . . I am so sorry poor old Lady Esher had a fall at the Drawing Room. I hope she was not much shaken. I know her pretty well as she and her husband often came from England to Homburg; she is French and a great friend of Count Hatzfeldt's. How very kind of you to say you will send the dolls to Princess Wied. She will be delighted. I think an Indian couple would be most acceptable if they could be had at such short notice – perhaps in the shop in London where only Indian things are sold. . . . It is such a source of pleasure and instruction to me to look at the book of

architecture you gave me for Christmas, by A. Gotch. Tino
and Sophie are also very fond of looking at it. We have been
to Frankfurt this afternoon to see some pictures. . . . I have
to go to the Confirmation of William's boys. . . . Dona seems
to wish it.

AFTER GLADSTONE'S DEATH

From the Empress Frederick
FRIEDRICHSHOF, MAY 21, 1898

[After birthday wishes] My offering consists in a Gothic
frame, carved, and of cherry wood. I have put an engraving
from a modern figure of Christ into it. I hope it may find a
place in, or before the Chapel at Osborne. I fancy one of the
walls between the windows is still empty and it might look
well there. . . . I am off to Berlin in half an hour. . . . Poor Mr
Gladstone[97] is at rest at last after having suffered very
much, I fear. Poor old Mrs Gladstone. . . .

From the Empress Frederick
FRIEDRICHSHOF, MAY 28, 1898

. . . I can quite well imagine how sad it must make you to
part from Beatrice even for a short while. I hope she will
derive great benefit from her cure at Kissingen and that little
Ena will have a nice time at Schönberg with Marie Erbach.
Sophie's visit to Berlin is going off all right and she has
been made *Chef* of the Königin Elisabeth Regiment which
gives her great pleasure [i.e. as a sign of reconciliation
with William II]. Little Georgie goes to Berlin tonight and
returns with Sophie and Tino on Tuesday. I shall be
represented at Mr Gladstone's funeral by Count Arco (of the
German Embassy) which I hope will be according to your
wishes. Poor Mr Gladstone was often your minister
and though it was impossible always to agree with him, yet

South-east view of Friedrichshof

Queen Victoria's carriage leaving Buckingham Palace for the Diamond
Jubilee procession, 22 June 1897

The Empress Frederick, 1900. (Photographer: T.H. Voigt)

he was a great Englishman and it is fitting to do honour to his memory as such. I had a letter from Henry dated April 22. Will you please tell Irène. He seems quite well, thank God! . . . Many thanks for sending the doll in Highland costume which I sent on immediately to Segenhaus to Princess Wied and am sure she will be delighted. I hope the Musselburgh Fishwoman will follow and also the doll in Indian costume. . . .

From the Queen
BALMORAL CASTLE, MAY 31, 1898

. . . I am so glad the Confirmation went off so well in *every* way. I had a very kind letter from William in which he expressed in the very strongest terms his great pleasure at your having been present. I am so glad Sophie and Tino's visit to Berlin went off so well, and that they went, and that Sophie wore the collar of the Regiment which shows all is being made up again. I only think, if it is *possible*, that in families all should be made up again, for life is so very uncertain. It was quite right of you sending Count Arco to represent you at Mr Gladstone's funeral. I cannot say that I think he was 'a great Englishman'. He was a clever man, full of talent, but he never *tried* to keep up the *honour* and *prestige* of Great Britain. He gave away the Transvaal, he abandoned Gordon, he destroyed the Irish Church and tried to separate England from Ireland and to set class against class. The harm he did cannot easily be undone. But he was a good and very religious man. The account of the funeral and above all one from Mrs Gladstone is very touching. . . .

From the Queen
WINDSOR CASTLE, JUNE 29, 1898

. . . Dear Marie L[einingen] left me to my great regret yesterday morning to return to Germany. She is really

better, not so thin or pale and does not intend to go to
Nauheim this year. We had a most successful performance
of Gounod's opera *Romeo and Juliet*, the music of which I
think quite heavenly – like *Faust*. Mme Emma Eames sang
most beautifully. She is American and a very charming
person and is now quite one of the best singers we have.
Edouard de Reszke and Plançon have both splendid voices
and sing and act well, but we were greatly disappointed by
Jean de Reszke, the great tenor, being taken ill and unable
to sing. His place [was taken] by a new tenor who[m] I do
not much admire. Louise [Aribert] has been here for two
nights, very far from well, but not in bad spirits. She is only
so weak and everything tires her. This dreadful war still
goes on and really ought to be stopped by the Powers. . . . I
am looking much forward to Tino and Sophie coming on the
2nd for two nights, returning about the 11th. I should also
be very glad to have them for a little at Osborne.

From the Empress Frederick
FRIEDRICHSHOF, JULY 9, 1898

. . . All you say about my Sophie and Tino gives me such
pleasure; nothing could give me greater pleasure than to
have them praised and appreciated. . . . They have gone
through so much. Yes, indeed, what is to happen? One must
be patient. I think a long regency for Tino would be a good
thing. The King is in a very difficult position. He could do a
great deal more than he does, if he were to exercise his
prerogative and use the power he has with more energy to
break with abuses and introduce reforms. On the other
hand, the King, who is very clever, has often had *la main
heureuse* [a happy touch] and often saved the situation when
it was full of danger, by his tact and conciliatory restraint
and by letting people have their own way. That policy is no
doubt wise and good, but does not always suffice and at the
present moment seems to me a misfortune. He is so just that
he does not like to *désavouer* [disavow] the Minister of War,

whom he has once taken into the Ministry. And this man has behaved so abominably to Tino . . . one wishes the King could take his son's part. . . . The army is on Tino's side. . . . I hope matters will improve and that Tino's and Sophie's views are a little too gloomy. . . .

[Ps.] I wish indeed you could see Sophie's children. The elder is a most interesting child. The second a really splendid child – enormous blue eyes with dark eyelashes, a steep forehead with wavy dark hair, a lovely mouth and a little turned-up nose and dimples in his pink cheeks. . . . Little Ellena (Sitta 'as they call her) is so sweet and pretty but very shy and a little fretful at times, which will wear off when she gets older.

From the Queen
OSBORNE, JULY 21, 1898

You will be greatly distressed at poor dear Bertie's *most* untoward accident [a broken kneecap] which though not dangerous is a serious one. For him especially who cannot be quiet a day, and who has so much to do requiring activity, it [is] most unfortunate. To be laid up now in London where the air is so bad and *now* is really very distressing. There is besides the fear that the leg may remain somewhat stiff. The accounts . . . continue quite favourable so far. He even was able to write to me. He is very patient I hear. Lenchen saw him yesterday. I hear Maria and Nicholas of Greece have arrived at M[arlborough] House. We expect Tino and Sophie tomorrow here. It is quite a mistake that Lord Salisbury is against a friendly understanding with Germany. He wishes it more than anyone, but he and I are most anxious also for a good understanding with Russia which is most important for the peace of Europe. . . .

From the Queen
OSBORNE, AUGUST 17, 1898

... Dear Beatrice opened a museum at Carisbrook[e] in remembrance of our darling Liko which is a memorial of the Island to his dear memory. The speeches were so pretty that I enclose an account of the whole for you and also return William's wonderful telegram. I certainly agree with you about the visit to Jerusalem which does indeed *fait le ridicule*. . . .

From the Empress Frederick
FRIEDRICHSHOF, AUGUST 26, 1898

On this ever dear day of truly blessed memory let me say how much my thoughts are with you and dwelling on the past, in the happy times. . . . Our dear beloved Papa would have been 79. . . . I do not give up all hope that for the good of both countries there may be a rapprochement. English, American and German trade are greatest in China, and if these nations stick together, and can carry Japan with them, I do not see what harm could come to anyone. No one would attack us and the danger of a clash – in short a war – would be effectively averted. I am sure dear Papa would have thought so too. I must end.

From the Empress Frederick
FRIEDRICHSHOF, AUGUST 31, 1898

I should like to say one word more about the Russian proposal [for what became the Hague Peace Congress, 1899] and all one hears. A great many people are delighted and take it *au sérieux* [seriously] and say what a blessing etc. . . . Of course nations have suffered and languished, and none so much as the German, under the tremendous strain of ever increasing armaments and no doubt socialism has grown in consequence or the country could [not] grow so rich [as it would have done], had the money been used for other purposes. Some again think that whatever the immediate result may be of this proposal, the idea of diminishing armaments, hitherto advocated by peace societies and peace-loving individuals without influence, or by democratic elements, now passes into a new phase, as it has now been taken up by an Emperor and a Government. . . . *I* cannot help thinking that the suddenness of this proposal, so little in accordance with Russian traditions, with their acknowledged national programme and their latest political moves, points to a sudden *fear* having arisen in their minds. The idea had floated about that the only barrier to their Asiatic plans of conquest would be a war with England or an alliance between England and Germany or England and America and Japan. This stroke Muraviev wished to parry and no doubt this has been done in a clever way. It brings Nicky to the fore; it lends importance and power to Russia and for the moment makes her the centre of European policy. Can she be taken at her word? I think she is only acting in her own interests and is far more astute than any of the Western Powers. . . . It is certain that for many decades Russia has been preparing for the final conflict with England for the supremacy in Asia. . . . Russia is not ready to fight England at present and afraid that events in China might run her into the danger of a war with England before she is fully prepared. This danger is averted by this manifesto. . . . Nicky is quite against constitutions or liberty for Russia. . . . An aura of peace seems hardly in accordance with the oppression and suffering of a race still governed by despotism. . . .

From the Queen
BALMORAL CASTLE, SEPTEMBER 5, 1898

. . . I have not answered what you say about Nicky's manifesto, but I have not heard from Lord Salisbury since. I think it is meant in a peaceable sense, only I don't see how it is to be carried out. Many, including ourselves, who have got such large possessions, and [these] overseas, exposed to attacks and wars, [cannot reduce armies.] But a reduction of the enormous armies of Germany and Russia and France would seem to be a good thing. The details of the victory [at Omdurman in Kitchener's reconquest of the Sudan] as far as we learn them by telegrams and newspapers are most splendid and comparatively speaking the loss has been small and all the wounded are doing well. But the Khalifa has not yet been caught which is unfortunate though I hardly think he can recover his prestige and power. He is being pursued and I trust will be caught. . . .

From the Empress Frederick
FRIEDRICHSHOF, SEPTEMBER 6, 1898

I would have written yesterday to thank you once more for your telegram and tell you once more how sincerely I rejoice at the success of our arms and what is, I hope, the termination of the Egyptian War and offer you my sincerest congratulations, but was prevented. The fact is, I had what might have been a very serious accident but I escaped with only a slight injury to my right hand. I was out riding with Mossy and Frau von Reischach when my horse took fright at a steam threshing machine in a field and shied violently. I tried to guide it and the groom got off to lead it past the machine but it reared in one moment and swung round throwing me off – happily on my right side and my habit caught in the pommel, which broke the weight of the fall. . . . However I got up and walked part of the way home and only felt shaken and stiff towards evening. . . . My right hand . . . was extremely painful. I went straight to my doctor. . . . I am all right today except for a headache. . . .

AFTER THE ASSASSINATION OF THE EMPRESS OF AUSTRIA

From the Queen
BALMORAL CASTLE, SEPTEMBER 11, 1898

I feel dumb with horror at this horrible event. Such too you must feel, having seen the poor dear Empress, whose sorrows have been great, so lately. What a fatality in her family. Her cousin drowned, her son murdered or committed suicide, her sister burnt and herself stabbed to death![98] How the poor, good Emperor, whose life has been so full of trials and sorrows [will bear it]. . . . It is too, too awful. It seems she did not see what happened and so was able to walk on board the steamer but soon after fainted and then a stain of blood was discovered on her dress. [They took her] to the hotel where she died in about two hours never recovering consciousness. I am so anxious for details. They say the poor Emperor bears up with wonderful fortitude. Many thanks for your last dear letter and the account of your dreadful fall. You have indeed had a merciful escape and you must never risk that horse again. . . . All [the] details of [the] great victory come in by degrees. It was a fearful battle and the memorial service [for General Gordon] in Khartoum must have been very touching. . . .

From the Empress Frederick
FRIEDRICHSHOF, SEPTEMBER 12, 1898

Only a line to say that I feel quite ill with horror and distress at the terrible death of the dear sweet Empress of Austria whom I have seen so lately. One's only hope is that she did not suffer much. She was so melancholy, so unhappy, so sick and tired of life and took such a sad view of existence that I am sure the fact of being at rest is a blessed one for her. . . . She was so kind and so simple and a straightforward, trustworthy character, courageous and independent. I was truly fond of her. . . . She had kept the traces of her extraordinary loveliness: her smile, her figure, her walk and her carriage, even now, though her face was lined and worn and she was terribly thin. She had not a grey hair, though the loads of chestnut plaits had become much thinner and no longer seemed too thick to dress and arrange and too long to fasten on her head. She was always so nice and good and kind to me. . . . She had strange eccentric habits, was shy, hated society. So people did not know that she was clever and gifted, which she really was. Her gardener arrived here two days ago to see my garden and copy some things for her. . . . The poor man heard the news from us. He said that his coming here had been the last wish she had expressed and he hoped her last orders would be carried out in her memory. . . .

From the Queen
BALMORAL CASTLE, NOVEMBER 5, 1898

Many thanks for your dear letters from Dalmeny where I am glad to see you liked Lord Rosebery's daughters. I trust the visit to Drumlanrig has been agreeable and pleasant. The visit of the Sirdar and Mr Balfour [to Balmoral] was particularly interesting. You must see both when you are at Windsor. . . . Mme Marchesi sang quite beautifully. Hollmann played especially well on the violincello. Thank God, the French have suddenly become reasonable *unberufen*. Why did they not do this [withdraw from Fashoda] long before? William seems to have been very prudent and civil and courteous to all denominations [in Jerusalem]. We hear the visit reported as a success. He telegraphed to me that he had visited the English Church. I hope you will find all clean and comfortable at Buckingham Palace.[99]

From the Queen
OSBORNE, JANUARY 11, 1899

Most beloved Child, I can't say how grieved I was to see you go. It was such a pleasure to have you all this time with us, and we shall miss you sadly. Pray don't refer openly about yourself [after a giddy fit at Dalmeny, cancer was feared] to Bertie; the fewer [who] know anything the better and safer. Better send your letters for Sir Francis L[aking] under cover to me or Beatrice and you had better write about your precious health on a *separate sheet*. I shall be most anxious to hear how Count Seckendorff bears the journey to London and whether he will be able to start tomorrow. You must not cross tomorrow if it is rough and you ought to hear early tomorrow about this. . . .

From the Queen
OSBORNE, JANUARY 12, 1899

. . . It is my greatest pleasure and happiness to be of any use to you, my darling, and to help and comfort others is the *one* object in life, when one has gone through so much sorrow as I, and indeed you have too. . . . Let me repeat, come to us whenever and wherever you like. I am so thankful you do not attempt to go today and you must not do so till the sea is calm and down. . . .

From the Empress Frederick
HOTEL ANGST, BORDIGHERA, JANUARY 23, 1899

. . . Today is Alfred's silver wedding [celebrated at Gotha in Coburg] and many affectionate wishes do I offer you, too, on the occasion. It seems but yesterday to me that I saw them married at Petersburg. I heard in a roundabout way, so I cannot help hoping and thinking that it is an utter mistake, that young Alfred's lungs are very seriously affected. It would be too sad for anything if this were the case. Have you heard anything to that effect? I trust that should his lungs be in the very least delicate they will take it in time and consult Professor Dettzila, the founder of the institution at Falkenstein for the care of diseases of the chest and a great authority on the subject. . . . My visit to San Remo yesterday was very painful. . . . I did not go near the Villa Zirio. . . .

From the Empress Frederick
HOTEL ANGST, BORDIGHERA, JANUARY 28, 1899

. . . I was so glad to see your handwriting so firm and clear too; quite like in former years which showed me that you were not tired when you wrote . . .[100]. There has been no need yet to send for a doctor. During this fortnight I have been following Sir F. Laking's instructions and have experienced nothing new or unusual, or I would immediately send for Dr A. Sturges. Pain comes and goes as it did at Osborne. My ear is much better but not altogether right again. I think the rest and quiet here, the good air etc. cannot but do my general health good and thus indirectly keep the evil in check which cannot be cured. . . . I had a letter from Irène from Hong Kong, who seems to like being there [where she had gone to join Henry] very much.

[Ps.] I have read through Aunt Elizabeth's Memoirs[101] with great interest. There are however some little mistakes, both in names and also facts, and some errors in spelling, which the editor ought to know of. I am very glad Sir J. Reid wrote to Dr Sturges and told him what he did, saying nothing more.

From the Queen
OSBORNE, JANUARY 30, 1899

... Lord Clarendon came here on Saturday and stopped till today. He gave an account of everything at Gotha. The loyalty and affection shown to both Affie and Marie was very great. He never saw poor Alfred, but Affie let me know he had borne the journey [to Meran] well. He [Affie] means to go over in a few weeks to see how he [young Alfred] is getting on. I will send you the report Dr Bankart has written. He is very clever and has great determination and Affie has unbounded confidence in him. I do not think his lungs have been attacked. I will mention the Professor's name to Affie, but I think he is quite satisfied with Dr Bankart and the German doctors he has consulted. ... I also hate this mania for building big hotels. ...

AFTER THE DEATH OF YOUNG ALFRED, HEIR TO COBURG

From the Queen
OSBORNE, FEBRUARY 8, 1899

I know how distressed you are at this awful misfortune – which is so far-reaching. But we must not [lose] heart or courage and God will help us. But oh, the poor, poor parents! To lose their only son, in whom their hopes and life were bound up, is fearful. I have three lines from poor dear unhappy Affie and Marie. Ernie of Hesse went to him and seems most kind and attentive, telegraphing to me several times. He describes poor Affie as in a dreadful state on first going to see the dear remains. But he could sleep and is quieter today. He telegraphed today: 'I have returned from praying near my dear boy who looks so peaceful. I am broken-hearted, but we start tonight with the remains for Gotha. Funeral on Friday.' They were going to have a blessing before they left. They won't have anyone for the funeral. Georgie was to have gone but they don't wish it. The poor boy is to be laid to rest at Gotha in the vault below the chapel at Friedenstein. I don't know why not at Coburg. . . . I got a long and most distressed report from Dr Bankart today, written on the 5th – the day before [the boy died]. . . .

From the Queen
WINDSOR CASTLE, FEBRUARY 15, 1899

I write a few lines only to send you the copy (typeprinted) [i.e. typewritten] of an interesting and touching letter from Sir C. Stephen, which please send on to Aunt Alexandrine when you have done with it. . . . You seem not to know that R. Catholics are excluded by the laws and customs of the Duchies of Saxe-Coburg-Gotha from succeeding to them. Young Arthur or Charlie *must* succeed [sons, respectively, of the Duke of Connaught and the Duke of Albany].

From the Queen
EXCELSIOR HOTEL REGINA, CIMIEZ, MARCH 29, 1899

. . . Leoncavallo played to us this evening, and beautifully, bits out of [the] new opera *La Bohème* and out of *I Pagliacci* – both lovely. He has an exquisite touch and such expression, but is very painstaking. It was such a pleasure to see you here.

From the Empress Frederick
HOTEL DE SAVOIE, GENOA, APRIL 4, 1899

. . . I was indeed sorry to leave dear Bordighera, especially to be again removed further from you. I think dear Beatrice enjoys seeing this beautiful city, as fine as any I know, and is struck with the situation, the noble palaces that have retained some of their ancient magnificence, the quaint narrow streets and enormously high houses. All so full of historical interest! The splendid views everywhere! Alas, it is becoming more and more a centre of trade, shipping and manufactories, but this is good for Italy, though most sad for the artist, historian and lover of nature. I wrote in the same strain to William as you did to me and said, while it was well in a quarrel to be the stronger and best prepared and have the best cause, still it did not justify provoking a quarrel, with all its terrible risks and the misery it would inflict on so many human beings. The 'great struggle' of which he speaks would indeed be dreadful, and it is well to 'keep one's powder dry' and be prepared, but I can see no impossibility of keeping it off altogether and this after all is the aim and object of all politics: viz. so to manage the affairs of a nation that there may be a minimum of sacrifice and suffering and a maximum of advantage. . . . What a startling telegram you have received from Sir Condie Stephen. . . .[102] I think Alfred has nursed the idea of having young Arthur and that he now feels it very difficult to abandon it and take up the other [i.e. of having Charles Edward as his heir in Coburg]. . . .

From the Queen
EXCELSIOR HOTEL REGINA, CIMIEZ, APRIL 10, 1899

. . .I cannot say what a blessing I think it that you were at Florence when Sir C. Stephen came to see Arthur. I think he was very sensible and very anxious. I feel it must have been a great trial for the poor parents and, on the other side, I felt what darling Papa would have felt and wished that the possible danger of losing the heritage was one not to be risked. And I hope and trust all will be settled and this idea of Arthur's going to see William is a very good one, though I do not admit that he has any right to be sore at not being consulted which we hear he is. They thought I ought to have written a sort of apologetic letter explaining why the family accidentally to a great extent met here. I have no time to say anything more except that I am so glad you went to the dear Palmieri which we were so fond of.

From the Empress Frederick
HOTEL BRITANNIA, VENICE, APRIL 17, 1899

. . . I hope you will not see fit to write an apologetic letter to William at all and think it would really be a great mistake if you were advised to do so. *Qui s'excuse s'accuse*. And it would be hard if the family could not meet by accident without being obliged to 'explain' it to William. He has nothing to do with the Coburg succession. It is all settled by law and it is only as a compliment or matter of courtesy that Arthur could go to see him, which is quite right. . . . I hear from Berlin that people are furious about Samoa, but it is really not just or fair. . . .

From the Queen
WINDSOR CASTLE, UNDATED [9 MAY 1899]

. . . Coburg is once more a great annoyance especialy as Affie seems to resist everything but having young Arthur [in Coburg] and as such pressure is put upon a decision, in England also, there is such agitation as to what Arthur is going to do, that he has to decide that he, and young Arthur also, can't leave England where they are much needed [and will renounce their rights to the Coburg succession]. So the whole family agree and I hear that Bülow told Sir Frank Lascelles that the succession concerned the family and Coburg only and that there could be no objection and it is therefore Affie only who makes that difficulty. It is not right indeed of Ernie to say he can't like Charlie who is a remarkably nice boy. William is very cross, declares Lord Salisbury to be his enemy and that he won't come to

England while he is prime minister. Then he will have to wait a long time. I want in thanking you for your two dear letters of the 7th and 8th [to say] pray don't ride without Sir F. Laking's permission and *do* come for my birthday. . . .

From the Queen
BALMORAL CASTLE, MAY 30, 1899

. . . I am rather helpless about important things without Beatrice or Lenchen, Harriet Phipps being also away, on account of her sister, who is so ill. . . . William has been very amiable about the Coburg succession, but very irate against Lord Salisbury in a letter which you shall see, and saying he can't come to Cowes. But I think if he came to *Osborne* with one or two people only, leaving the others on board, as a visit for my eightieth birthday, the difficulty could be got over. . . . I can't say how I admired *Lohengrin*! It was beautifully sung by those marvellous brothers [Jean and Edouard de Reszke] and Mme Nordica and, oh, how beautiful the music is! So poetic in feeling and I might almost say religious. The lovely *motives* always returning as the subjects return.

[Ps.] I must say the way in which William attacks Lord Salisbury and my Government is almost unpleasant[?]. I should never dream of writing a line about his ministers in that way.

From the Empress Frederick
FRIEDRICHSHOF, JUNE 21, 1899

I wonder whether you have heard anything more from William and whether any reply has been given to the remarks you sent? The excitement in France seems as great as ever and the difficulty as great to form a ministry. The military party seem quite determined to set at nought the

decision of the *Cour de Cassation* [that the case of Captain
Dreyfus should be retried]. It seems to me a very dangerous
game. No doubt the generals are the stronger and the army
would follow them and could upset the Republic if they
liked, but on so wrong a cause – it would indeed be a shame.
However I am convinced that all Frenchmen will do their
utmost to prevent the risk of ruining the success of their
Exhibition next year, and that is about the only guarantee
one has that peace will not be disturbed. The Peace
Conference at the Hague does not seem to create much
interest or be keenly followed by anyone. The day after
tomorrow Tino and Sophie go to Kiel. . . . I am very glad to
hear that you have satisfactory accounts of Marie of
Mecklenburg's future husband [found for her by Aunt
Augusta]. . . . I do not know Count Jametel so I was
concerned at the thought and am glad to hear that the
person who told me was misinformed. . . . We ought to hear
of dear Alicky's safe confinement very soon. I do hope all
will be well, and that it may be a boy this time. I shall
indeed be disappointed and distressed if I cannot manage to
see Beatrice somehow or other while she is at Boppard. She
would be running no risk [of catching smallpox] in coming
here I think. . . .

[Ps.] My house is very full just now and it is very difficult to
find time for all the guests who are always asking to come.
Fischy is going to return to active service as a captain in the
82nd Regiment of the Line at Frankfurt. . .

From the Queen
WINDSOR CASTLE, JULY 12, 1899

Your sad first telegram about the poor Duchess of Rut-
land's hopeless state shocked me much. I telegraphed at
once to the good Duke and received a touching answer from
him that she had passed away at seven. We saw so much of
her when we were abroad in '89, '90, '91 and '92, and she

was always so kind to me and mine that, despite all her eccentricities, I deeply regret her and above all [feel] for the poor, dear Duke whom she watched over so carefully. I know how sad you will be and they were devoted to you. And now poor Lady Salisbury has had a slight stroke though they don't generally [announce] it. There is much trouble in this world. Poor George of Russia's death comes rather suddenly and is a great blow to poor Minnie [his mother]. I now revert to the idea of the Prince of Hohenlohe Bartenstein. You could find it out much better than me, through the Rei-schachs. It sounds well but the great difficulty and anno-yance mixed marriages cause now would make it absolutely necessary to know before. . . . Lenchen did not dislike the idea but Tora wishes it to be clearly understood what would be done about the marriage. Else, as she said, if she should like him and great difficulties arise afterwards about the religion, it would be very unpleasant and painful. It there-fore would be very kind if you could find this out before anything more is done. I have been asked to try and find a *parti* for Clémentine [of Belgium] and it struck me that if this prince did not do for Tora, he might for her? Angeli is still here. He has painted a most admirable and beautifully painted picture of me.[103] It is the best and likest he has painted of me. He has also painted a very pretty one of Daisy – only head and shoulders. Mine is half-length.

From the Queen
WINDSOR CASTLE, JULY 21, 1899

. . . Helen has not decided anything about Charlie's school or where she will stay. She wishes to see and choose for herself but he will not read anywhere. It would not do after Eton. Poor dear Helen feels the uprooting of her happy and first home terribly and Charles feels leaving Eton very much. It is most stupid and ill-judged of them both to take the poor boy away in the middle of his education and before he knows German enough to be able to *learn* in German.

William unfortunately set this idea going. On the 4th the dear boy (who is very popular at Eton) will be Confirmed quite quietly in St Gecrge's and then leaves for Reinhardtsbrunn the next day. May I again remind you of the small medal for my poor Abdullah (the one in Scotland) who was promised it when you gave the one to Ismael?]. . .

From the Queen
OSBORNE, AUGUST 7, 1899

Many thanks . . . for the medal for Abdullah with which he will be delighted. Also many thanks for the prints of the royal family. . . . I must at once tell you that poor Helen and her darling Charlie have met with a very cordial reception at Reinhardtsbrunn from all and Affie writes to me that they will do all to make it pleasant. The Confirmation on Friday was very touching and very sad and the poor dear little boy cried afterwards most bitterly which was very distressing to see. Helen and Alice were also much distressed.

From the Empress Frederick
FRIEDRICHSHOF, AUGUST 22, 1899

. . . I was so dead tired yesterday, as I went to the parade at Mayence and had to leave here very early; after having taken William to the station. The cold, high wind and burning sun together gave me a headache and made me feel very giddy. Ducky kindly let me drive with her. All parades are now, as you can imagine, sad and painful to me when the one figure I used to watch is gone and I do not see others in his place that can compare to him. . . . William's visit to me went off very well. He told me he was going to take Dona to England. He seems pleased to go there. He is looking very well but gets more like Uncle Ernest in figure and manner etc. each time I see him. How strange that is! I wish he was as like our beloved and beautiful Papa, or his own dear father. Still he looks very nice on horseback and manages to ride quite well, as you know, in spite of his arm. I did not tell you that poor Marie Münster has been through a terrible operation. For the moment she appears cured, but I have not much hope for the future. Poor dear Marie! . . . We are deeply interested in the Dreyfus trial. All these generals exercise such pressure on the Court Martial that I feel, in the face of truth and justice, they will not dare to acquit the poor innocent victim. This row in Paris has been very disgraceful,[104] also: the murder of two French officers in the Soudan by two of their comrades. I heard from a very good source that the French talk seriously of having a war with England in 1900! How and where and what for, I wonder. They are really too mad. . . .

From the Empress Frederick
FRIEDRICHSHOF, AUGUST 26, 1899

On this our beloved Papa's birthday my thoughts are more than ever with you, and returning to the bright past, since which so many years have rolled past. Time cannot rob us of our precious recollections nor make the love and gratitude die in our hearts. . . . I too wondered at Count Münster being made Prince, but the official world at Berlin and William think him a wonderful ambassador at Paris. . . . I am not quite so convinced of this . . . though I like him personally very much. . . . I remember dear Papa buying some of Mr Varley's pictures, amongst others the one over the looking glass and mantelpiece in dear Papa's former dressing room at Windsor, now Beatrice's boudoir. It is a very pretty landscape which I am sure you remember. . . .[105]

From the Queen
BALMORAL CASTLE, SEPTEMBER 3, 1899

I much grieve to hear from Bertie that you have a feverish attack which I trust will soon pass off. It is so tiresome for you. . . . I am sorry that you do not approve of the Princess of Wied as *Mitrath* for Helen [i.e. as co-trustee with Helen for her son in Coburg as heir presumptive]. She chose her herself, but I shall tell Sir R. Collins in confidence. I hope to see him as he is coming over for a few days. I hear he is very depressed. . . . The news from the Transvaal are very fluctuating. Yesterday they were not good and today they are much better. There has been an unpleasant rising amongst some Dervishes and Arabs on the Blue Nile. The Khalifa is still a danger. If only we could get him. . . .

From the Empress Frederick
FRIEDRICHSHOF, SEPTEMBER 7, 1899

. . . I am all right again (so to say), up and about, but shaky and must still take care and cannot do a great deal. It was more than provoking to have been laid up just when dear Bertie was here etc. Alas, he leaves today and I was to have gone over to Darmstadt and Wolfsgarten with him, but I do not feel up to it which is most provoking, as we wanted to go to the mausoleum together and carry wreaths there. . . . Bertie seems very well and active and to have had a successful cure at Marienbad. I hope the Gathering will go off well – such a pretty sight. My thoughts are so much with you in dear Scotland. . . . The Transvaal must be a fearful anxiety to you – these constant fluctuations of prospects. Those awful people at Rennes seem to wish to spin out the Court Martial at Rennes until poor Dreyfus may no longer be alive to hear his sentence. They say he is very much exhausted. . . . How one admires MM Labori, Picquart,

Hartmann, Freystätter, Scheurer-Kästner and Trarieux, almost all Alsatians. I have no words to say what I think of the Generals. . . . All strict Catholics (Clericals) and indeed Conservatives are against Dreyfus here, but everyone else, unanimously, for him and the whole case excites the keenest interest.

From the Queen
BALMORAL CASTLE, SEPTEMBER 9, 1899

. . . I am so thankful that you are better but am so sorry that this should happen just when Bertie was with you. Still he managed to see a great deal of you. I am quite *boulversée* [overcome] by the news of poor martyred Dreyfus's new condemnation [when his case was retried]. It is the greatest disgrace to France and the army which could take place.

September 10. . . . The perjury, lying and wickedness of the officers appearing before the court martial, of so many of them called as witnesses, is beyond words. I cannot tell you what I feel about it and I see by your dear letter received yesterday that you do the same. . . . I think that marriage of Isabelle Paris's very pretty third daughter to her cousin Jean d'Orléans, whose eldest brother was an idiot and the other is a shocking lump, is very sad, for the fathers were brothers and the mothers are first cousins. What will the children be like? The only exception to this rule is the Jews, who do not become stupid by perpetual intermarriage. One thing I must not omit to mention which I had from Helen, which is that William has been extremely kind about her and Charlie and very strict [that] she must be protected and her boy left solely in her charge. She is very pleased and so am I. I thank God that your pain is not so constant.

From the Empress Frederick
FRIEDRICHSHOF, OCTOBER 10, 1899

... Anxiously one watches for news and my British heart
beats with anxiety and is often tortured, and yet feels a sort
of confidence in the persons who guide the affairs of the
dear old country and in all the sound common sense and
practical wisdom they have access [to] which cannot be
shaken. I cannot help thinking the right thing will be done.
The clamour and fury of the press of other nations springs
from ignorance on the one hand and jealousy on the other;
but even this is a paroxysm which will pass and give room to
calmer thought. The news are not worse so that all chances
are not over of a peaceful solution still being found though
the likelihood of war is greater, I fear. So many thanks for
kindly saying you will contribute to the little fund for raising
a monument to the Landgravin Elizabeth. . . .

[Ps.] My lumbago is no better. . . . Professor Renvers has
been to see me today and seemed very much satisfied,
though I am feeling anything but well and suffer much
pain. . . .

AFTER THE SOUTH AFRICAN WAR BEGAN

From the Empress Frederick
[?]OCTOBER 12, 1899

So war has really begun! How sad! It could not be avoided
after Kruger's violent reply. Our strength and greatness
does not please our rivals and neighbours. Their disposition
is more spiteful and jealous than the English temper which
is honest, open and kind. They enjoy seeing us in a fix and
each is thinking what he can gain by it. Never mind – I think
of what John of Gaunt says in *Richard II* (Shakespeare) –
'Nought shall us rue, so England to herself doth bide but

true'.[106] I think all our rivals in turn egged on Kruger, to see what we should do, and get us into a tight corner, abuse us for being cowardly and weak, unable to fight and afraid of the Boers if we did not make a stand as they now abuse us for our violence, tyranny and rapine. . . . We must now hope that the struggle may be short and that we shall win the day as soon as possible and with as little bloodshed as possible. I do so feel for you now you have this new anxiety which must be so great. I only wish I could be with you. . . . Willy of Greece was here yesterday on his return from Copenhagen. . . . My lumbago is worse than ever and defies all remedies. Today I could hardly get up and down stairs. Kissing your dear hand . . .

From the Queen
BALMORAL CASTLE, OCTOBER 22, 1899

Beloved and darling Child, I could not write for I have spent these two last days in receiving and sending telegrams. We have had two most desperate actions and our soldiers, including two Irish regiments, held an almost inaccessible position with most marvellous success [at Glencoe Camp]. The two actions took place yesterday. But, alas, our losses were very heavy. In the one [at Talana Hill] on the 20th we had ten officers killed and twenty-two wounded, in all two hundred and fourteen. In yesterday's we had taken guns and waggons from the Boers who fought desperately. . . . But we do not know our loss. Poor Sir W. Symons is a little better.

October 23. Nothing new today. I was much shocked to hear of poor good Marie Münster's death which will be a great sorrow to you. I will telegraph to the poor old father. We were so sorry to lose dear Franzjos and Anna on Saturday. She is charming. . . .

From the Empress Frederick
RUMPENHEIM, OCTOBER 24, 1899

Your telegram yesterday caused great joy. With all my
heart I congratulate you on the brilliant success. Alas, it
seems to have been dearly bought and brave valuable lives
have been lost. . . . [The Boer] numbers must have been
very overwhelming. I only hope Mr Rhodes is safe. . . . I am
so distressed to hear of poor General Symons being mortally
wounded. Is there really no chance of his recovery?] . . . It is
pleasant to read the Italian and Austrian papers in contrast
to the French, Russian and German. . . . I cannot help
hoping in Spring you will go to Italy and not to France,
really the French have been too nasty. I wonder how it will
be with William's visit? His foolish telegram to Kruger [in
1896], after all, has to answer for a very great deal, and it is a
great satisfaction to me that the German Government
should in some ways have to eat their words. . . . My
lumbago is still very bad and I do not look forward to the
journey and the shaking of the railway. . . . Professor Renvers . . . wants me to be out of doors and have as much sun
as possible. To leave Mossy and the children for so long is of
course a great wrench. . . . I had a letter from poor old
Count Münster: who is really going back to Paris after my
poor dear Marie's funeral. . . .

From the Empress Frederick
IMPERIAL HOTEL, TRENT, NOVEMBER 2, 1899

The sad news of the reverse at Ladysmith has made me
dreadfully unhappy and I can imagine how it must distress
you and what anxiety it must cause you and everyone in
England. Our forces were indeed too slender, at that place,
to oppose such an enormous number. I can only hope and
trust that we shall be able to inflict a signal defeat on those

dreadful Boers elsewhere and that our success will not be doubtful in the end. If only part of our fleet were in Delagoa Bay and reinforcements could reach Ladysmith from another quarter. So much advice is given the Boers from German, French and Russian and Dutch sources that of course they know quite well what to do and where our weakest points are. You cannot think how I feel being far away and not knowing what is going on, except in snatches and from the abominable German papers, as *The Times* and *Daily Telegraph* arrive so late. It does not do to lose heart.... My doctor arrived yesterday and today I am going to begin the electricity and massage cure for this awful lumbago which till now has yielded to nothing. The constant pain is so wearing and the helplessness very trying. My only comfort in not being with you now is that I should be a trouble and an encumbrance in your house in my present state. Poor Lenchen must be in a state of great excitement and suspense about Christle and May about her brother and the Gleichens about Eddy Gleichen. I wonder whether Cecilia Downe's son is out there?...

From the Queen
BALMORAL CASTLE, NOVEMBER 9, 1899

I am most thankful to say that the Samoan affair is quite satisfactorily settled between the German Government and ourselves and William telegraphed to express his great satisfaction. We leave tomorrow and on Saturday morning after I arrive I shall take leave of the squadrons of Life Guards and Blues, who are going out immediately, at the barracks. It is always affecting to bid them goodbye when they go on active service....

From the Empress Frederick
IMPERIAL HOTEL, TRENT, NOVEMBER 17, 1899

. . . I shall be anxious to hear whether you are not tired after the interesting visit to Bristol. I am relieved to see in the papers that Sir R. Buller has arrived at Durban. How wicked of those wretched Boers to go on shelling the hospitals and places in which the women have taken refuge – at Kimberley ignoring the Red Cross flag. They are such cruel brutes. I only hope they may soon have to rue all they have done. I am rather sorry a statue has been erected to Oliver Cromwell.[107] He was a great historical figure, a remarkable statesman, and did great things, but he was a regicide and a murderer, and his qualities as a public man do not counterbalance the crime he committed, though he was of great use to his country and one ought not to underrate the services he rendered his nation, yet I do not think he can be held up to admiration. My poor Charles I – how often you used to laugh at my affection for his memory. It is quite unaltered to this day. He is a martyr in my eyes. . . .

From the Queen
WINDSOR CASTLE, NOVEMBER 25, 1899

I trust you will forgive my not having written before, but my time has been so taken up by the visit [of William, Dona and two sons] and the terribly sad event of darling Marie L[einingen]'s sad loss that I could not write before. What her loss is to me I cannot tell you. She was like a sister and daughter and dearest friend and her dear quiet visits were the greatest pleasure and comfort to me and the thought that I shall never see her again on earth is quite terrible. For poor Ernest, but still more for her poor blind daughter to whom she was all in all – it is too grievous. Many, many thanks for your dear sweet letter of the 21st. I am so glad you liked the cross and shawls. Many thanks also for the one received today. The visit has been a really great success. Both William and Dona were extremely amiable and kind. And I had a god deal of talk with William on all subjects and found him very amiable and *most* anxious that all should go well between the two countries and that they should be on the best of terms. Count Bülow, whom I think most agreeable and amiable, spoke very openly to me and quite in the same sense. He spoke with the greatest devotion of you. I will say more another day. Dona was also very nice and kind and not stiff at all. The dear boys are delightful, well-behaved children and took great interest in all they saw. We had large dinners over in St George's Hall which I still went to. The day of the sad news I did not appear, but I made the great effort to dine on Thursday and Saturday, but had no bands and went away after dinner yesterday.

[Ps.] I asked Count Bülow to write to you.

From the Queen
WINDSOR CASTLE, UNDATED [? 20 DECEMBER 1899]

I received your dear letter of the 14th only on the 18th. Many loving thanks for it and for all the kind words it contained for that double, sad anniversary. The music was beautiful and the Dean had written a very pretty prayer. We have had some reverses but there is no alarm.[108] Still as there is much going on, telegrams received and sent, I put off going to Osborne till after Christmas (a sacrifice, as the fogs and darkness here are quite dreadful). There have again been many sad losses. Poor Lord Roberts losing his only son, supersession of Sir R. Buller [by Lord Roberts] but an appointment sad as it is, no one could resist. Lord Kitchener goes with him. Poor Lord Roberts has lost his only son in this last failure to cross the Tugela River. I telegraphed to dear Sophie 'thank you' for so kindly sending things to our brave soldiers; and how kind of you to be knitting socks for them. I hope the lumbago will be better. . . .

From the Empress Frederick
LA MARIGOLA, SARZANA, DECEMBER 22, 1899

. . . I thought you would perhaps give up going to Osborne for Christmas at this critical time when business of all kinds must be so pressing. I have had an inkstand made for you; it is an attempt to produce majolica at Kronberg and I venture to hope that this piece is worthy of your acceptance, as no second will be made and the artist has taken great trouble. All my Christmas prayers and wishes and blessings I find it difficult to express. . . . I am no better. Indeed the pain seems even more acute at times. No doubt the violent wind which is cold and cutting has a deal to do with it. Vicky and Adolf are here since two days. Vicky is helping me, getting the things together for South Africa for the sick and wounded and has put in her contribution. I sew and knit in bed by the light of a rather sorry petroleum lamp, but, alas, one cannot effect as much as one would like.

From the Empress Frederick
LA MARIGOLA, DECEMBER 29, 1899

. . . As I am completely in bed and unable to move you must excuse my letter being very badly written. . . . Poor Lord Roberts, how extremely trying for him to go out after the death of his only son. I pity Lady Roberts so much. . . . I am very glad Arthur is going to Ireland [as Commander-in-Chief]. It is a good thing in every way I think. Did you read how two hundred and fifty Greeks are anxious to volunteer for South Africa, to fight for the English? Considering the country is small and poor and has been through such troubles and misfortunes, I think it quite touching. Gratitude is so rare and always a real pleasure to meet with. I found the Greek people never forget a kindness. They have warm hearts. . . . I shall be very pleased to see Sir F. Laking in February and hope to be better by then and up and about again. It is a shame to be laid up in this lovely country and climate and not to be able to enjoy the beauties of the scenery. . . .

From the Empress Frederick
LA MARIGOLA, JANUARY 1, 1900

The first words this morning and my motto for the century – 'God Save the Queen'. Never was this prayer breathed more lovingly and devotedly, nor from a more grateful heart. One hates parting, even from an imaginary bit of a past so precious, and one loves not beginning a new phase and embarking on the unknown, though we do so every day of our lives, without thoughts as solemn as those with which we enter upon a new year and this time even a new century. . . . I hope the news from South Africa are more reassuring. William wrote me a card saying he hoped 'peace would soon be made and this useless bloodshed put an end to'. These sentiments in this form I cannot echo. Heaven knows that each drop of precious British blood seems a drop too much to be shed, but to allow ourselves to be driven into giving up a struggle which was unavoidable and forced upon us at the very moment when it is most unfavourable to us, I should think most deplorable and disastrous and mistaken all round. . . . My opinion is that England will come out of this contest, which she was bound to undertake as part of her mission in the spread and establishment of civilisation, stronger than she went in. She will see who are her friends and who her foes; she will also see what defects there are in her armour and will reform whatever is faulty. The Empire will be welded more firmly together than ever by having faced a common danger. England will put forth her strength and I doubt not weather the storm. I am able to be up for a little in an armchair and on the sofa. The pain is still very acute.

Professor Renvers is coming to see me tomorrow, and new endeavours will be made to cure this severe and tedious attack which causes so much suffering. . . .

From the Queen
OSBORNE, JANUARY 15, 1900

. . . I am quite shocked to hear that my Christmas presents arrived only on the 10th. I tend [to forget] that everything goes so slow in Italy. I am glad you like the watercolour painting. You said in one of your letters that you had two or three books of poor King Charles.I. Would you not rather I exchanged it for something else? Just tell me. Your lovely inkstand is on my table in dear Papa's room where you know I always sit in the morning. We are in expectation of some great results near Ladysmith tomorrow. [General Buller's second attempt to relieve Ladysmith failed.] It makes one very anxious. But all you say about the war and the good it is doing England and the Empire is most true. The want of preparation and knowledge is indeed terrible. I don't know what Hatzfeldt thinks; old Münster does not hold that language to William. . . . I wonder that you are pleased at Irène's having a third boy. There are far too many princes in Prussia and only two girls – William's and Fritz Leopold's. Irène did so wish for a daughter. Affie went today to Russia with Sandra and Ernie. He was anxious to be away from Gotha at this time and Missy is going on very well.[109] Tora is here since the 10th and we expect Lenchen on the 22nd and Louise on the 23rd. You will think of darling Beatrice and her children and me on the 20th. It was 8 years yesterday since poor Eddy's death. On the 13th was young Alfred's and today dear Drino's birthday. I was so thankful to hear you were a little better and hope this will continue. My intention *unberufen* is to go to Bordighera in the middle of March.

From the Empress Frederick
LA MARIGOLA, JANUARY 27, 1900

On this day your first grandchild was born, to you and dear Papa, 1859. . . . The news you have kindly allowed Sir A. Bigge to telegraph to me is very depressing and fills me with double anxiety because one fears that the relief of Lady-smith is delayed and that operation thrown back, and that there have been heavy losses again. Still, on the other hand, the occupation of Spion's Kop, even if it had to be abandoned, may have been a very useful reconnaissance, and to hold it longer without guns (as it was too steep to get any pieces of artillery up) seems to have been quite impossible. One only dreads the Boers having reinforced strongly and making a final rush on Ladysmith, while our forces have retreated. It is no use to be discouraged or despondent, but one does tremble for fear of new misfortunes to our brave and heroic troops whose devotion to their duty nothing could surpass. . . . One wonders whether if Lord Lansdowne [War Secretary] gave up his place to Lord Wolseley [Commander-in-Chief] it would be an advantage, and Arthur were Commander-in-Chief?]. . . It is significant that Dr Leyds should have predicted what has happened twenty-four hours before. I suppose Bertie is not coming out to Cannes this year and that but few English will go to the Paris Exhibition. . . .

From the Empress Frederick
LA MARIGOLA, SARZANA, FEBRUARY 10, 1900

On this your dear wedding day my thoughts are always so much with you! It is my precious Waldie's birthday and the remembrance of my darling is always so vivid on this day and the pain of having lost him. Another sad remembrance takes me back to San Remo and beloved Fritz's operation –

that dreadful time. . . . Henry arrived [from China] on the 7th. It was such a joy to see him, and find him looking so well and in such good spirits. Alas, I was in bed, in tortures of pain, so that it was a sorry welcome for him – poor boy. He is just leaving. He goes to Vienna and thence to Berlin where there will be a reception (no doubt a general airing of Chauvinistic sentiments which rub me up the wrong way). Then he goes on to Kiel where there will be another reception as it is his home and he started from there. I think it most natural and right the people there should give him a nice welcome home. What joy for him and Irène to be together again and for him to see his children and make the acquaintance of this new baby! . . . Sophie writes to me as follows: '. . . How is dearest Grandmama bearing all this; it is so trying for her. If only no surprises are in store for us! The Russians for instance are our terror. Here the sympathy for England increases every day. People keep sending small sums of money and wine to Sir A. Egerton for the wounded soldiers . . .' I think this is very touching, considering how poor the people are there. I too feel anxious about the Russians and feel convinced (Henry shares my opinion) that they are driving at having Pekin – that they will have it sooner or later. . . . Henry thinks the Japanese are very 'cheeky' just now and rather wish to come to blows with the Russians, but that they would be quickly and completely beaten. Today is very fine and Henry has steamed away back to Genoa. . . . Vicky and Adolf have gone with him. . . . I am up and about again. . . .

From the Empress Frederick
LA MARIGOLA, SARZANA, FEBRUARY 17, 1900

Only one line to say how truly thankful, happy and delighted I am to hear by your telegram yesterday evening that General French has gone into Kimberley. It is wonderful news.

From the Empress Frederick
LA MARIGOLA, SARZANA, FEBRUARY 27, 1900

... How delighted I am to hear this most important and excellent news of Cronje's surrender with seven thousand men to Lord Roberts. I cannot say how thankful I feel for you, for Lord Roberts and Lord Kitchener, for the army in general and for all England. I am sure it is part of a great load off your mind. Now one's only wish is that Ladysmith and Mafeking should be relieved, General Joubert beaten and Bloemfontain and Pretoria taken and the war ended. . . .

From the Queen
WINDSOR CASTLE, MARCH 7, 1900

... I cannot tell you how grieved I am not to go and see you at Bordighera, or how I pine for the sunny, flowery south, but with the abuse against England and even me, and the war still going on and much to be settled, I feel I could not, with safety almost, go abroad. But do try and come here by very slow stages. All could and would be done to make it comfortable and easy for you. You will be startled when I tell you that I am going early next month to visit Ireland. It is entirely my own idea as was also my giving up going abroad. It will give great pleasure and do good. The people want to give me a great reception in London tomorrow. I am going for two nights but not for a Drawing Room. I hope the weather is fine in the south now. I do feel not going there much, after doing so every Spring for fourteen years.

From the Empress Frederick
LA MARIGOLA, SARZANA, MARCH 9, 1900

. . . You have not been to Ireland for many years and it will be quite an event and most interesting in every way. Lord Cadogan has given himself so much trouble as Viceroy that I am so pleased for him too, as it will be a great satisfaction for him, I am sure. I have still a piece of the train you wore at Dublin for the Drawing Room years ago. I am so thankful for the news that all is going on satisfactorily in South Africa. . . . Today it is very fine and I shall go on board the *Loseley* and see whether we can take a little trip, perhaps to Leghorn which is three hours from here. The air is very chilly but the sun fine and warm and no wind. Beatrice has written to me. How more than kind and good you are in assisting me in paying Sir F. Laking's fee. I am more touched and grateful than I can say. . . .

From the Queen
VICEREGAL LODGE, PHOENIX PARK, DUBLIN, APRIL 6, 1900

. . . Everything went off admirably on the 4th – enormous crowds, great enthusiasm, beautiful decorations. But what a merciful escape dear Bertie has had from a very real danger.[110] The indignation felt everywhere is very great, but it shows the harm such atrocious vilifications of us, including even me, have [done] and the totally mistaken idea of the war which affects the minds of weak, ignorant and ill-disposed people. I am thankful I did not attempt to go abroad; it was a fear of something happening on the road which made me give up going. I am in despair to hear of your having been again so suffering. How I wish I could be of any use! There was rather an unfortunate affair the other day under Colonel Broadwood, but Lord Roberts does not consider that it has at all affected his plans seriously. We lost some guns unfortunately, as our troops were again led into an ambush. Mafeking can hold out still. I think they do get some provisions in. We are very comfortable here, but the weather is not very pleasant though the two last afternoons were fine. The Cadogans do extremely well here. Arthur and Louischen and children (who only came over on Thursday and Friday) met us at Kingstown and came up here early yesterday morning. May and the boy are doing well. He is to be called Henry, a fine old English historical name and very dear to us [as Prince Henry's name], William after Willy, Frederick after Lord Roberts, Albert, and is to be christened at Windsor on my return. [The future Duke of Gloucester was christened on 18 May.]

From the Queen
WINDSOR CASTLE, MAY 9, 1900

. . . I forgot to say that the King and Queen of Sweden, whom I saw on Friday, asked much after you and if you were well again. I only answered that you were not very well yet. They are staying at Roehampton and their youngest son has been very ill. I am sending you today some photographs of our reception in Ireland and of the inspection of the naval brigade you might like to have. . . . The accounts from South Africa are good but it will be slow. I also send you a white silk embroidered coverlet for your sofa or bed which I brought from Ireland where it was worked which I hope you will like and use.

From the Queen
WINDSOR CASTLE, MAY 15, 1900

. . . I think I mentioned to you that I am godmother to three poor little babies, all boys, who were born after their fathers were killed in this terrible war. One, Mrs Donne, whose very gallant husband was killed at Elendslaagte in October, I saw on Saturday last with her very fine baby. The child was born six months after the father was killed. He was in the Gordon Highlanders. What, however, I think will particularly interest you is that she is the daughter of an Archdeacon Dealtry who read English with William and Henry at Cannes in '70, or rather in '69 and '70, to whom you and Fritz gave a handsome inkstand with an inscription. He is dead but his son, Mrs Donne's brother, possesses the inkstand. She is pleasing and quiet in her overwhelming grief. The other one, Mrs Elgar, her husband was taken prisoner and exchanged for Joubert but lost his leg and died as soon almost as he was liberated. And the third is a Mrs Lomas. Her husband was in the Welsh Fusiliers and she could not be told of her loss before her confinement. My standing sponsor helped her. It is touching. It is very striking that they should all be boys, as if the life taken was given back again. Amongst the privates and sergeants, too, so many of the wives have had boys. We have today had very good news which I telegraphed to you, but not yet from Mafeking. . . .

May 16. There [is] good news from Sir R. Buller today. But the treachery of the Boers in hoisting the flag and concealing themselves and then firing on our men has again been practised and is too monstrous. We are going after an early luncheon to Netley to see the poor sick and wounded this morning. Georgie and May, Athur, Louischen and children arrive this evening. The christening is tomorrow at one. Abbat arrives early tomorrow and comes on here. I hope and trust you are feeling more comfortable? . . .

From the Empress Frederick
FRIEDRICHSHOF, MAY 18, 1900

. . . Indeed, it does interest me very much to hear that you have seen a daughter of Archdeacon Dealtry (Archdeacon of

Madras). I did not know he was dead. Dear Alice and I used to like him very much and see a good deal of him at Cannes. His little girl used to be carried about by an Indian servant called Francis, whose portrait I tried to paint there. I had no idea of course that the daughter was married to an officer and that her husband was killed, poor unfortunate woman, but what a blessing and comfort for her that you have become sponsor to her little boy. William and Henry remember quite well having had lessons from Archdeacon Dealtry. The other poor widows must have been equally grateful to you. How nice the babies should be boys. Indeed, England will want many, many boys in place of the precious lives lost in this war. . . . I am sure Abbat was quite delighted to have been sent to the christening. . . . On your birthday there will be a gathering of your grandchildren here. I only hope I shall be well enough to entertain them. . . .

From the Queen
WINDSOR CASTLE, MAY 21, 1900

. . . The relief of Mafeking has filled the whole country with wild delight. We have no official account of it, but it is undoubted. Everything is really going on well now everywhere, and Sir R. Buller has been very successful. Our visit to Netley was very interesting and very sad. So many very bad cases! But so uncomplaining and patient. One man has lost arm and leg. The christening next day went off extremely well. The baby is a very pretty little thing. . . . Abbat was very amiable and Alix most civil to him. On Saturday we went to Wellington College where I had not been for upwards of thirty years if not more, and where Drino is now. They have got an excellent headmaster, a Rev K. Pollock, great nephew of the celebrated General and godson of the Judge. He talked of your visit there. I will not be able to write by messenger, but shall afterwards. I am sending you a photograph taken at the Viceregal Lodge of

251

me with my little Doggie. I am going this afternoon to wish God Speed to more of the drafts and must end for today.
[Ps.] The relief of Mafeking is confirmed by the Colonial Office. On the 17th it took place. The people were quite wild on Friday night and Saturday. . . .

From the Queen
WINDSOR CASTLE, JUNE 24, 1900

. . . We had a good journey and the news from South Africa are very encouraging. But China is very alarming and makes one very anxious. Dear Marie Coburg [Alfred's wife] arrived yesterday with baby B[eatrice] grown a pretty girl with a very pretty figure. Poor Marie talked very openly to me about her sorrow. Affie has been very unwell at Hercules-bad, with a very bad throat. The cure was too strong. We have had a great alarm about the poor Khedive[111] who, they fear[ed], was going to have diptheria. But it is not, as it [is] only a very bad relaxed throat. He is still on board the *Osborne*, but it is hoped will land on Tuesday and come here at the end of the week. Affie is not coming over now. . . .

From the Empress Frederick
FRIEDRICHSHOF, JULY 4, 1900

. . . I am sure you too are shocked that the death of the poor German minister at Peking, Baron Ketteler, turns out to be true after all. He seems to have been murdered in the streets. His poor mother was a great friend of Fritz and a playfellow of his. . . . I fear the Germans have been much too go ahead in their doings in China which has alarmed the Chinese and made them turn against all foreigners fearing that their independence is threatened as one Power after another was seeking to obtain a footing there. . . . What a controversy these letters [to *The Times*] of Sir C. Burdett

Coutts have raised about the hospital arrangements in South Africa. . . . It seems hard that before all the world our arrangements should be denounced as bad, defective, careless, inefficient, etc. . . . Tino returned yesterday from Paris and seems to have had an interesting time there and have seen some remarkable people. He is so intelligent and has such a marvellous memory that when he travels he hears and sees a great deal. . . . I am about again but in great pain . . .

From the Empress Frederick
FRIEDRICHSHOF, JULY 28, 1900

. . . I am indeed quite unhappy that you are anxious about dear Affie. What can be the matter with him? Is it gout? or eczema? or are the kidneys not right? I hope he has been prudent lately? If I were not so helpless just now, I should ask to be allowed to go over to Coburg to see him. But I am afraid I could not well travel as I am now. . . . I am in much pain today and could not go down to luncheon. The news still seems contradictory about the Peking massacre. If it has taken place, as was at first said, then it is strange that the fact is not yet officially confirmed. How very good Mr Chamberlain's speech in the House was. I grieve to see that the conduct of the Liberals has not been as patriotic as one would wish; it is carrying party feeling too far, I think. I was especially sorry to see Mr Bryce join Mr Campbell Bannerman and Mr J. Morley in the attack on Mr Chamberlain, who is decidedly the ablest statesman in Europe at this moment, even though lacking the ways and methods of the aristocrat such as British Ministers have usually excelled in and Lord Salisbury possesses so fully. . . .

From the Queen
OSBORNE, JULY 31, 1900

I little thought when I wrote yesterday giving a bad account of our beloved Affie that the end was so near. It is too terrible and, I fear, must be a great shock to you. We have been kept quite in the dark and he, poor dear, in writing to poor dear Marie never mentioned his health even though already some time ago he was very ill. The end was most peaceful. It is hard at eighty-one to lose a third grown up child in the prime of life. . . .[112] Poor Muther was finally very sorry to go, but he was determined to leave. I have got a very nice gentlemanlike and *fähige* [capable] successor, Herr von Pfiffer whom I like very much. In the midst of my great grief for our beloved Affie I omitted to say how dreadfully shocked and grieved I was at the murder of the dear kind King of Italy, always a true and kind friend. It is awful, but he never took any sort of precautions. I always feared this happening. The poor, poor Queen, how I feel for her! God bless you, darling child, protect and guide you.

From the Empress Frederick
FRIEDRICHSHOF, JULY 31, 1900

I really do not know how to begin these lines. The thought of your grief is an agony to me. That this blow should fall on you in the midst of the trials and anxieties of our war is too cruel. Could I but be with you, dearest, beloved Mama! At present I am no use. But hope to be better and able to go to you later. To think of our darling beloved Alfred being taken at this time – at his age – is too dreadful. . . . He was an ornament to our glorious navy and he had already done a deal of good to dear Coburg and has left his mark on the place. . . . What can have been the matter with him? . . . He seems to have passed away in his sleep without pain or distress. Unhappy Marie, how I feel for her and the poor girls. . . . What a difficult position for Helen and little Charlie! . . .[113] It is too heartrending, three of your nine have gone home and followed beloved Papa. . . .

From the Queen
OSBORNE, AUGUST 26, 1900

This is a day which makes me think so particulary of you, darling child, and of former very bright happy days and all our dear ones once with us. They are [memories] very dear and cast a reflection of the past on the present very altered life. I have been thinking very much of that day which we spent at lovely St Cloud, with its beautiful avenue and flags when the Emperor gave dear Papa the beautiful picture of La Rixe and the Empress that lovely carved cup. . . .[114] Dear Alix has written so kindly to me, telling me how you spend your day. I am so glad you saw Sir C. Stephen and heard many details from him. He will return by Homburg hoping to see you and Bertie again. Is Sophie leaving you soon? I hope not. Henry was to have followed Irène and remained some little time. Now William has stopped that and only allowed [sufficient time] to bring her or that he may come back again to fetch Irène which he cannot do. I asked William to allow him to stay on a few days as I had not seen him for so long, but he refused and said he must stay for the manoeuvres! . . .

From the Empress Frederick
FRIEDRICHSHOF, SEPTEMBER 18, 1900

So many loving thanks for your dear letter and the photograph done at Osborne, such a pretty group though your dear face has not come out as well as it should and as the others have. What a look of poor Liko little Leopold has and

Ena seems so much grown. So many thanks for sending it. I will certainly send some of Sophie's sweet children, but there are none that do them justice. I think Lord Roberts's proclamation [of the annexation of the Transvaal and Orange Free State] excellent and hope it will have the best effect in the Transvaal. The general elections will be a moment of great anxiety and interest and excitement. I am very glad Lord Salisbury is home again. Chinese affairs seem to hang fire. I do hope some good arrangement can be made before Count Waldersee arrives as I do not see what his military command of 'all the international troops' is to come to. How sad is poor Henry of Hesse's death. How lonely it must be for Ernie to be the only remaining representative of his family. It is more than ever to be wished and hoped that Ducky may have sons. . . . Mossy has gone to Wolfsgarten today. . . . I have had more pain again these last few days.

From the Empress Frederick
FRIEDRICHSHOF, OCTOBER 1, 1900

. . . I am still laid up in bed with a worse attack than I had in Italy. I hope however it has reached the climax and that the violent spasms will become less acute. . . . I cannot say how much touched I am by the dear Empress Eugénie's more than kind offer of her lovely house, Cyranos, close to Cap Martin. Such a position and view and such a comfortable house! Unfortunately it would be too small for the party I am obliged to bring about now, and it is a little close to the very large hotel and the high road. At the Château Malet, which is not half so fascinating, I can stow [away] everyone and also it is completely shut off from the high road which runs below. I have already accepted their offer which I could not now throw over.

From the Queen
BALMORAL CASTLE, OCTOBER 2, 1900

I have the very best news of the election. There never were so many unopposed elections of Conservatives and Liberal Unionists and where there was opposition, the numbers with which the Government candidates have come in is greatly increased. . . . Today Albert of Belgium's wedding takes place. I believe the bride pretty and nice. I hear George of Greece is making a tour of visits to different countries. . . . I am sending you a telegram about the elections. God bless and protect you.

From the Queen
BALMORAL CASTLE, OCTOBER 30, 1900

. . . I cannot write but a few words as we are in such distress about dear beloved Christle's loss. It is too terribly sad to have gone through such hardships and dangers and not far from his return home to get that awful illness and be lost when all thought him safe. He had, alas, malarial and enteric fever. We hoped to the last. Poor dear Lenchen bears up wonderfully; so too does poor dear Tora who leaves for Cumberland Lodge today . . .

From the Queen
WINDSOR CASTLE, NOVEMBER 19, 1900

Accept my most earnest wishes for your dear birthday and for every blessing God can bestow and many better returns to come. My presents I hope you will like. The one is a locket which can be worn as a bracelet in remembrance of dear Affie. As there was no hair unfortunately, I have put a little photograph [of him inside the locket]. The other is a medal by that clever artist (or sculptor) called Fuchs which he calls a Peace Medal, which is somewhat too early, but I think you will admire, as the design and composition are really very fine. . . .

From the Queen
OSBORNE, DECEMBER 27, 1900
Dictated to Beatrice

I must dictate these few lines to you as I am not well able to write myself, and wish to thank you for your last dear letters. I am so delighted that you are plesased with my gifts and that you are a little less suffering. A thousand thanks for the most beautiful and tasteful magnifying glass which I shall always use in thinking of you. I have not been very well myself, but nothing to cause you alarm and I have not a bad pulse. I have also been able to get out a little most days. This Christmas has been one of the saddest I ever remember, excepting '61, and you are I am sure as horrified as I am at the loss of my good beloved Jane Churchill, who died in her sleep on Christmas Day. What her loss is to me I cannot describe or even realise yet, and that it should happen here is too sad, but it is I think what she would have wished, excepting for the trouble and sorrow it has caused. Poor Lenchen, Christian and their children have borne up wonderfully, but poor Christian is terribly aged. . . . As your sisters have written to you and given the very uninteresting news from here, I will end for today, hoping to be able to write myself next time.

From the Queen
OSBORNE, JANUARY 6, 1901[115]

I am so grieved to see by your dear letters that your hands trouble you so. It is very troublesome [that they] hurt you so much. I attempt to write myself [instead of dictating]. I don't suffer from my eyes, only the sight is rather bad since I have been rather poorly but I hope it will soon be much better. I gave your message to Lord Roberts who was greatly gratified. There were great crowds to receive him and both Beatrice and Arthur went out to receive him. He is looking well and was greatly gratified. Then I gave him the Garter and told him he was to be an earl. . . . I must, I fear, end for today to save the post. God bless you, darling child.

Notes

1 By Edna Lyall who was, ironically, an ardent Home Ruler. In the Royal Library at Windsor there are copies of third editions, 1886, with on the flyleaf of *Donovan* in the Queen's hand: 'Read to me by Beatrice 1886 VRI', and on the flyleaf of *We Two*: 'Read to me by Beatrice 1887 VRI'. Both came from the library at Osborne where they were found in 1901.

2 For medical details showing that the Empress Frederick's impression that William's instability as well as his shortened arm were caused by something which happened at his birth was true, see John C.G. Röhl, *Kaiser Wilhelm II* (Schriften des Historischen Kollegs, München, 1989, p. 6).

3 Goethe's *Faust* in translation, staged by Henry Irving at the Lyceum where he was actor-manager.

4 A landscape painted in 1860, two years before he died, still at Osborne.

5 Died by his own hand after his neglect of the state and extreme indebtedness had caused him to be declared incapable of ruling. His brother, Otto II, succeeded, but his uncle, the Prince Regent Luitpold, ruled. Queen Mariechen, mother of Ludwig and Otto, was a Hohenzollern, a cousin of the Emperor William I.

6 Published anonymously as *Co-Regents and Foreign Influence in Germany*, asserting that the Crown Princess was too much in league with her mother.

7 i.e. of Prussia in 1866 in the war against Austria. The Schmalkalden forest was a detached part of Hesse-Nassau which Prussia annexed, lying south-west of Gotha. The papers had been sent by the Queen on 30 June 1886, with her comment, 'Uncle cannot alter the *Fidei Comiss* [entail] without the consent of the agnates'. She proposed to send copies to Prince Alfred, the heir to Coburg.

8 In November Swoboda was sent to India to paint people and landscapes. These paintings are now at Osborne House. The Indians and others referred to in the next letter were in London for the Colonial and Indian Exhibition.

9 The Prince of Wales was to represent the Queen at the celebration of William I's ninetieth birthday on 22 March.

10 Where her husband, Prince Leopold, Duke of Albany, died in 1884 at the Villa Nevada.

11 Laurits Tuxen. A detail from the painting (of some fifty relatives, children and grandchildren of the Queen grouped in the Green Drawing Room at Windsor) is reproduced on the dust-jacket.

12 The Queen had received six Addresses, one from the *Society of Friends*, represented by John Bright, whom the Queen sent for afterwards. Bright had stayed at Osborne in 1868 and at Balmoral in 1871.

13 Of fifty stanzas, see *Nineteenth Century*, vol. 21, June 1887, p. 781, beginning:

> Eight hundred years and twenty-one
> Have shone and sunken since this land
> Whose name is freedom bore such brand
> As marked a captive and the sun
> Beheld her fettered hand.

14 Philippe of Orleans, son of the comte de Paris, was concerned about his brother, who had defied the decree of banishment from France and stood for election to the French Chamber.

15 The laying of the foundation stone of the Imperial Institute.

16 i.e. the two eldest Connaught children and the two Albany children, all between the ages of three and five.

17 In an unprinted letter of 1 September, still from the *Victoria and Albert*, the Crown Princess recommended the installation on the yacht of 'electric light, steam steering and a couple of baths'.

18 Suspect to Bismarck as a princess of the Orleans family though married to Augustus of Coburg.

19 Karim al Ali, who came in March 1888 and went in October 1889.

20 As an expression of sympathy the ladies normally received at court walked in single file between a double line of pages past the Empress, curtseying deeply. All wore black and the rooms were hung with black: see *Das Tagebuch der Baronin Spitzemberg*, R. Vierhaus (ed.) (1963), pp. 226–7.

21 Or Hanoverian party. Bismarck called them, as he called the representatives in the *Reichstag* of the Polish provinces, *Reichsfeinde*, or enemies of the Empire. Prussia had annexed Hanover in 1866.

22 On 2 July the Empress Frederick wrote: 'Yesterday I had to give up the cuirasse, and helmet and sword, white coat, boots and spurs to the colonel of the regiment. . . . He wore it for the last time at your Jubilee.'

23 '. . . here I and sorrow sit; Here is my throne, bid Kings come bow to it'. (Shakespeare, *King John*, Act III, Scene I, lines 73–4.)

24 Presumably a German painting returned to Germany after the exhibition, since it is not known in England.

25 Relating to the Mayerling tragedy, where her husband, Crown

Prince Rudolph of Austria, took his own life (or was murdered) and
that of Marie Vetsera on 30 January 1889.

26 The hospital of St Katherine was a charity founded in the Middle
Ages of which the Queen of England, whether regnant or consort,
was always patron; several letters in the correspondence relate to
vacancies there for English ladies retiring from the service either of
the Empress or the Queen. It was then in one of the Terraces in
Regent's Park.

27 Manuscript marginalia by Lord Sydney entered in Queen Victoria's
copy of Henry Reeve's edition of the *Greville Memoirs* (1865) now at
Windsor and transferred to the volumes sent to the Empress
Frederick, possibly by Princess Beatrice or a lady-in-waiting; part
published as an appendix to the edition by L. Strachey and R.
Fulford (1938).

28 Italian 'Protestant' community made familiar to Englishmen by
Milton's sonnet 'Avenge oh Lord, thy slaughtered saints', but it
went back to an anti-sacerdotal movement originating with Peter
Waldo in the second half of the twelfth century. The Empress
Frederick sent her mother a letter on 11 June from the Scottish
minster in Genoa asking whether the Queen would send congratulations through her ambassador in Rome on their celebration
of the bi-centenary of the return of the community to the Savoyard
valleys from which they had been expelled. Sir Henry Layard
attended the celebrations and reported to the Queen that no
message of congratulation ever arrived.

29 The Queen in fact wrote 'Friedenskirche', but can only have meant
Friedrichskron, the former home of the Empress Frederick which
William II had now taken over, much to her distress, and changed
its name back to Neues Palais.

30 Introduced by George III.

31 *'Edel sei der Mensch, hülfreich und gut! Denn das allein unterscheidet ihn von
allen anderen Wesen die wir kennen.'* This is the first verse of *Das Göttliche*.
In English: 'Let man be noble, charitable and good! For this alone
distinguishes him from all other forms of life we know.'

32 The photographs are in the Royal Archives at Windsor but the
painting itself is of course not in the Royal Collection.

33 Prince Alexander had married an Austrian singer and, taking the
name of Count Hartenau, had settled in Austria early in 1889.

34 A portrait of Frederick painted by Weber and now at Buckingham
Palace; see illustrations.

35 William II had summoned a conference of representatives from
European governments to consider labour problems.

36 The duc d'Orléans was the grandson of King Louis Philippe. He
landed in France despite the edict of expulsion and was duly
arrested. He and the Orleanist claims he represented suffered a

setback with the collapse of the Boulangist movement.

37 The long letter of 19 February, with its continuations of 21 and 22 February, was printed by Ponsonby, pp. 405–8. It tells the Queen that Sophie expects a child in August and describes a visit of Prince and Princess Bismarck to her in which Bismarck deplored the initiative of William II over the labour conference and spoke of his own resignation soon. The Queen writes '52nd anniversary' but she must mean 42nd.

38 A method of printing photographs on paper prepared by various chemicals including platinum.

39 An entry in the Queen's Journal for 7 May 1890 indicates that this painting was for her regiment of Prussian Dragoons, to whom it was presumably sent. It is referred to in her letter of 12 February 1890.

40 The day originally fixed for Moretta and Adolf's marriage so that it might be on the Empress Frederick's birthday, but it was put earlier, on the 19th, so as not to clash with the anniversary of Adolf's grandfather's death.

41 The Empress Frederick was Koch's patron. She wrote on 9 December 1890, 'I have taken a great deal of trouble to put English, Italian, Greek and Austrian doctors *en rapport* with Koch: they have applied to me' over his treatment of tuberculosis. *The Times* on 17 November had a long article headed 'Cure for Consumption'.

42 *Waterfall near Gastein*. This Christmas present is still at Osborne.

43 William II had raised objections to his sister Sophie's entry into the Orthodox Church.

44 Died 24 April, aged 90.

45 Brother of Tsar Alexander II, 1855–81.

46 The German Emperor and Empress were to pay a state visit to England from 4 to 14 July 1891.

47 Victoria Battenberg, wife of Ludwig, eldest of the Battenberg brothers, arrived from Malta, where Ludwig was serving in the Royal Navy. Louis was her father and Alicky her sister.

48 She escaped from the massacre at Manipur.

49 He had referred to Napoleon as 'that Corsican upstart'.

50 Correctly, 'He who first met the Highlands' swelling blue', and continuing, 'Will love each peak that shows a kindred hue'. (*The Island* (1823), stanza xii, canto 2.)

51 He was then intriguing to bring about a reconciliation between Bismarck, to whom he was related, and William II.

52 Prince Albert Victor, Duke of Clarence (Eddy), died 14 January 1892. The Queen means 'go to Windsor'. She did not attend the funeral in St George's Chapel. His tomb is in the Albert Chapel at Windsor. The memorial there was made by Sir Alfred Gilbert, a pupil of Böhm.

53 Died 12 March 1892. Ernie succeeded as Grand Duke of Hesse Darmstadt.
54 A visit to Queen Victoria would have been embarrassing if Eddy, who had wished to marry her (see p. 108), had not died.
55 William II still refused to see them, though he knew they were with the Empress Frederick.
56 Respectively Frederick Charles's mother and sister.
57 Where he, now ultimate heir to the throne and created Duke of York, 24 May 1892, went for two months in September–November to study German.
58 Harcourt had not looked forward to the visit either, but it passed off agreeably with an exchange of engravings of his grandfather, Archbishop of York 1807–47. See A.G. Gardiner, *Life of Sir William Harcourt* ii (1923), p. 198.
59 See Hallam Tennyson, *Alfred Lord Tennyson. A Memoir* (1899), p. 778: 'Two anthems were sung; both were settings of words by my father; one, 'Crossing the Bar', by Dr Bridge; the other, 'Silent Voices', a melody in F minor by my mother, and set by her at my father's express desire'; for two letters from the Queen to Hallam Tennyson, 6 and 19 October, see ibid., pp. 798–9.
60 Dr Hans Blum published in a German newspaper a series of three interviews with Bismarck. The last contained a diatribe against the Anglo-German exchange of Heligoland for Zanzibar by the 1890 treaty.
61 Gladstone argued that to keep the Irish Home Rule question open must provoke the continual growth of the evil called democracy. The Queen's answer was a snub.
62 Because Rosebery was by devious means evading Gladstone's opposition to its annexation.
63 This is probably, in the light of what the Empress Frederick wrote later (see p. 159), *The Lovers*, now hanging at Hampton Court.
64 The Royal British Nurses' Association, of which Princess Helena (Lenchen) was President, had addressed a petition to the Queen for a Charter of Incorporation to allow it to keep a register of qualified nurses. The Privy Council heard the petition in November 1892. Florence Nightingale's case against it was based on two grounds: that it was too soon and that registration and paper qualifications were inappropriate because of the personal qualities expected in a nurse. The decision of the Privy Council was given in May 1893. It allowed the Charter and a list but not the word 'register'.
65 The second Titian, *Landscape with a Herd of Sheep*, is still in Buckingham Palace Gallery.
66 This enterprise had been initiated by the Prince of Wales as a permanent memorial to the Queen's Jubilee. As such it failed, but it eventually became part of London University, losing its connection

with the Empire. The Queen had laid the foundation stone and opened it. The reference here is to a social occasion where the Prince of Wales was host.

67 Relating to the Empress Frederick's complaint of the state of the tombs.

68 Of Coburg, where Ernest II, brother of Prince Albert, had died on 22 August.

69 The Duchess of Edinburgh (Marie) was concerned about Missy's relations with Elisabeth of Roumania, wife of King Carol (Charles) but then living with her mother, the Princess of Wied. Roggenbach, liberal politician of Baden, had an acknowledged position as *Hausfreund*. Gossip said that he was secretly married to the Princess and acknowledged as her husband on his deathbed.

70 Named after Sir George Couper, Controller to the Duchess of Kent, who once lived there; now renamed Karim Cottage.

71 The Empress Frederick had met the Queen at Coburg at the marriage of Ernie of Hesse Darmstadt and Affie's second daughter, Ducky. Princess Alice's daughter, Alix or Alicky, and the future Tsar of Russia, Nicky, were engaged to be married.

72 The future Edward VIII (abdicated 1936), familiarly David, born 23 June, christened in the drawing room at White Lodge Edward Albert Christian George Andrew Patrick David.

73 Tree's company from the Haymarket played *The Ballad Monger* by Sir Walter Pollock and Sir Walter Besant, adapted from a French play by Theodore de Bainville, and *The Red Lamp* by William Outram Tristram. Neither play was ever published; their manuscripts were deposited with the Lord Chamberlain.

74 Meaning a general understanding among the European states concerned, Russia, Germany, France and Britain, as to the outcome of the war between Japan and China.

75 Hermann von Hohenlohe succeeded his cousin when the latter succeeded Caprivi as Chancellor.

76 Married on 26 November 1894 to Nicholas II; assassinated with him by the Bolsheviks.

77 Some half-dozen Russian groups were active in Ethiopia between 1891 and 1895. They were 'slavophils' interested in the Russian mission as heir to Byzantium to bring all eastern Christians within the fold of the Orthodox Church. See C. Jesman, *The Russians in Ethiopia* (1958).

78 Ponsonby had a stroke during the night of 6/7 January, 1895.

79 The Queen's remarks were prompted by the duels arising from the von Kotze affair. He was accused of sending anonymous and insulting letters to members of the court but cleared in a court of law. The last duel between Kotze and Schrader is referred to by the Queen on 4 April 1896. Duels were forbidden by the Reichstag on 20 April.

80 Duke Waldemar of Lippe Detmold had died. His will appointed Adolf of Schaumburg Lippe regent for his brother, the Duke's heir, who was insane. The will was contested and in 1897 he was obliged to leave Detmold. Count Ernst of Lippe Biesterfeld then became regent.

81 Uncle George, then seventy-six, who had been Commander-in-Chief since 1856, was superseded by Field Marshal Lord Wolseley, but the affair was not settled until just before the Government fell on 21 June.

82 The last of William II's annual visits for the Cowes regatta. On this visit William's new yacht *Meteor II* outdid the *Britannia* of the Prince of Wales.

83 The Villa Hohenlohe bought from Hermann of Hohenlohe-Langenburg on his succeeding to the title in 1872. The Empress Frederick had written to her mother from Baden (18 October) where she had stopped on her way to Wörth.

84 When he was offered the throne eventually accepted in 1863, after Otto's reign, by William of the Danish royal house, who became King George.

85 Whippingham Church was the parish church of Osborne House.

86 The reference is to William II's telegram of congratulations to President Kruger on the restoration of order after armed bands – the Jameson raid from South Africa to the Transvaal – had broken into his country.

87 The Queen was told by telegram on Friday 10 January that Prince Henry was suffering from fever and could not join the Ashanti fighting. He died at sea on the way home.

88 Fritz, Eddy and Liko were the three princes; Fritz, Louis of Hesse Darmstadt and Liko were the sons-in-law.

89 The day when the Queen had reigned longer than any other British sovereign.

90 Where the Empress Frederick was from December 22 to 28, going on to Berlin and then to England.

91 This letter and the following one from the Empress Frederick are copies, filed in the Royal Archives under Eastern Question H.39. She was again in England during the last fortnight of June for the Queen's Diamond Jubilee.

92 Of the five daughters of Nicholas I of Montenegro, two had married Grand Dukes of Russia and Helen had married the Crown Prince of Italy, after 1900 King Victor Emmanuel III. Anna was the fourth daughter.

93 To Detmold. The lawsuit over the succession had gone against them, and they returned to Bonn.

94 The Queen wrote 'mystical' but must have meant mysterious. The reference is to the Mecklenburg–Strelitz affair. Marie, daughter of the heir to the duchy and his wife Elisabeth of Anhalt, was with child by a married footman.

95 William II, in taking leave of Prince Henry at Kiel, on 15 December, proclaimed 'imperial power is naval power' and threatened with 'the armed fist' any who did not acknowledge Germany's power. Prince Henry made a fulsome reply.

96 Son of Henry (still in China) and Irène, suffered from haemophilia. Leopold, second son of Princess Beatrice, had also shown signs of the illness.

97 Died 19 May; lay in state in Westminster Hall, 26–7 May; buried in Westminster Abbey, 28 May 1898.

98 Elisabeth, Empress of Austria, was assassinated at Geneva; her cousin was Ludwig of Bavaria (drowned in 1886); her son was Rudolf of the Meyerling tragedy; her sister Sophie, duchesse d'Alençon, was burnt in a fire at a charity bazaar in Paris.

99 The Empress Frederick was in England and Scotland from 1 October, when she arrived at Balmoral, to 14 January 1899. She visited Dalmeny (3 October–4 November), Drumlanrig Castle (4–7 November), Buckingham Palace, Sandringham, Windsor, and was at Osborne for Christmas. She arrived at Bordighera on 15 January 1899. She complained of giddiness when at Dalmeny and later of trouble with her ear.

100 The Empress Frederick is now writing 'in dark ink with a broad pen and words far apart' so that the Queen, whose sight was beginning to fail, could read it more easily.

101 *Letters of Elizabeth, Landgravin of Hesse-Homburg*, edited with notes and an introductory chapter by P.C. Yorke (London, November 1898).

102 Reporting the intended renunciation of his rights to the Coburg succession by the Duke of Connaught, both for himself and for his son, 'young Arthur'. This raised a fresh difficulty that an effective renunciation could only be made by young Arthur himself after he was twenty-one.

103 Reproduced as the frontispiece to *QVL*, 3rd ser. iii; see also illustrations.

104 There had been serious rioting in the Belleville district of Paris with some three hundred injured before order was restored.

105 *Evening Landscape*, acquired in 1841 by the Prince Consort, still at Windsor.

106 Correctly, '. . . Nought shall make us rue, If England to itself do rest but true'. (Shakespeare, *King John*, Act V, Scene VII, last lines of the play.) One supposes that the Empress Frederick has mistakenly placed the lines in John of Gaunt's famous speech in *Richard II* (Act II, Scene I, lines 40 ff.): 'This royal throne of kings, this scept'red isle . . . This blessed plot, this earth, this realm, this England.'

107 There was a *fin de siècle* revival of interest in Cromwell. Since 1895 Rosebery had promoted the project for this statue, erected in time for the tercentenary celebration of his birth in November 1899.

108 This, surprisingly, is the Queen's summary of the so-called Black
Week, Monday 11 December to Saturday 16 December. The week
opened with General Gatacre's defeat at Stormberg in Cape
Colony. Next came General Methuen's defeat in his attempt to
clear the road from the Modder river to besieged Kimberley at
Magersfontein ridge (13 December). The climax was the defeat of
General Buller in his attempt to cross the Tugela river on the way to
Ladysmith, at the battle of Colenso (15 December).

109 A daughter, Marie, who married Alexander of Yugoslavia, was born
to Missy and Ferdinand in Roumania the day before a son, Henry,
was born to Henry and Irène (7 and 8 January 1900).

110 He was shot at by an Italian on leaving by train from Brussels. He
and Princess Alexandra were sitting in the railway carriage but
were not hurt.

111 He was received at Windsor on 30 June and 1 July and at
Marlborough House by the Prince of Wales on 2 July 1900.

112 Prince Alfred, Duke of Edinburgh and Duke of Coburg, died on the
night of 31 July/1 August 1900.

113 Who now succeeded as Carl Eduard, Duke of Saxe-Coburg-Gotha.

114 The Queen and Prince Albert with the five eldest children visited
Napoleon III and the Empress Eugénie in Paris, 18–27 August
1855. *La Rixe* by Meissonnier now hangs in a corridor in
Buckingham Palace.

115 This is the Queen's last letter. The last letter preserved of the
Empress Frederick is a dictated letter of 5 October 1900. She died
on 5 August 1901. Queen Victoria died on 22 January 1901.

List of Anniversaries

14 January	Death of Prince Albert Victor (Eddy), 1892
20 January	Recovery of Prince Henry (Liko) reported, 1896; death next day
25 January	Marriage of Princess Victoria to Crown Prince of Prussia, 1858
10 February	Queen Victoria's wedding day (1890, golden wedding anniversary)
27 March	Death of the Crown Princess's son, Waldemar, 1879
28 March	Death of Prince Leopold, 1884
25 April	Princess Alice's birthday
24 May	Queen Victoria's birthday
15 June	Death of the Emperor Frederick, 1888
18 June	Death of the Crown Princess's son, Sigismund, 1866
20 June	Queen Victoria's accession
21 June	Jubilee day, 1887
17 August	Duchess of Kent's birthday
26 August	Prince Albert's birthday

29 September	The Princess Victoria's engagement day
15 October	Queen Victoria's engagement day
18 October	Frederick III's birthday
9 November	Prince of Wales's birthday
21 November	The Crown Princess's birthday
14 December	Death of Prince Albert in 1861 and of Princess Alice in 1878

Index

The index refers to the letters only. Abbreviations used are as follows: dau. = daughter of; Pr. = Prince; Qu. = Queen Victoria.

Index

Grand Duke Frederick of Baden, last chancellor of the German Empire (1918), 145

Badeni, Count Casimir, minister president in Austria (1895–7), 194

Bagshot Park (Duke of Connaught), 122, 146

Baird, Admiral, 95

Balfour, Arthur, 1st lord of the treasury, visit to Balmoral, 222

Bankart, Dr, physician, 225, 226

Barber, Charles Burton, painting from 1873, 174

Baruda, the Gaikwar and Maharani of, 59–60

Battenberg, Princess, mother of the four Battenburg brothers

Baudoin, Pr., elder son of Philippe and Marie Flanders, heir presumptive to his uncle King Leopold, 120, 121

Bayonne, Qu.'s visit to, 82

Beatrice, Princess, Qu.'s youngest dau., married to Pr. Henry of Battenberg (Liko): birth of her daughter, 87; golden wedding gift to Qu., 104; at Florence, 67; at Grasse, 126; Qu. on her absence, 214; birth of 2nd son, 133, 173; appears in tableaux vivants, or acts in plays, 103, 154, 167; goes to the opera, 161; at Oberammergau, 114; reads articles for Qu., 178; visits and admires Friedrichshof, 180; and Pr. Henry's (Liko's) illness and death, 187, 188, 197; remembers Duchess of Kent, 193; goes to Kissingen, 192; opens museum at Carisbrooke, 218; at Genoa, 226; at Boppard, 230; Qu. helpless without her, 229; writes for Qu., 248, 258

Bell, D. Courtenay, official of the Privy Purse, 63

Benckendorff, Count Paul von, marshall of Russian court, 195

Bergmann, Professor Ernst von, surgeon, 79, 164

Berlin, 49; Empress Frederick's journey to (1888), 63–4, (1890) 101; Empress Frederick's visit to market of, 70; gift to Empress Frederick, 79; few connoisseurs at, 124

Bernardines, convent of, 82

Bertie, Albert Edward, Pr. of Wales, Edward VII (1901): represents Qu. at William I's 90th birthday, 46; at William I's funeral, 65; advises Qu. 47, 126; speech at unveiling of Qu.'s statue at Aberdeen, 56; friendly and kind, 56; silver wedding, 64; much graver, 105; unwell, 91, 93; at Athens, 97; visit to Germany with Georgie, 142; and gambling, 123; and Eddy's illness and death, 138–9, 142; does not go to Mossy's or Missy's wedding, 152; visits Empress Frederick, 131–2, 142, 234–5; accident (1898), 217; shot at, 248

Bigge, Major Sir Arthur, later Lord Stamfordham, assistant secretary, later private secretary to Qu., 49, 88, 154, 245

Bigio, Francesco, painting by in Buckingham Palace, 159

Birmingham, Qu.'s visit to, 46

Bismarck-Schönhausen, Count Herbert von, son of the German chancellor (1867–90), alleged friend of Lord Rosebery, 66, 91, 96

Bismarck-Schönhausen, Otto Edward Leopold von, Pr., German chancellor, 'the great man', 'the wicked man': Qu.'s conversation with, 68, 71; on

Index

Index

Gounod, Charles, French operatic composer, 132, 169, 216

Grande Chartreuse, Qu.'s visit to, 50

Grandmama, see Kent, Duchess of

Granville, 2nd Earl, foreign secretary (1868–74, 1880–5), 28

Greco–Turkish war, 200–4, 205, 210

Greece: and Bulgaria, 145; and Crete, 133, 179, 183, 190–1, 199–200; and Macedonia, 118, 183, 199–200; dislike of Italians, 122; domestic politics, 121–2, 175; financial crisis, 169; gratitude to England, 194; tour by Empress Frederick, 98–9; supports Britain in South African War, 246

Grenfell, General Sir F., 191

Greville's Memoirs, 87

Grieg, Edvard, composer, played before Qu., 209–10

Grimwood, Mrs, heroic escape on north-west frontier of India, 128

Guelf party, 69

Haggard, W.D. 1st secretary of legation at Athens, 101, 112

Hague Peace Congress, 218–20, 230

Hamilton, Lord George Francis, 1st lord of the admiralty (1885–6, 1886–92), secretary for India (1895–1903), 29

Hampton Court, treasures at, 60

Harcourt, Sir William G.G. Venables Vernon, home secretary (1880–5), chancellor of the exchequer (1886, 1892–5), 148 and note 58

Hartington, Spencer Compton, styled Marquis of, 8th Duke of Devonshire (1891), prominent in Derbyshire, 36, 127

Hatzfeldt, Paul, Count von, German ambassador in London (1885–1901), 44, 45, 59, 93–4, 96, 145, 154, 213, 244

Hatzfeldt, Princess, *Oberhofmeisterin* (mistress of the robes) to the Empress (1888), 68

Helen, Princess of Waldeck and Pyrmont, Duchess of Albany, widow of Pr. Leopold, 123, 231, 232, 234, 255

Henriette, dau. of Philippe and Marie Flanders, niece of Leopold II of Belgium, sister of Pr. Baudoin, 120

Henry, Pr., 2nd surviving son of the Empress Frederick: engagement and marriage to Irène of Hesse Darmstadt, 41, 44, 46, 48, 71, 159; visit to Qu., 170, stopped by William II, 255; given Order of the Garter, 92; naval posting to China, 209, 210; returns from China, 246

Herschell, Sir Farrer, later 1st Baron, lord chancellor (1886, 1892–5), 149

Hertel, Albert (1843–1912), painter, 119

Hewett, Admiral Sir William, 71

Hindustani, lessons of the Qu. in, 63, 124

Hohenlohe, Qu.'s villa at Baden, 182

Hohenlohe Bartenstein, Pr. of, 231

Hohenlohe-Langenburg, Hermann von, son of Aunt Feodora, father of above, succeeded to the title (1872), Stadthalter of Alsace-Lorraine (1894–1907), 172, 173

Hohenlohe-Schillingfürst, Chlodwig von, Stadthalter of Alsace-Lorraine (1870–94), German chancellor (1894–1901), 172, 186

Hollmann, musician, 222

Index

Kruger, Paul, president of Transvaal Republic, 236–7
Kruger telegram, 186, 238

Labouchere, Henry, Radical MP, proprietor of *Truth*, 147
Labour conference, 104, 105
Ladysmith, fighting at, (1899–1900), 238–9, 244, 245, 247
Laking, Sir Francis, physician in attendance on Empress Frederick, 223, 224, 229, 242, 248
Landseer, Sir Edwin Henry, painter, 61, 119
Lansdowne, Henry Charles Keith, 5th Marquis of, secretary for war (1895–1900), 245
Lascelles, Sir Frank, successively consul-general in Sofia, minister in Bucharest and ambassador in Berlin, 40, 228
Lathom, Edward Bootle-Wilbraham, 1st Earl of, lord chamberlain (1885–6, 1886–92), 51
Launay, Eduardo, conte di, Italian ambassador at Berlin (1867–92), 61
Leighton, Frederick, painter, 123
Lenchen, Princess Helena, 3rd dau. of Qu., married to Pr. Christian of Schleswig-Holstein: trouble with her eyes, 78; at Baden, 148; her work for nursing, 156; *parti* for her dau. Tora, 231; and her son Christle during the South African War, 239, 257, 258
Leoncavallo, Ruggiero, composer of *I Pagliacci*, 226
Leopold, 2nd son of Princess Beatrice, 213, 255–6
Leopold I, King of the Belgians, Uncle Leopold, 78, 148, 183
Leopold II, King of the Belgians, 102, 121

Leyds, Dr, successful Boer propagandist from Brussels and Berlin, 186, 245
Liko, Pr. Henry of Battenberg, brother of Alexander (Sandro), 2nd of the four Battenberg princes, husband of Princess Beatrice: and Sandro's kidnapping, 39; absent at Christmas, 100; returns from holidays, 104, 132; his regiment in Germany, 111; Ashanti campaign and death, 184, 187, 188–9, 198; painting of, 158, 189; Empress Frederick on, 192–3
Lily of Hanover, Princess Frederica, dau. of George V, last King of Hanover, 58, 86, 192
Liszt, Franz, pianist and composer, had played at Drury Lane before George III, 32, 38
Liverpool, Lady, friend of Qu.'s youth, 42
Liverpool, Qu.'s visit to (1886), 32–3, 167
Lobanov-Rostovsky, Alexis Borisovitch, Pr., Russian minister for foreign affairs (1895–6), formerly ambassador in London, 179, 180
Loch, Emily, 129
Loë, General Walter von, Baron, Field-Marshal, member of the Crown Prince's liberal circle before he became Emperor, 197
Lords-in-waiting, three scientific, 151–2
Louis, Grand Duke of Hesse Darmstadt (d. 1892), 110, 139–40
Louischen, Louise, Princess of Prussia, Duchess of Connaught, wife of Pr. Arthur, 229; *see also* Arthur
Louise, Princess, 4th dau. of Qu.,

281

Index

Index